The Northern Ireland p‹

Manchester University Press

The Northern Ireland peace process

From armed conflict to Brexit

Eamonn O'Kane

MANCHESTER UNIVERSITY PRESS

The right of Eamonn O'Kane to be identified as the author of this work has been asserted by them in accordance with the Copyright, Designs and Patents Act 1988.

Published by Manchester University Press
Oxford Road, Manchester M13 9PL

www.manchesteruniversitypress.co.uk

British Library Cataloguing-in-Publication Data
A catalogue record for this book is available from the British Library

ISBN 978 0 7190 9083 7 hardback
ISBN 978 1 5261 7909 8 paperback

First published 2021

Typeset
by Sunrise Setting Ltd, Brixham

For Bridget O'Kane

Contents

Acknowledgements

This book owes a great deal to the community of scholars who research, discuss and disagree over the events and interpretations it examines. Paul Dixon, Christopher Norton and Mike Cunningham have been hugely helpful over many years. They may not agree with my conclusions, but if they do not, they should have done a better job of convincing me of the alternatives. The Irish Politics Specialist Group of the Political Studies Association has long been a forum for the debates which have influenced my thoughts on the peace process. I am extremely grateful to my co-convenor, Alan Greer, and a wide cast of people who have made academic life more enjoyable and enlightening. This includes, amongst others: Máire Braniff, Feargal Cochrane, Aaron Edwards, Cathy Gormley-Heenan, Will Hazelton, Tom Hennessey, Stephen Hopkins, Jim McAuley, Martin McCleery, Shaun McDaid, Marisa McGlinchey, Catherine McGlynn, Cillian McGrattan, Henry Patterson, Graham Spencer, Jon Tonge, Graham Walker and Sophie Whiting. I also owe a significant debt to all the politicians and officials who agreed to be interviewed over the years for my research, some of whom are quoted in this book, but all of whom helped me to clarify my thoughts on the topic.

I have been extremely fortunate in working with a great group of people and students in the Department of History, Politics and War Studies at the University of Wolverhampton and I am grateful for the support of the university's Centre for Historical Research, which provided the sabbatical that helped me complete the book.

Good friends and family have been a welcome distraction from the process of completing this work. Thanks to Siobhain O'Kane; Jackie and Danny Doherty; Jane Anthony and Kevin Allsobrook; Peter, Judy, Chris and Karen Anthony; Brian, Brendan and Tony Walsh; Dennis Roxborough; Linton Williams; Martin Perry and Paul Maguire. In Worcester, thanks to Mark and Kay Weaver, Matt Buttler, Lisa Tye, Sarah and Mark Poole and the Redhill Dropouts for the beers and banter.

This book has taken too long to come to fruition, and I am grateful to Tony Mason, Jon de Peyer and Rob Byron of Manchester University Press (MUP) for their patience and keeping faith with the project.

My main debt, however, is to my lovely wife Bridget, and my children, Thea, Niall and Dylan. That they did not share my obsession with the peace process makes their toleration of it all the more generous.

Finally, I would like to also thank all the above for agreeing to buy this book in hardback; there's a few sold, MUP.

Abbreviations

AIA	Anglo–Irish Agreement
APNI	Alliance Party of Northern Ireland
DSD	Downing Street Declaration
DUP	Democratic Unionist Party
FWD	Framework Documents
GFA	Good Friday Agreement
IRA	Irish Republican Army
NIA	Northern Ireland Assembly
NIO	Northern Ireland Office
NISS	Northern Ireland Secretary of State
NSMC	North–South Ministerial Council
PSNI	Police Service of Northern Ireland
PUP	Progressive Unionist Party
RUC	Royal Ulster Constabulary
SDLP	Social Democratic and Labour Party
STAA	St Andrews Agreement
UDA	Ulster Defence Association
UDP	Ulster Democratic Party
UFF	Ulster Freedom Fighters
UUP	Ulster Unionist Party
UVF	Ulster Volunteer Force

1

The origins of the peace process

The peace process in Northern Ireland resulted in an outcome that few expected – a sustained power-sharing government headed by the Democratic Unionist Party (DUP) and Sinn Féin, via a route that no one envisaged. The fact that the peace process period resulted in such an apparent success in Northern Ireland, ending Europe's longest running post-war conflict, explains the interest that the case has attracted. Yet what is most striking about the politics of Northern Ireland in the last decade of the twentieth and the first decades of the twenty-first century is how ad hoc and 'messy' the process was. Given the time that has now elapsed since the origins of the peace process, a fuller picture is emerging which makes it possible to explain and evaluate the factors that caused, sustained and, on occasions, nearly destroyed, the fundamental changes that Northern Ireland witnessed during the period.

One of the main ambitions of this book is to seek to examine the peace process in the context of the times that the decisions were taken. There is a real danger of 'reading back' into the peace process its outcome. In recent years several accounts have, with some justification, critiqued decisions taken by participants and argued that mistakes were made in both the design and implementation of the peace process. These range from the necessity or desirability of concessions to Sinn Féin and the Irish Republican Army (IRA), or later, to the DUP, the failure to protect the leadership of David Trimble and the Ulster Unionist Party (UUP), a lack of support for the Social Democratic and Labour Party (SDLP), an unwillingness to exclude Sinn Féin from government, the imposition of new preconditions during the peace process and the design of the institutional structures that it resulted in. At different stages of the peace process different criticisms were to the fore, and no party to the quest for a solution to the conflict was immune from censure. Given the complexity of the peace process, and the competing agendas and aspirations of those involved, it is unsurprising that different interpretations of the process and different prescriptions for its advancement exist. As a result of the new evidence that has become available to scholars in recent years, reinterpretation of the period and how it was handled is both inevitable and desirable. However, it needs to be remembered that such evidence may not have been available to all parties during the peace process. The reason that this is notable is that criticism of actors' and parties' actions (or inaction) has on occasion been based upon a knowledge that the parties did not have at the time that decisions were taken. This does not, of course, invalidate criticism; reflection and reinterpretation are essential activities for historians and political scientists. Where such criticisms are problematic is when commentators seek to extrapolate lessons from Northern Ireland which are based on scenarios that were unrealistic given the available evidence at the time. This is why this work seeks to examine the peace process in the context of the time that decisions were taken. It does offer a critique of decisions taken by actors when the evidence suggests that such decisions were not only unhelpful or counterproductive but, crucially, when such decisions were taken in the face of available evidence that meant actors should have been cognisant of the likelihood that the decisions were unlikely to be beneficial.

Examining (and critiquing) the peace process is also made more difficult as the parties to the process had competing and, at least ostensibly, incompatible objectives. This has resulted in differences between commentators regarding what the desirable outcome or advisable action may have been during the process, in terms of its overall outcome. There are several reasons for such differences of interpretation. In part they are a result of differences over the significance and availability of evidence. Different writers will place differing weight on particular evidence, and this will inevitably lead to competing conclusions. There are also ideological differences between authors, which may well feed into how they prioritise evidence and the critiques they offer (from which this author is obviously not immune). What this book seeks to do is explain the peace process, and evaluate its progress and outcome.

Defining the peace process

The term 'peace process' emerged to explain the changes occurring in Northern Ireland in the early 1990s and has remained commonly used ever since. Indeed, Northern Ireland appears to have had a perpetual peace process that has lasted for over almost three decades. The term itself has become a symbol of Northern Ireland's 'success' but its meaning has always been somewhat opaque. Northern Ireland's politics in the third decade of the twenty-first century are clearly significantly different from the situation the region faced in the early 1990s. Yet the term continues to be used by many to describe Northern Irish politics. The term itself is not completely value-neutral and its usage has differed over time and between parties. In the early 1990s the term was invoked to describe the process of seeking to entice the IRA away from violence. During the time of the Brooke–Mayhew talks there were frequent references to a 'talks process' seeking to secure peace in Northern Ireland. However, given the exclusion basis of these talks, these were different to what became known as the peace process. The peace process became the label attached to the objective of seeking to secure an end to the violence in Northern Ireland and a move towards all-inclusive talks including those who were associated with groups that had advocated the use of violence to secure political ends (primarily Sinn Féin but also those associated with loyalist paramilitary groups). Republicans themselves frequently invoked the term. In August 1991 (three years before the cease-fire) Sinn Féin President, Gerry Adams, stated that his party 'believe that peace can be achieved, we are prepared to take political risks, we are prepared to give and take, we are committed to establishing a peace process' (English, 2003: 270). The term, though, tended to have less resonance with the unionist community in Northern Ireland. Whilst it was frequently invoked by nationalists, the British and Irish governments and international commentators, unionists took to talking of a 'political process' distinct from a peace process. The reason for this distinction is that for many unionists the 'peace process' came to represent the granting of undue concessions to republicans in a dishonourable attempt to ensure that the IRA did not return to violence.

Dating the peace process

The dates of the peace process are contested. It can be dated from the first IRA ceasefire of August 1994, or to the British and Irish governments' Downing Street Declaration (DSD) of December 1993, which was designed to persuade the IRA to end their violence and participate in inclusive political dialogue. However, both the ceasefire and the DSD were only possible due to the contacts between the two governments and the IRA that had existed for several years. So, whilst the 'visible' peace process emerges post-1993/94, an 'invisible' one had been in operation before this. Debate continues as to when these contacts began. The difficulty here lies in the fact that a channel of communication had existed between the British government and the IRA since the early 1970s. This was an indirect channel that had been used sporadically during the Troubles period, notably in the early 1970s, in the run-up to the 1974–1975 IRA ceasefire, during the 1980/81 hunger strikes and then in the run-up to the peace process (Ó Dochartaigh,

2009). The British government's account suggests that the 'backchannel', as the link was known, was reactivated in 1990 as the person who had been the contact on the British side, Michael Oatley of MI5, was about to retire. Peter Brooke, the Secretary of State for Northern Ireland (NISS), gave approval for the backchannel to be reactivated so Oatley's replacement, 'Fred' could be introduced to the Derry businessman who acted as the link to the republican movement, Brendan Duddy. It is clear that, from this period, there was relatively frequent contact between the British government and the republican movement via this backchannel (Sinn Féin, 1993; the Duddy Archive, Galway). Ed Moloney, however, has dated the links back further than 1990 and suggests that the contacts that existed between Gerry Adams and the then Secretary of State, Tom King, via Fr Alec Reid, of West Belfast, at the end of 1986 were instrumental in creating the peace process. This contact, which predated that acknowledged by the British, according to Moloney, necessitates 'a fundamental reassessment of the genesis and origins of the peace process' (Moloney, 2002: 249). Given the secrecy behind such contacts it is difficult to know either the extent or impact of any exchanges between the British government and the republican leadership via the intermediaries. It is interesting that, on occasion, the government appeared to be rather equivocal on the possibility of contacts. For example, on 24 November 1987, Mrs Thatcher told the House of Commons, 'I think most of us believe that no one in this House should have contact with the IRA or Sinn Féin'. Labour's Ken Livingstone then challenged the Prime Minister to give assurances that 'there has been no further contact between the IRA and members of her intelligence services, MI5 or MI6, during the last eight years'. In reply Thatcher merely stated, 'Ever since 1979, the policy of the Government has been that we have no contact at ministerial level with the IRA or other terrorist organisations' (Thatcher, House of Commons, 24 November 1987, vol. 123, cols 137–139), thus not explicitly stating that there had been no indirect contact with the republican movement via intermediaries below ministerial level. The years that immediately followed these earlier exchanges were, however, as Moloney notes, 'a turbulent and violent period in Northern Ireland, encompassing the smuggling of huge amounts of Libyan arms to Ireland, and an intensification of IRA violence' (Moloney, 2002: 249). Henry Patterson has questioned Moloney's interpretation of the importance of Adams's attempts to engage Tom King. He has pointed out that it had long been a tactic of the IRA to seek dialogue with the British whilst continuing the violence; and this element of continuity has been downplayed. According to Patterson the 'fact that Adams opened up a line of communication with King should not therefore be seen as a radical innovation which kick-starts the peace process' (Patterson, 2011: 98–99). Evidence from the Irish government's actions in that period suggests that Dublin did not see a potential major shift by the IRA at that stage. Whilst Adams was making overtures to the British government, he was also, again via Fr Reid, seeking a dialogue with Charles Haughey's Irish government. Although this led to two instances of direct talks between Haughey's advisor, Martin Mansergh, and republicans in Dundalk, the Irish government stopped the process as there was no commitment from the IRA to bring the violence to an end and so, according to Mansergh, the dialogue 'could not be prudently sustained' (Mansergh in Elliot, 2007: 110). So, whilst these earlier discussions and contacts may have been useful in setting the background to the peace process, it is the contacts and interaction that occur from 1990 onwards that appear to have been more influential. As a result, this work is primarily concerned with the period from the early 1990s.

Dating the peace process is also further complicated by the fact that it did not so much 'begin' as emerge. What became known as the peace process was just one of three initiatives that were in play in the early 1990s. The contacts with republicans that were to form the basis of the peace process were being pursued concurrently with the inter-party talks between the 'constitutional' parties and an intergovernmental dialogue about a possible joint declaration. The embryonic peace process was just one of three shows in town and, as will be discussed, at the time appeared to be less likely to be pursued than the other options.

The state of play at the outset of the peace process

In the period preceding the peace process, the parties to the conflict in Northern Ireland appeared to be polarised. It is worth briefly outlining the apparent views and aspirations of the main players in the conflict at the end of the 1980s/beginning of the 1990s.

The British government

The policy of the British government at the end of the 1980s was, at one level, the same as it had been since the early stages of the Troubles in the 1970s. British policy was driven by a commitment to upholding the principle of consent (the undertaking that the constitutional status of Northern Ireland could not be altered without the agreement of the majority of Northern Ireland's citizens). In addition to this commitment, British policy was shaped by three other, interrelated, aspirations: to try and significantly reduce if not eradicate the violence resulting from the conflict; restore devolved government to Northern Ireland; and prevent the issue from disrupting the wider British political agenda to a problematic degree. Since Northern Ireland's parliament was prorogued in 1972 it had been the stated aspiration of successive British governments to try and restore devolved government to Northern Ireland. The 1970s and 1980s were littered with failed initiatives in this regard. The Sunningdale Agreement of 1973 was the closest that the objective came to being fulfilled, with an Assembly created and a power-sharing Executive sitting for a few months in 1974, but this was to be short-lived, brought down by the Ulster Workers' Council Strike in May of that year (McGrattan and McCann, 2017). In 1982, a plan for 'rolling devolution' to a new Assembly failed as nationalists boycotted the institution and it was finally wound up in 1986. In 1990 the British government had begun a new round of talks aimed at trying to broker agreement between the 'constitutional' parties in Northern Ireland (those that rejected the use of violence) that would enable the restoration of devolved government. These 'Brooke–Mayhew' talks (named after the Secretaries of State that oversaw them) ran between 1990 and 1992 but failed to achieve their objectives.

The failure to achieve sustained devolved government in Northern Ireland by the mid-1980s had led the government to pursue a slightly different tack. In 1985 the government signed the Anglo–Irish Agreement (AIA) with the Irish government. This agreement, which was registered as an international treaty at the United Nations, gave the Irish government a right of consultation over Northern Ireland. It was designed to not derogate from British sovereignty over Northern Ireland but the rationale behind it can be seen as an attempt to address the British objectives in Northern Ireland of reducing violence and the issue's impact on wider British politics. For elements within the British government (notably the Prime Minister) the main purpose was to improve security cooperation with the Irish government against the IRA; for others in the government the desire to reduce international criticism or attention of other states on Britain's government of Northern Ireland was a factor. The objective of creating an agreement as a tool to coerce the unionists to agree to share power in Northern Ireland with nationalists is less persuasive as an explanation for the AIA (Aughey and Gormley-Heenan, 2011).

What is notable about Britain's position towards Northern Ireland by the end of the 1980s (and arguably long before this) is the pragmatism of policymakers. There were serious and fixed limits to this pragmatism, the most important of which was the commitment to the principle of consent, which was spelt out in Article 1 of the AIA. However, as long as consent was upheld, Britain's policy towards Northern Ireland was largely a quest for an initiative that would reduce the violence and the impact of the issue at Westminster. At times, this pragmatism caused annoyance for the unionist community who often doubted the commitment of the British to uphold consent and feared that they would abandon the Union or seek to 'persuade' the unionists to agree to a united Ireland. The failure to make progress towards their desired objectives in Northern Ireland caused frustration in British policymaking circles and periodically this frustration spilled over into the public domain. In an unguarded moment in 1993 the Secretary of State, Sir Patrick Mayhew, told a German interviewer, 'Most people believe we would not want to release Northern Ireland from the United Kingdom. To be entirely honest, we would with pleasure' (O'Clery, 1999: 215). This was more a manifestation of frustration at the lack of progress than an indication of a weakening of commitment to the Union. However, as the frequent repetition of the principle of consent indicated, the commitment to the Union was conditional rather than absolute. It had long been the stated British policy that they would accept a united Ireland. This was again acknowledged in the AIA which asserted that in the event that 'a majority of the people in Northern Ireland clearly wish for and consent to the establishment of a united Ireland' the British and Irish governments would 'introduce and support in the respective Parliaments legislation to give effect to that wish' (AIA, Article 1c). For the British, ideology played a lesser role in policy formation than for many other parties. In general, almost any outcome would have been acceptable to the British state as long as it did not breach the consent principle, served to lessen the violence and, ideally, insulated British politics from the perceived negative influence of the Irish question. But it is important not to extrapolate indifference from pragmatism. Although there was an element of fluidity to British policy this was not insouciance. Consent was a real and serious condition for the British. Whilst by the late 1980s (if not for a considerable period before) there was no widespread emotional and ideological attachment to unionism of the Ulster variety amongst British politicians, there was a sense of commitment and obligation to both uphold consent and seek to defend the people of Northern Ireland. This necessitated trying to end or dissipate the violence they faced from non-state actors, notably the IRA. Again, though, pragmatism was evident here, and, as will be discussed, it was to be a contentious but key aspect of the emerging peace process.

Despite protestations of not talking to terrorists, as noted above, the British had periodically had indirect communication with the IRA, and indeed direct talks in 1972 and 1975. The British did not have a policy of never talking to republicans; the refusal to engage in direct dialogue was based on a belief that the IRA's violence was illegitimate and by its use the republican movement had absented itself from the political process. It was the methods rather than the aims of the IRA that meant the British state would not engage in talks with its representatives. The result of this was that

British policy was based on exclusion. Except for the AIA, the initiatives launched by the British throughout the Troubles were variants on the model of seeking an agreement between the constitutional parties. The aim of the initiatives was to get these parties to agree to a political accommodation that would bring stability to Northern Ireland and further isolate those that advocated violence. In this regard they were unsuccessful. By the late 1980s the British were beginning to contemplate a move to an inclusion-based approach which rested on enticing the IRA to abandon their armed campaign and enter all-party talks. Overtures were beginning to be made by the end of the 1980s aimed at this outcome. On 3 November 1989, Peter Brooke gave an interview in which he recognised 'the fact ... that in terms of the late twentieth-century terrorist, organised as well as the Provisional IRA have become, that it is difficult to envisage a military defeat of such a force' and suggested that the government could enter into talks with them if the violence ended (Patterson, 1997: 218). However, it was far from clear as that decade closed that the IRA would end the violence or that a peace process was likely.

Republicanism

There is an issue of terminological difficulty which needs to be noted here. The label 'republicans' during the Troubles in Northern Ireland was largely used as a shorthand for groups that wanted to achieve a united Ireland and were willing to use or support violence to achieve this end. However, such use has been criticised for 'implying the only republicans in Ireland are those who support or have supported the "armed struggle"' (Swift, 2020). This is a logical position and a case can be made that the term should not be surrendered to armed groups, as to do so is to equate republicanism with support for violence (and implicitly suggest that those who did not support the campaign of groups such as the IRA were not 'real' republicans). However, having noted this, the practice has been common in academic literature on Northern Ireland for many years, and for convenience the practice is adopted in this work. Its use should not be taken as an endorsement of the view that support for a united Ireland necessitated endorsing an armed struggle or that those who rejected the use of violence were not republicans in the literal sense of the word.

The stated objective for the main armed republican group, the Provisional IRA, throughout the Troubles had been to 'militarily' drive the British from Ireland and create a united 32-county Irish Republic. The Provisionals had emerged in 1970 from a split within the Official IRA, based on a belief that the movement was becoming too political and not prioritising military activity. In terms of the IRA's rhetoric, the position was still the same by the end of the 1980s. However, there were signs that the movement was not as dismissive of politics as it had been in the early 1970s. During the 1981 hunger strikes the IRA prisoner, Bobby Sands, and after his death his electoral agent, Owen Carron, were elected to the House of Commons, and two further hunger strikers were elected to the Irish parliament. This caused some reflection within the republican movement over the role of politics. From this emerged what became known as the 'Armalite and ballot box' strategy based on Sinn Féin's Danny Morrison's question during the 1981 debate on whether Sinn Féin should contest elections. 'Who here really believes we can win the war through the ballot box? But will anyone here object if, with the ballot paper in one hand and the Armalite in the other, we take power in Ireland?' (Bew and Gillespie, 1999: 160). In 1986 the party went further and voted to drop their policy of abstention in the South of Ireland, deciding they would take their seats in the Dáil if they were elected. However, care needs to be taken to make sure that not too much is read into these changes. Although by the 1980s the republican movement was not as categorically opposed to participation in electoral politics as it had been in 1970, this was not necessarily a clear signal of a movement towards what would later be the peace process. Evidence does indicate that there was a debate emerging within the republican movement by the late 1980s regarding the viability and productivity of the 'armed struggle'. However, it was far from apparent that the decision had been, or was likely to be, taken that the IRA would end the use of violence and pursue their objectives by exclusively peaceful means. Many within the IRA continued to hold a deep scepticism towards politics and saw the military approach as the only way to achieve their goals. The argument originally made was that the political route was to be used to advance support for the armed struggle, not as an alternative to it (Alonso, 2007: 118). Gerry Adams had stated in 1986 that if Sinn Féin disowned the armed struggle before the British presence in Ireland was removed, 'they won't have me as a member' (Bew, 2007: 537) and as late as 1990 an IRA spokesperson told an interviewer, 'We can state absolutely, on the record, that there will be no ceasefire, no truce, no cessation of violence short of a British withdrawal' (Adams, 2003: 95). There was also a real fear that a move towards exclusively peaceful means and the abandonment of the armed struggle could lead to a significant split within the movement (a perennial concern within republicanism). Therefore, publicly at the end of the 1980s the Provisionals remained committed to pursuing the armed struggle to achieve their goal of a united Ireland.

By the early 1990s, however, there were different noises beginning to emerge from within the republican movement. It began to appear that they were reappraising the utility of violence, in line with the stalemate thesis (discussed below), and whether a move away from the armed campaign might enable them to cooperate with constitutional nationalism (those parties who aspire to a united Ireland but reject the use of violence to achieve it, including the SDLP in Northern Ireland and most political parties in the Irish Republic) and potentially international actors, particularly in the US. It must be stressed that their objective remained a united Ireland, but a re-evaluation of how it might be achieved (and whether the armed campaign was a hindrance towards that objective) appeared to be underway at the outset of the peace process; and indeed, this may well have been the fact that made the process possible. As a result, the objectives for republicans by the early 1990s were to end the violence on relatively favourable terms; increase their influence; advance politically; and make progress towards a united Ireland.

The SDLP

The leader of the SDLP, the main nationalist party, John Hume, had long argued that the armed campaign was counterproductive as it increased division between nationalists and unionists in Northern Ireland. The party had been buoyed by the 1985 AIA. Hume had been closely consulted by the Irish Government during its negotiation. The AIA was in part designed to help the SDLP and to try and stem the apparent rise of Sinn Féin after its decision to begin contesting elections. Sinn Féin had achieved 10.1 per cent of the vote in the 1982 Assembly elections and 13.4 per cent in the 1983 general election but fell back slightly to 11.8 per cent in the May 1985 local elections. The mechanisms created under the AIA to allow the Irish government to act as a spokesperson for northern nationalists were designed, according to the former Irish minister for foreign affairs, Peter Barry, to ensure that the SDLP could 'achieve things for West Belfast through a political circle, that Gerry Adams couldn't achieve through a gun' (O'Kane, 2007: 76–77). The AIA was viewed favourably by the SDLP as it acknowledged a role for the Irish government in Northern Ireland, examined the issue in a wider remit than an internal British problem, and could be seen as denying unionists a veto on political developments in Northern Ireland (Murray and Tonge, 2005: 141–142). This last point was seen as important by Hume. In an *Irish Times* interview in 1988 he argued it was not possible to resolve the differences in Northern Ireland 'if one section has its hands on all of the power or if it has a veto on what a British government is going to do, and I think that we are now on an equal footing' (Millar, 2009: 8). The Agreement could also be read as an indication that the British were neutral on Irish unity, as Hume later argued in his talks with Gerry Adams. However, the reaction of unionists to the AIA meant that the chances of creating a devolved power-sharing government backed by an Irish dimension, which the SDLP favoured, were reduced rather than increased in the short term. Unionist anger at the AIA was genuine, deep and bitter. The association of the SDLP, and Hume in particular, with the project reduced the willingness of unionists to consider sharing power with that party. As a leading UUP MP, John Taylor, explained in 1989, what they perceived as the 'greening' of the SDLP ruled out devolved government. For Taylor, the SDLP had 'become a very green party, with a very rabid anti-security image, anti-UDR, anti-police, wanting a united Ireland or nothing' (Millar, 2009: 61). As the chances of a deal with unionists receded after the AIA, in 1988 Hume and the SDLP began a dialogue with Sinn Féin. Although at that stage the fundamental differences between the two parties on whether Britain was neutral over Northern Ireland and whether the armed struggle was necessary or counter-productive, could not be resolved, the dialogue was important. McLoughlin has argued that the talks led Hume to believe that 'the republican movement was in a state of political transition' and required greater evidence that the British were neutral on Northern Ireland (McLoughlin, 2010: 146). Hume increasingly became focused on seeking to provide republicans with this evidence and to persuade them into the political process rather than working to reach an agreement with unionists that excluded them. The exact series of events remains slightly unclear. The question of whether Hume's dialogue with Adams was primarily due to the requests made by Fr Alec Reid for him to talk to Adams; a result of his belief that the AIA had indeed transformed the situation in Northern Ireland; a result of unionists' unwillingness to enter into dialogue with his party; or a combination of such factors is still open to debate. What is apparent is that by the end of the 1980s the SDLP was encouraged by the AIA, viewed the prospect of power-sharing with unionists as remote and was beginning to believe that the republican movement might be amenable to altering its approach. As a result, their objectives as the peace process emerged were to persuade the IRA to end their violence, embark on progress that would lead to all-party talks and advance nationalism's interests.

Unionists

The AIA cast a long shadow over unionist politics post-1985. Unionists viewed the AIA as, at best, granting a foreign government an unacceptable level of influence in the internal affairs of the United Kingdom, and at worst, part of a plan to oust Northern Ireland from the UK and into a united Ireland. The clearly genuine negative reaction, and highly visible rejection of the AIA by unionists in Northern Ireland, caused consternation and surprise in sections of the British government. The decision by the two main unionist parties to effectively withdraw from political life in an attempt to force the abandonment of the Agreement, meant that progress towards a deal that would enable power to be devolved back to Northern Ireland was impossible. The problem that unionists faced, however, by the late 1980s was that their attempts to bring down the AIA had failed, and concern was beginning to grow amongst sections of the unionist leadership that their hard-line position was isolating them without advancing their cause. In 1987 a review of the campaign against the AIA, undertaken by three prominent unionist politicians, led to the report *An End to Drift* which was submitted to the UUP and DUP leadership. The report argued that 'protest can be no substitute for politics' and advocated a dialogue with the British government towards securing devolved government back to Northern Ireland. The report was at pains to stress that it was not advocating accepting the AIA and insisted that an alternative to it must be achieved. For the authors, devolved government was essential to protect unionist interests and if this was not possible as part of the United Kingdom then independence might need to be considered (*The Task Force Report. An End to Drift*, Conflict Archive on the Internet (CAIN)). Whilst the report was contentious (the failure of the two leaders to respond to it led to the departure of one of its authors, Frank Millar, from unionist politics), it was an indication that there was a growing debate within Unionism as to how to make progress after the AIA. This reflection did not, at that stage, incline the main unionist parties to seek to share power with the SDLP whilst the AIA existed. The unionist leaders met the NISS in late 1987 but the boycott of dealing with Northern Ireland Office (NIO) ministers by unionists would continue until 1990. Whilst the Thatcher government was disappointed with aspects of the Agreement (Thatcher, 1993: 410–415) the government was not willing to abandon the accord.

The unionist parties did take part in the Brooke–Mayhew talks with other constitutional parties and the two governments from 1990 but their position in the early 1990s remained one of mistrust. This mistrust was of most of the other parties to the conflict: the two governments and the nationalist SDLP. Unionists saw themselves as having been betrayed in 1985 by their government, facing a Republic of Ireland which they saw as having achieved an unacceptable institutionalised say over Northern Ireland, an SDLP seeking to politically further undermine the Union and a republican movement seeking to destroy it by violence. The fear of further marginalisation and the failure of the anti-AIA campaign had led the unionists to re-engage in the political life of Northern Ireland and, as Paul Bew has argued, during the Brooke–Mayhew talks unionists were 'in effect, conceding in principle both power-sharing and an Irish dimension' (Bew, 2007: 539). This was thought to be with the constitutional SDLP, and the Irish dimension unionists proposed was less formalised and extensive than that which Dublin had secured in 1985. However, the peace process that emerged was to alter the situation significantly. As the outline of the peace process started to become apparent, unionists were faced with a significant challenge. Their primary objective was to protect the Union and, given the impact that the AIA had had on them, to minimise Dublin's input into Northern Ireland affairs. But they also had to decide how to deal with the emerging role of Sinn Féin in the process. On this issue they differed; the UUP chose to participate in the peace process, although not to engage directly with Sinn Féin, in the hope that devolved government could be achieved which would see them primarily share power with the SDLP. As will be seen, their objective towards Sinn Féin was to minimise their role and force them to progress away from the armed struggle, whereas for the DUP the goal was to exclude Sinn Féin from government.

Loyalists

Like 'republican', the term 'loyalist' is problematic. It is most commonly used to denote the variant of Unionism that was willing to use, or support the use of, violence to maintain the Union with Britain. This use of the term is, however, contentious. There are those who would argue that such a depiction is too narrow and fails to appreciate the strand of 'transformative loyalism' whose focus is more progressive and whose primary loyalty is to the Protestant working class (Shirlow, 2012: 13–15). Beyond this, the narrow association of loyalism with support for an armed campaign to protect the Union can be seen as problematic in wider terms. Peter Taylor, for example, argued in his study of loyalism that Ian Paisley was the 'one dominant loyalist figure who runs through the entire history of the current conflict' (Taylor, 1999: 29). Yet Paisley was, of course, the leader of the DUP, a political party that was not directly associated with loyalist paramilitarism. However, most studies of loyalism (including Taylor's) in relation to the Troubles period have focused upon the groups and individuals associated with loyalist paramilitarism. The consideration of loyalism in this book, in a similar fashion to the consideration of the republican movement, is on loyalism's use and support for violence and its attempts to move away from its own armed struggle to a more political role.

Loyalists shared the anger of the wider unionist community with the AIA and their fear that the British were considering a move towards disengagement from Northern Ireland (an enduring concern). This fear was instrumental in the increasing levels of loyalist violence in the late 1980s and early 1990s. Loyalist groups had been undermined to an extent by the supergrass system of the early 1980s which led to a significant number of key figures being imprisoned, and their levels of killing had decreased notably from the mid to late 1970s levels. But the anger that the AIA had wrought, and the emergence of new leaders and activists, saw a marked increase by the late 1980s. These developments were also assisted by new arms that were procured by the main loyalist paramilitary groups from Lebanon in 1987 (Taylor, 1999: 189–192). By 1993, loyalists were killing more people than republicans (McKittrick et al., 1999: 1476). The relationship between loyalist paramilitary leaders and mainstream unionist politicians had deteriorated in the run-up to the peace process. In the immediate aftermath of the AIA, loyalist groups and their leaders had cooperated with the politicians of both the UUP and the DUP in a concerted effort to force the British government to abandon the accord. There was a precedent for this, given the success of similar cooperation in bringing down the 1974 Sunningdale Agreement. Relations between loyalist paramilitaries and unionist politicians came under great strain, however, as the AIA proved to be more resilient than Sunningdale (not least because, unlike the power-sharing devolved government that underpinned Sunningdale, the AIA was an intergovernmental accord and was not dependent upon unionist participation to survive). (For a discussion of the relationship between the AIA and the peace process see Aughey and Gormley-Heenan (2011).) Loyalist leaders felt they had been used by unionist politicians, who had made speeches, such as Paisley's claim at an Ulster Clubs rally in June 1986 that 'we are on the verge of civil war … We are asking people to be ready for the worst and I will lead them' (Taylor, 1999: 187). However, when violence occurred or, as in 1987, evidence emerged of loyalists arming themselves, unionist politicians criticised them and distanced themselves from such groups. This led to an increasing scepticism of unionist politics by loyalists, who believed that such leaders simply saw loyalists as 'cannon fodder' (Ulster Defence Association (UDA)'s Jackie McDonald, Liddle Hart Centre for Military Archives (LHCMA)) and that loyalists should not allow themselves to be 'used' again by mainstream political leaders (David Ervine, LHMCA).

The challenge for loyalists, then, was how to respond to what they saw as an increasingly precarious situation for the Union. By the mid-1980s they believed they were at risk of being betrayed by the British government, which had given the Republic of Ireland an institutionalised right of consultation over the affairs of Northern Ireland; they had little faith in their elected (unionist) politicians and faced the continuing threat from republicans determined to destroy the Union by violence. The response of loyalism took several, somewhat contradictory, forms which reflected both the diverse challenges they believed they faced as well as the internal divisions within loyalism. The belief that the Union was at risk as a result of the AIA, and the anger that the accord had generated, led to an influx of new recruits to loyalist paramilitary groups (McDonald, LHCMA) and an increase in the violence perpetuated by the groups. Some of this was targeted at republicans but much was simply sectarian attacks on random Catholics. In addition to this violence, however, there was an increasing belief within both the UDA and the Ulster Volunteer Force (UVF) that loyalism needed its own political voice and political agenda. To this end, elements within both groups began to explore what the political strategy of loyalism should be. The Ulster Political Research Group, which was closely linked to the UDA, published *Common Sense* in 1987. The document was seen as comparatively progressive, with its call for 'co-determination' between Catholics and Protestants in Northern Ireland, a written constitution, proportionality of seats on a new executive and committees in a devolved assembly, a bill of rights and a written constitution (*Common Sense. Northern Ireland – An Agreed Process*, CAIN). At the same time, key people within the Progressive Unionist Party (PUP), the political party associated with the other main loyalist paramilitary group, the UVF, were debating the need for a political strategy in addition to the paramilitary one. People such as Gusty Spence and David Ervine sat on the UVF's 'Kitchen Cabinet' and were tasked with providing the 'political analysis' of the situation for the UVF (Ervine, LHCMA; Edwards, 2017). The relationship between the military and political agendas that were in play within loyalism was far from settled and it is certainly not the case that all within loyalism saw a need for increasing political engagement or questioning their variant of the 'armed struggle'. The situation in the post-AIA years meant that there was an increasing belief that violence was both necessary and justified. The procurement of arms by loyalists was portrayed as a defensive response to the activities of the IRA. As Jackie McDonald argued, 'we felt under threat and you couldn't very well defend your area with rolled up copies of *Common Sense*' (McDonald, LHCMA). This tension between the increasing use of violence by loyalist paramilitaries and the less obvious political debate taking place amongst (some) loyalists would bedevil loyalism for many years but the emerging political debate was to ensure that loyalism played an important (and perhaps underappreciated) role in the peace process that subsequently emerged.

At the outset of the peace process, loyalist objectives were to seek to defend the Union but also to do so not just by the use of violence but by developing a political analysis and voice which better represented what they felt was the (largely working-class urban) constituency, a constituency they believed was poorly represented and ill-served by traditional unionist parties.

The Irish government

The Irish government's position by the late 1980s was also highly influenced by the AIA. Dublin saw the institutionalised consultative role that it had secured in 1985 as significant and was not willing to give up this advance lightly. Although unionists saw the role of Dublin as predatory – pushing constantly for advances towards unification and seeking to use the AIA to advance these objectives – the reality was a little different. Although rhetorically (and, given Articles 2 and 3, constitutionally) the South was committed to reunification, practically their priorities were somewhat different. In some regards the position of the South mirrored certain aspects of the British government's attitude to Northern Ireland. For Dublin, a key concern was to reduce the violence in Northern Ireland, remove its ability to disturb the political and social life in the South (as it had done during the 1981 hunger strikes) and assist constitutional nationalism in its struggle with violent republicanism for the position of spokesperson for northern nationalists. This should not be overstated; the desire for unity was real within the South but it had become highly conditional. For a long period, the primary concerns of political leaders in the South had been the establishment and advancement of the Irish Free State/Republic. This had led to an attitude in the South that the former Fine Gael leader and Taoiseach, Garret FitzGerald, described in 1989 as 'Augustinian'.

> Most people in the Republic prefer to distance themselves from Northern Ireland. Apart from times of real crisis people want to switch off, forget about it, get on with their own affairs and hope it will go away. This is totally disguised by the rhetoric of anti-partition, which suggests that people down here are deeply concerned. The aspiration to unity exists everywhere at a certain level, but it has changed a great deal. It's an Augustinian situation – unite us, O Lord, but not yet. (*Independent*, 7 June 1989)

This was not indifference to the plight of Northern Ireland but a question of priorities. For the South, the North was a concern, and during times of heightened tension and violence this concern had a sense of urgency. The issue itself, though, had little electoral impact in Southern polls and Southern politicians had long used the rhetoric of unity to mask the reality of policies that were designed to reduce the ability of the issue to undermine stability and politics in the South. There was an apparent difference between the two main political actors in Irish politics in the 1980s, Garret FitzGerald and the leader of the largest party, Fianna Fáil's Charles Haughey. Whilst in opposition Haughey had rejected the AIA on the grounds that it recognised British sovereignty over Northern Ireland and suggested he would seek its renegotiation once returned to power. When he became Taoiseach in 1987, however, there was little change in the Irish government's approach to Northern Ireland. Haughey's government reiterated their commitment to an Irish dimension in any 'settlement' of the Northern Ireland conflict. Whilst the Irish position was that they would contemplate the replacement of the AIA, the government informed the opening session of the Mayhew round of talks in July 1992 (by which time Haughey had been succeeded as Fianna Fáil leader and Taoiseach by Albert Reynolds) that the AIA was 'a formal acceptance that the Irish Government have both a concern and a role in relation to Northern Ireland. We would expect that any broader agreement, which might be reached, would incorporate these elements in full measure' (Opening Statement on behalf of the Irish Government, Strand Two, Brooke–Mayhew talks, 6 July 1992).

The Haughey government, along with John Hume, had been contacted by Fr Alec Reid in 1987 which led to the Mansergh–Sinn Féin meetings of 1988. Mansergh argues that ideologically, given its republican origins, Fianna Fáil was actually closer to Sinn Féin than the SDLP was. He also argues that Haughey's government was not as convinced of the neutrality of the British government as the SDLP were, stating that Fianna Fáil were 'decidedly sceptical' of the political neutrality of the British government towards Northern Ireland. At the talks, Mansergh made the case to Sinn Féin that 'we considered that violence was counterproductive and that it actually weakened and divided the nationalists in the North'. According to Mansergh, at that time there were 'no immediate proposals by the republican leadership to renounce violence' and so 'it wasn't obvious that [the dialogue] was going to lead anywhere immediately' and given the continuing violence in 1988 Fianna Fáil decided 'it wouldn't have been responsible to continue the dialogue', although they kept a 'line of communication' open through Fr Reid (Mansergh, LHCMA). The position of the Irish government in the late 1980s/early 1990s was that the AIA was to be protected, and if replaced it must contain a strong Irish dimension, reduce the violence in Northern Ireland, improve the plight of nationalists living there and, in the words of FitzGerald, get them to 'settle down in a Northern Ireland which will for an indefinite future be part of the UK' (AIA Witness Seminar, 1997) and reduce its impact on the politics of the South.

Explaining the emergence of the peace process

Given the apparently inauspicious circumstances noted above, with division between the parties in Northern Ireland, unionist disenchantment with the British government and continuing violence by republican and loyalist paramilitaries, why did the peace process emerge in the early 1990s? As noted, the key characteristic of the peace process was the attempt, and subsequent success, in getting the IRA to end their violence and enter a political process with the other parties to the conflict. But the key issue is why did the IRA begin to move in this direction in the early 1990s and why did the two governments, along with the SDLP and (to an extent) the US government believe this was a possibility at this time and begin to strive for the outcome? The literature on the peace process highlights differing factors to explain the changes undertaken by the republican movement in this period (discussed at the end of this chapter). But it was the emerging reconsideration over tactics, if not objectives, within the republican movement that was the key to the peace process.

The approach of the British and Irish governments altered in the early 1990s from one of exclusion to one of inclusion. The peace process marked a move by the governments who sought to entice those associated with violence (primarily the IRA) to abandon the armed struggle and enter the political process. Some accounts suggest that this was not actually a notable departure on the grounds that it had always been Britain's position that Sinn Féin were entitled to join the political process if the IRA ended their violence (Neumann, 2003: 187; Clancy, 2010: 58). Whilst strictly speaking this is correct, it overlooks the efforts that the two governments made in the peace process period to actively encourage this change in policy by the republican movement. It was the concerted action and focus by London and Dublin in achieving this outcome, and the overtures they made to republicans, that was the contrast from the earlier period and marked a significant departure from exclusion to inclusion. The sporadic exchanges between the government and Sinn Féin via the backchannel from 1990 played a role in this. The channel for communication between the British government and Sinn Féin via a three-person 'link' based in Derry had existed since the 1970s but had, according to McGuinness, 'been dormant until mid-1990' (Sinn Féin, 1993: 9). The official reason for its reactivation had been the retirement of the British end of the link, Michael Oatley, in that year and the desire by the British to introduce his replacement to the republican movement. What is interesting about this early period of the reactivation of the backchannel is that it was clearly the British who were the more proactive in using the channel to send messages to Sinn Féin. Hennessey notes that in the period up until February 1991 'the British government courted the republicans' (Hennessey, 2000: 70).

This reactivation by the British government of the backchannel was one of a series of dialogues with republicans (discussed in more depth in the next chapter). In addition to the backchannel communications, Gerry Adams's dialogue with John Hume had continued after the 1988 Sinn Féin–SDLP talks ended, and contacts between the Dublin government and republicans (via Fr Alec Reid) had also endured after the 1988 Sinn Féin–Fianna Fáil talks officially concluded. There was something of a Whitehall farce element about these interactions as in many cases the participants were unaware that others were also in dialogue with Sinn Féin and recriminations and criticisms occurred when links were subsequently revealed. Hume was consulting with the Irish government and informing them of his ongoing discussion with Adams. In addition, indirect contact between Sinn Féin and the Irish government continued via Fr Reid, who Adams claims 'was travelling to and fro between me and the Irish government' (Adams, 2003: 110). These indirect contacts with the Irish government became direct contacts once more after the new Taoiseach, Albert Reynolds, approved secret meetings between Martin Mansergh and Martin McGuinness in October 1992, which Hume was unaware of (Reynolds, 2010: 250). The discussions between Sinn Féin and both the Irish government and the SDLP centred on several issues: the role of the British government, the issue of self-determination, the related issue of the necessity of unionist consent and the possibility of a common approach between 'nationalist Ireland' in relation to the issue of Northern Ireland. It was on these issues that dividing lines between the republican movement on one side, and the Irish government and the SDLP on the other, were evident.

Pan-nationalism?

The talks that Sinn Féin were holding (separately) with the Irish government and the SDLP were designed to try and find common ground between the variants of Irish nationalism that the three sides represented and enable the combined forces of Irish nationalism to put pressure on the British and unionists. This was a constant theme of Sinn Féin's pitches to the SDLP and Dublin in the period. During the exchange of documents with the SDLP in the 1988 talks, Sinn Féin made their case for a pan-nationalist approach. For Sinn Féin the key was to secure a declaration from the British government to withdraw and an undertaking from them to persuade the unionists of the necessity of a united Ireland. This, Sinn Féin argued, would be best achieved by a united approach from nationalists:

> As a step towards such a strategy ... we propose that Sinn Féin and the SDLP jointly issue a call to the Dublin and London governments for them to consult together to seek agreement on the policy objective of Irish reunification. Having agreed this, both governments would issue a public statement outlining the steps they intend taking to bring about a peaceful and orderly British political and military withdrawal from Ireland within a specified period.
> The adoption of such a position by Sinn Féin, the SDLP and Dublin government would advance the situation, concentrate everyone's mind, not least the unionists, and put the responsibility where it belongs – with the British government. (Sinn Féin, 1988: 15)

This is one of the earlier statements of what became known as a 'pan-nationalist' approach. Republicans were making similar points in their internal debates in 1994. The TUAS document (originally believed to stand for 'Totally Unarmed Strategy' but later it was claimed that the acronym stood for 'Tactical Use of Armed Struggle') was circulating within republican circles in 1994 and was revealed by the *Sunday Independent* in April 1995. The document stressed the need for concerted action with other actors to advance republicans' (unchanged) goals of 'a united 32-county democratic socialist Republic'. The problem was that 'republicans at this time and on their own do not have the strength to achieve the end goal. The struggle needs strengthening most obviously from other nationalist constituencies led by SDLP, Dublin government and the emerging Irish-American lobby, with additional support from other parties in the EU rowing in behind and accelerating the momentum created.' The republican leadership argued that factors were more conducive to such cooperation than had been the case in the past. 'It is the first time in 25 years that all the major Irish nationalist parties are rowing in roughly the same direction. These combined circumstances are unlikely to gel again in the foreseeable future' (TUAS document, CAIN).

Despite the desire of republicans to create a united nationalist movement there were major differences between the three main branches of Irish nationalism as to both the conditions and purposes of any increased cooperation. Throughout the early stages of what became the peace process, these divisions remained apparent. It was Sinn Féin's objective to seek greater cooperation with the SDLP and the Irish government to pressurise the British into making their declaration to withdraw and become persuaders for Irish unity. The SDLP suggested that they were amenable to a united approach to the issue of resolving the conflict and advocated that the Irish government should invite all Northern Ireland's parties (including the unionists) to a conference 'to try to reach agreement on the exercise of self-determination in Ireland and on how the people of our diverse traditions can live together in peace, harmony and agreement'. However, it 'would be understood that if this conference were to happen that the IRA would have ceased its campaign' (Sinn Féin, 1988: 12). The SDLP were not, however, merely buying into Sinn Féin's agenda. The parties had fundamental differences over many aspects. The SDLP argued strongly that the IRA's violence was counterproductive as it increased the mistrust between unionists and nationalists in Northern Ireland. The SDLP were also fundamentally opposed to Britain making a declaration of intent to withdraw, which they argued would create a power vacuum that would lead to increased inter-communal violence in Northern Ireland and be 'likely to ensure that the peace and unity of Ireland would never come' (Sinn Féin, 1988: 8). The issue of the necessity for unionists to agree to a united Ireland also divided the SDLP and Sinn Féin. Republicans argued that it was desirable to have unionist agreement for unity but not a prerequisite; to insist that unionists needed to agree before unity could be achieved was to give them a veto that was unjustified in the face of the majority of people in Ireland favouring unity. The SDLP argued that 'the unionists have a natural veto since they live on this island and since their agreement is essential if unity is to be achieved' but they shared the objective of persuading the British government to favour unity. Britain could then use 'all its influence and resources to persuade the unionist people that their best interest lies in a new Ireland which accommodates their interests to their satisfaction, and which has a new relationship with Britain' (Sinn Féin, 1988: 16).

To an extent, the Irish government also favoured creating conditions that would allow greater cooperation with Sinn Féin. The secret talks between Mansergh and Sinn Féin in 1988 under Haughey and the authorisation by Haughey's successor, Albert Reynolds, for further direct talks in 1992 were early signs of a willingness to engage with republicans. Whilst Martin Mansergh may have argued that ideologically Fianna Fáil were closer to Sinn Féin than the SDLP were, they too had significant differences with Sinn Féin over the use of violence. When he had met with Sinn Féin in 1988 Mansergh had made the case to Sinn Féin that, historically, 'when there was a political consensus between nationalists, the nationalist position was at its strongest'. However, what united Dublin and the SDLP was the belief that the use of violence was counterproductive and divisive. The term 'pan-nationalist front' was also seen as problematic as 'front' had an 'aggressive connotation'. The Irish government were seeking to 'establish a democratic nationalist consensus from which violence would be excluded' (Mansergh, LHCMA).

Although there was some substance behind the arguments around a 'pan-nationalist front', the term suggests an unrealistic level of cohesion between the constituent parts of nationalism in Ireland in the run-up to the 1994 ceasefire. The issue of the use of violence was a factor that divided republicans from the SDLP, the Irish government and indeed important elements of the Irish-American lobby that Sinn Féin sought cooperation with. These divisions were factors in encouraging consideration of an exclusively political approach within republicanism in Northern Ireland. The wariness that constitutional nationalists felt towards republicans in the early 1990s, and the differences that existed between them, meant that on its own the desire to create a pan-nationalist front was not a persuasive explanation for the emergence of the peace process. Although Catherine O'Donnell makes an interesting case regarding the emergence of pan-nationalism, her claim that the peace process 'was spawned from within nationalism and the British government was only involved at a point which the participants of the pan-nationalist alliance deemed necessary' is imparting too much importance and coherence to the quest for cooperation between republicans, the SDLP and the Irish government (O'Donnell, 2007: 102).

Stalemate

The explanation for the emergence of the peace process in the early 1990s and the willingness of the IRA to consider a non-violent path that has been most influential is that associated with the stalemate thesis. The idea of stalemate as a motivator for conflict resolution has been influential in the theoretical literature and is primarily associated with Zartman. According to Zartman, conflicts become 'ripe' for resolution when a mutually hurting stalemate is reached. The key is 'when the parties find themselves locked in a conflict from which they cannot escalate to victory and this deadlock is painful to both of them (although not necessarily in equal degrees or for the same reasons), they seek a way out' (Zartman, 2000: 228). Whilst elements of Zartman's theory are open to question, notably his claims that it has a predictive capacity (O'Kane, 2006), the idea that the IRA was inclined towards considering a non-violent path due to the realisation that they could not achieve their objectives via the armed struggle is persuasive. Evidence exists that there were voices being raised within the republican movement in this period questioning the efficacy of the armed struggle. Sinn Féin's former director of publicity, Danny Morrison, recorded in his prison diary in February 1990, 'There are young lads in here, still in their teens, who are facing life sentences; they will *serve* life sentences unless our political problems are resolved. The British government is in the luxurious position of sitting the whole thing out; the cost to them appears tolerable' (Morrison, 1999: 31). This suggests that he did not believe that the British were unduly troubled by the continuing armed campaign. In November 1991 Morrison argued in a letter to Adams that, 'I think we can fight on forever and can't be defeated. But, of course, that isn't the same as winning or showing something for all our sacrifices' (Morrison, 1999: 241). Such sentiments are fully in line with the stalemate thesis. Publicly in 1990 the IRA were arguing 'we can state absolutely, on the record, that there will be no ceasefire, no truce, no cessation of violence short of a British withdrawal', though they did state that they would engage in dialogue with the British if it was genuinely sought by the government (*Independent*, 31 November 1993), but privately debate was occurring.

The stalemate thesis raises certain questions, however, and has been criticised by some (Bew et al., 2009; Edwards, 2011; Tonge et al., 2011). An obvious question is why did the IRA perceive themselves in a stalemate and act to bring the armed struggle to an end in the early 1990s and not before? Arguably it had been apparent for some time that the IRA would not be able to force the British from Ireland using violence. The British state had demon-strated its ability to withstand the IRA's violence throughout the Troubles. The IRA was unable to deliver its proposed escalation of violence in the late 1980s – its equivalent of the Tet offensive (Moloney, 2002: 20) – and there seemed to have long been an awareness by some in the higher echelons of the movement that there was little progress being made. In 1978 when an IRA spokesperson was asked by an Irish magazine if the violence had been worth the cost, he replied, 'Of course not ... Virtually nothing has been achieved' (Smith, 1997: 225). This begs the question why stalemate took so long to result in a peace process. There are several reasons for this. First, as the IRA spokesperson went on to explain in 1978, 'We can't give up now and admit that men and women were sent to their graves, died for nothing' (Smith, 1997: 225). To call off the campaign with nothing to show for it would be an admission of defeat and risk splitting the movement. Rogelio Alonso's study of the IRA makes a powerful case against the decision of the IRA to continue with its campaign after it accepted that it was unlikely to succeed. Alonso argues that morally this was unacceptable. He puts forward a strong argument that once it is decided that you are not going to succeed using violence, continuing the use of violence results in people dying for a better negotiating position. For Alonso this is immoral, 'the IRA lacked this expectation of success many years before it finally decided to end its campaign and, therefore, applying the republican movement's own logic the only conclusion that can be reached is that the violence was immoral'. Based on extensive interviews with IRA volunteers, Alonso argues that the early 1980s were the key period wherein there was a growing awareness amongst some in the leadership that they were fighting for a victory 'which they knew they would never achieve' (Alonso, 2006: 144). Alonso is highly critical of Adams and McGuinness, who he believes had accepted by 1988 that the armed struggle would not succeed; once they realised this, 'the logical con-sequence would have been to stop the violence or to leave the IRA if the group failed to take such a decision' (Alonso, 2006: 149). Alonso's argu-ment of the immorality of continuing a campaign that you believe will not succeed is philosophically persuasive, but clearly other issues beyond moral-ity weighed more heavily in republican calculations. The IRA was not a completely unified movement; although there may have been an increasing awareness amongst (sections of) the leadership that the violence was unlikely to secure their goals this did not, for them, equate with defeat (discussed below). As a result, pragmatism and realpolitik did indeed lead them to attempt to do what Alonso criticises them for: to extract as strong a position as possible in return for the ending of violence. As Danny Morrison put it, 'it was now time to cash in the chips of the "armed struggle"' (Edwards, 2011: 234). Morally, on an individual basis, the decisions of particular leaders, who doubted the efficacy of the armed struggle but continued to support/acquiesce to its continuance, can be questioned. However, looking at the wider picture, would the decision of individual leaders to distance themselves from the IRA once they had come to this conclusion have resulted in the end of the IRA's campaign sooner and led to a reduced overall death toll in Northern Ireland? Or would the departure of the 'politicos' on such terms merely have resulted in the continuance of the armed campaign for an even longer period, led by the more hard-line ideologues and resulted in a larger death toll in Northern Ireland, preventing or seriously delaying the emergence of a peace process? At another reading, for republicans such as McGuinness and Adams, the peace process was actually an attempt to stop the violence, as Alonso advocates they should have done, but on terms that would provide some justification for past actions. Rather than simply walk away with nothing to 'show' for a quarter of a century of armed struggle they sought a deal that would allow them to claim that advances had been achieved by their campaign. This is clear from the narrative that republicans offer to explain the peace process and to argue that the ceasefire was the result of new opportunities. In this narrative the armed struggle was not without achievement. The achievements that are claimed for the armed struggle are clearly not in line with what the IRA had long claimed was their objective: to secure British withdrawal and create a 32-county socialist Republic in Ireland. What is claimed now is that the campaign was instrumental in bringing about advances for the nationalist population in Northern Ireland. The veteran IRA man, Tommy McKearney, argued that

> Insurrectionary republicanism had advanced the political agenda to a stage that parliamentary practice failed to match. Northern Catholics now have opportunities to participate in local political, social and economic life to an extent that earlier generations could only have dreamt of. Republicans may have failed to break the Union but they certainly smashed the one-party state of James Craig, Basil Brooke and the Ulster Workers Council. (McKearney, 2011: 206)

This statement is open to challenge for its claims that the civil rights advances in Northern Ireland were the result of the IRA's violence, a claim that other non-violent components of the civil rights movement and the SDLP would, with a great deal of justification, refute. Similarly, the argument that it was the violence of the IRA that brought down Stormont is highly questionable. But that aside, the narrative argues that the tactics have changed but not the objectives. The argument is that the armed struggle *was* necessary in the past but by the early 1990s its continued use was counterproductive, due to the stalemate. The advances that the IRA had secured meant that the situation had altered to the extent that the objective of a united Ireland could be better pursued via politics rather than the military campaign that was *no longer* necessary.

The stalemate thesis is an important explanation of the situation that the IRA, and the British government, found themselves in at the turn of the 1990s. In an interview in 1989 Peter Brooke accepted that it 'was difficult to envisage a military defeat' of the IRA (Taylor, 1998: 316) and, as noted above, the IRA were increasingly aware that they could not bomb the British from Northern Ireland. What was different in the early 1990s was not necessarily the existence of the stalemate, which had arguably been evident for some time, but that the parties to the conflict took action to break out of the stalemate and create a new path. This may have been because there was an increasing appreciation of the stalemate, or of the possibilities that alternatives existed/could be created via a peace process, what Zartman terms the existence of mutually enticing opportunities. The most likely explanation for the decision for the IRA to end their violence and embark on a peace process is that the 'military' situation (stalemate) had closed the opportunity of 'victory'. There was an emerging belief that conditions were increasingly favourable for them to end the armed struggle in terms that could be presented as honourable and they could claim were adjustments of tactics rather than objectives.

Defeat theory

Although the stalemate thesis as an explanation for the ending of the IRA's armed campaign has been the most influential, in recent years a debate has emerged regarding whether, rather than being in a stalemate situation, the IRA had effectively been defeated by the British by the early 1990s. Such a conclusion would have significant implications for the stalemate thesis. David McKittrick wrote at the time of the IRA ceasefire in 1994,

> What is clear is that this is not an IRA surrender. The organisation has the guns, the expertise and the recruits to go on killing: it has not been militarily defeated. Rather, it has allowed itself to be persuaded that in the circumstances of today it stands a better chance of furthering its aims through politics rather than through violence. These are violent people, but they are also proud people, with high self-esteem, who over decades have had much violence inflicted on them. What has led them to this point is not the activities of the Army, the SAS, the RUC or the intelligence agencies: it is a sense that a real alternative to terrorism is now on offer. (*Independent*, 1 September 1994)

This is the argument that underpins the stalemate thesis: the IRA had the capacity to continue the war but decided to take the political route to further its aims. However, some now question this view and argue that the situation the IRA found itself in by 1994 was far more precarious than comments such as McKittrick's above would suggest. The most extreme variant of the thesis is to be found in William Matchett's 2016 book, *Secret Victory: The Intelligence War that Beat the IRA*. Matchett suggests that it was possible to have completely defeated the IRA, quoting former cabinet minister Norman Tebbit, who was seriously injured in the IRA's bombing of the Grand Hotel during the Conservative Party's 1984 conference in Brighton. Tebbit argued that Airey Neave, who was to have been NISS under Margaret Thatcher but was killed by the Irish National Liberation Army (INLA) before the 1979 election, had intended to achieve 'the total and complete military defeat of the IRA' but the project failed as 'sadly Major and Blair fell for the IRA's "ceasefire" gambit to save the skins of their leaders'. For Matchett this complete military defeat, 'was not the annihilation of the IRA but winning the intelligence war plus forcing the IRA to say sorry and what they did was wrong' (Matchett, 2016: 258). Even leaving aside that Thatcher had over a decade to achieve what apparently Neave would have done (and the fact that it was Thatcher that authorised the reopening of the backchannel between the British and the republican leadership that was a key component of the peace process) Matchett's account is not convincing. There is little to suggest that his variant of 'complete military defeat' was achievable. He also seems to see the IRA's influence as being incredibly widespread, asking 'Did the IRA inspire 9/11?' (Matchett, 2016: 253). As Ed Moloney has argued, 'His analysis, as deficient in its way as the "Blair–Ahern brought the Provos to peace" theory of the peace process, entirely leaves out of consideration the reality that the terrorism which he describes had a political foundation and that it could not be brought to an end solely or even mostly by security methods' (Moloney, 2017).

A more nuanced variant of the thesis is offered by Bew et al. who have argued that the stalemate thesis needs to be re-examined as it takes too little account of 'the impact of hard power' on the IRA. They argue that the failure to pay adequate attention to the impact that the use of informers by the British and 'the highly effective unofficial war against the republican movement that was being carried out by the intelligence services' could lead to a tendency 'to see the 1990s peace process in Northern Ireland as something entirely removed from the war that preceded it' (Bew et al., 2009: 246–247). The authors are clearly correct when they argue that the role of factors beyond dialogue need to be considered if we are to understand what happened in Northern Ireland. They engaged in debate with Paul Dixon on the issue of defeat versus stalemate, claiming they did not argue that the IRA were defeated and that Dixon claims they have been contradictory on this point and have drawn lessons for Afghanistan and Iraq (Bew and Frampton, 2012). The reason why this debate is important is because it has potential implications for what Northern Ireland may demonstrate about how states should deal with terrorism.

The debate regarding whether the IRA were defeated is somewhat hindered by the competing evidence available and problems over what 'form' the defeat took (and when it was apparent). The British army's own review of the Northern Ireland conflict concludes

> It should be recognised that the Army did not 'win' in any recognisable way; rather it achieved its desired end-state, which allowed a political process to be established without unacceptable levels of intimidation. Security force operations suppressed the level of violence to a level which the population could live with, and with which the RUC [Royal Ulster Constabulary] and later the PSNI [Police Service of Northern Ireland] could cope. The violence was reduced to an extent which made it clear to the PIRA that they would not win through violence. This is a major achievement, and one with which the security forces from all three Services, with the Army in the lead, should be entirely satisfied. (Ministry of Defence, 2007, para 855)

There is, of course, ambiguity in this statement and discussion could be had on the differences between 'winning' and achieving your 'desired end-state', but the point does suggest that the army did not see itself as having 'defeated' the IRA. The observation that the IRA were made to realise that they would not win using violence is useful but can, again, be interpreted several ways and is not incompatible with the stalemate thesis. The army's own view of their role echoes the observation of Peter Brooke that the army and Royal Ulster Constabulary (RUC) were 'holding the ring' whilst the search for a political solution was conducted (Brooke, LHCMA).

Much of the discussion, and differences, over whether the IRA were defeated ultimately come down to how 'defeat' is defined. If by defeat one means a situation where the IRA were effectively destroyed as a fighting force (in a similar fashion to the fate of the Tamil Tigers in Sri Lanka in 2009) then clearly such a charge is not supportable. The IRA had the capacity to continue an armed campaign and sought to use violence to pressurise the British and send a message that they were not negotiating from a position of weakness in the run-up to the 1994 ceasefire. Whilst involved in the backchannel communication, the IRA launched a mortar attack on Downing Street (February 1991) and Heathrow airport (March 1993), detonated huge bombs at the Nat West Tower in London (April 1993), outside Belfast's Grand Opera House (May 1993), in Newtonards (July 1993) and Armagh (September 1993). In addition to this they were also conducting regular lower profile attacks. Not all of these attacks had the impact that the IRA desired; the killing of two young boys in Warrington in March 1993 provoked a wave of protests and John Major felt the episode 'had put the IRA very much on the back foot' (Major, LHCMA). The IRA's attempt to kill the leadership of the Ulster Freedom Fighters (UFF) by bombing a fish shop on the Shankill Road resulted in the deaths of nine Protestant shoppers (and one of the bombers) and increased inter-communal tensions with eleven people killed by loyalist attacks in the following week. But the IRA still had the capacity to operate and kill in the early 1990s.

Although the IRA were not therefore defeated in pure military terms, others argue that they were defeated in strategic terms. Smith claimed, 'the truth was that by the time of PIRA's ceasefire, the organisation's overall military position was one of relative decline. Talk of a surrender may be wrong. But one can make a distinction between surrender and *strategic failure*'. Smith defined strategic failure as 'the inability to attain designated ends with chosen means' (Smith, 1997: 215). This argument is made on the grounds that the IRA were effectively forced to realise that they could not win using force. Thomas Hennessey has argued (and Bew and Frampton concur) that 'the PIRA were not defeated militarily, but the British only needed a draw to win' (Hennessey, 2000: 220; Bew et al., 2009: 246). By denying the IRA victory, the British ultimately forced them to end their violence, which was a primary British objective. What these authors, and others such as Aaron Edwards, suggest is that this is different from the stalemate thesis, as the latter theory suggests that the IRA had more options and free will in the 1990s than was the case. This school of thought argues that the actions and successes of Britain's campaign against the IRA, particularly the intelligence-led approach and the counterterrorist operations carried out by the SAS, are 'under-played' by the stalemate thesis, the proponents of which 'attribute more autonomy to the IRA's position in the early 1990s than is actually the case' (Edwards, 2011: 232; also see Dingley, 2009).

These arguments are questioned by Thomas Leahy in his recent in-depth study of the role of intelligence in the campaign against the IRA. Leahy concludes that the 'IRA's campaign was never in terminal decline because of the intelligence campaign against it' (Leahy, 2020: 5). For Leahy this was due to the fact that several (often rural) units of the IRA were not fundamentally undermined or penetrated; the core leadership of the movement was cut off from the wider movement so even the high-profile agents that were in place were not party to the decision-making or knew the leadership's 'core strategic vision' (Leahy, 2020: 232). For Leahy although there was intelligence infiltration of the IRA and republican leadership, its importance and impact has been overstated by some commentators. His account raises similar objections as Dixon had before him, although somewhat surprisingly he does not engage with Dixon's analysis (Dixon, 2012, 2019). Leahy's work is a largely convincing challenge to the accounts that suggest that the IRA were defeated/forced into the peace process, though he perhaps overstates the importance of Sinn Féin's electoral advancement as a motivator for the move away from the armed struggle.

The competing explanations of stalemate versus defeat have opened an intriguing and important discussion that has serious implications for our understanding of the emergence of the peace process. The problem is that the evidence is presently inconclusive. The debate, as it is emerging, is often based on hindsight and evidence that appears to have come out in recent years, notably the revelations of highly placed informers within the IRA such as Scappaticci and Denis Donaldson, and presumably more evidence will emerge when access to the official records is allowed. What is striking when looking through the discussion of the possibility and actuality of an IRA ceasefire in the period itself is that there is very little to indicate a belief within British circles that the IRA were defeated, strategically or militarily. The actions taken by British policymakers, which will be examined throughout the book, are commensurate with a belief that the IRA needed to be enticed away from violence and might well revert to violence in the future. The peace process, from the British point of view, was primarily an exercise in wooing the republican movement away from the armed struggle and onto the purely political path. British policy was not commensurate with accepting or delivering the defeat of the IRA. When the British received the 'conflict over' message in 1993, for example, (discussed in the next chapter) their reaction is interesting. The existence of such a message could have been taken as an indicator of 'defeat' by the IRA, given the British claims that they believed the message to be genuine and from McGuinness. However, the immediate British reaction was not one of vindication and victory; the most pressing concern for the Major government was whether 'this was a dangerous trap' by the IRA (Mayhew, LHCMA). The then Home Secretary, Kenneth Clarke, recalled discussion over the risk that engagement with the republicans as a result of the message could become 'a tremendous political coup for the republican movement by demonstrating a weak British government approaching the IRA and making reckless offers to them, which they would then expose in order to shatter confidence in the rest of the Irish community and the rest of the British government' (Clarke, LHCMA). The journalist Peter Taylor 'subsequently asked Sir Patrick Mayhew whether he regarded the "message" as a signal from the trenches that amounted to a flag of surrender. He said he most certainly did not' (Taylor, 1998: 330).

Given these factors, the stalemate thesis is a far more convincing explanation for the emergence of the peace process and the considerations that were in play *at the time*. The IRA knew that they could continue an armed campaign (though undoubtedly it was more difficult for them given the intelligence war of the British and the levels of infiltration) and, importantly, the British also appeared to have structured their policy based on the belief that the IRA could, and indeed might, continue the armed struggle. The claims that the British had strategically defeated the IRA by the early 1990s are interesting, but they were not generally being made contemporaneously with the emergence of the peace process. The British policy only makes sense in this period if it is viewed through a prism of attempting to persuade an active paramilitary organisation to move away from violence. The concessions and pragmatism that are the hallmark of the peace process suggest that this view was largely shared. As will be examined in the coming chapters, a constant complaint made during the peace process was that too many concessions were being offered to the IRA. Whether this was the case will be examined, but it is the arguments that underpin the stalemate thesis that best explain the emergence and progression of the peace process, and the actions of all the main participants. The following chapters will examine how the objectives of the parties, and the context in which they found themselves operating, shaped the peace process and the trajectory that it took over the coming decades – a trajectory that resulted in a political outcome in Northern Ireland that was largely unanticipated and, at times, highly problematic.

2

The emergence (and collapse) of the peace process, 1990–1997

The peace process took further shape and was given momentum by the Downing Street Declaration (DSD) signed by the British and Irish governments on the 15 December 1993. The DSD was the culmination of sporadic talks over two years between the two governments and wider consultation with the parties in Northern Ireland. By December 1993 the governments had prioritised the peace process and the main objective had become the quest to secure an undertaking from the IRA to end their violence in an effort to facilitate their entry into the political process and secure a wider negotiated settlement. The DSD effectively marked the end of attempts to secure agreement between the constitutional parties in the hope that this would further marginalise the groups that advocated violence as a political tool. Although periodically there were suggestions that a new exclusion-based talks process would be launched, by 1994 the chances of successfully doing so were negligible. By that stage, as John Chilcot argued, things 'had gone too far forward really. Too much progress had been made. The only game in town was to get the real result, which was peace, however imperfect and perhaps not permanent but nonetheless to get it and, with that, some kind of political settlement' (Chilcot, LHCMA). However, getting to that declaration had been fraught.

The Brooke–Mayhew talks

The movement towards a ceasefire by the IRA was slow and unclear in the early 1990s. The public pronouncements emanating from republicans were often discouraging. The behind-the-scenes messages that were being passed between the British government and Sinn Féin were unknown to the other parties and the public focus was on the Brooke–Mayhew talks, the last attempt to secure a deal solely between the constitutional parties. The NISS, Peter Brooke, and his successor, Patrick Mayhew, convened two rounds of talks between April 1991 and November 1992. The participants were the two governments and the UUP, DUP, SDLP and the Alliance Party of Northern Ireland (APNI). The structures that were designed to underpin the initiative were based on a three-strand model. The strands dealt with the internal government of Northern Ireland (Strand One), the relationship between Northern Ireland and the Republic (Strand Two) and the relationship between the Republic and the British government (Strand Three). The talks were conducted on the basis that nothing was agreed until everything was agreed, to prevent any party securing advantage on issues they wanted progress on and then failing to agree to the other strands. This was a widespread concern of all the main parties. Both the three-strand approach and the necessity for agreement on all elements of it were to be key features of the subsequent all-party talks that led to the Belfast/Good Friday Agreement (GFA) in 1998. Launching the first round of talks had been difficult and they marked the re-emergence of Ulster Unionism from its self-imposed, post-AIA isolation. Brooke held a series of meetings with the party leaders from early 1990 to launch the wider talks process. The Ulster Unionists originally argued that they were unwilling to deal with the Irish government whilst Ireland's constitutional claim to Northern Ireland (Articles 2 and 3) remained. In reality, there was no chance that the Irish government would remove the claim unilaterally. The issue had long inflamed unionists who argued that the claim was illegal and hostile. For nationalists, though, it represented a commitment from the Irish government to unity and for the Irish government; whilst the articles were arguably of little practical significance, they became seen as a bargaining chip. Coincidentally, at the time that Brooke was attempting to launch his talks, there was a debate in the Irish parliament, brought by the Workers Party TD (Teachta Dála), Proinsias de Rossa, on amending the articles. This was the first such debate in over fifty years. The discussions illustrated the differing opinions in the Dáil on the issue but the motion was defeated seventy-four to sixty-six (*Irish Times*, 13 December 1990). The case for amending the constitution was based on the idea that the articles were divisive and offered succour to the IRA. The arguments against amending the articles were that they offered hope and demonstrated solidarity with the nationalists in Northern Ireland. In explaining the government's opposition to the amendments, the Taoiseach, Charles Haughey, claimed that the move would be detrimental to constitutional nationalism in the North:

> What signal are we to send to those who have struggled to uphold the values of constitutional nationalism? Are we to say that, after all, expressions of nationalism have come to embarrass us in the South, that we no longer feel comfortable with a Constitution which gives full expression to the Nationalist idea? Is that what we want? I would submit that the day we made such an

admission will be one not just of disappointment and disillusionment for Northern Nationalists but also … a day of comfort for the men of violence in Northern Ireland – they will assert that constitutional nationalism has been fatally weakened, that the claim to nationhood has become the exclusive property of them, the men of violence. (Debates, 6 December 1990, vol. 403, cols 1316–1317)

But Haughey also suggested that he was unwilling to see the articles abandoned unilaterally, especially as they would be an issue in any future talks with unionists.

The point that the articles had value as bargaining chips was made even more strongly in the debate by the Labour Party leader, Dick Spring (although the party supported the amendment for symbolic purposes whilst arguing that a referendum should not be held). Spring argued, 'A concession on so fundamental a symbol to so many people as Articles 2 and 3 deserves to be part of a process of give and take, to put it at its very mildest. If such a concession is now made, why should unionists come to the table looking for it?' (Debates, 6 December 1990, vol. 403, col. 1324). The utilitarian value of the articles was put more colourfully by the next Taoiseach's press secretary, Sean Duignan, when he noted that Albert Reynolds's view of the articles was that they were 'pearls beyond price, what are they worth to you?' (Sean Duignan, author interview, 2000).

The unionists also claimed that they could not enter talks without the AIA being suspended; this was not something that the two governments would countenance. They did state that whilst they would not abandon the AIA, they were willing to negotiate its replacement. In January 1990 Charles Haughey said, 'Nobody has ever suggested that the Anglo–Irish Agreement is there for all time. It is an international agreement between two governments and can always be substituted by agreement' (*The Times*, 22 January 1990). In May of that year Peter Brooke wrote an open letter to the UUP leader, James Molyneaux, affirming that the proposed talks would consider proposals for an alternative to the AIA (*The Times*, 7 May 1990). The two governments also agreed that the talks would take place in a gap between meetings of the AIA's Intergovernmental Council (rather than formally suspend the Agreement).

Procedural difficulties, however, dogged the talks process over issues such as when the Irish government would enter the process – their desire to participate in Strand One was rejected on the grounds that the unionists would not agree to their participation in plans for the internal government of Northern Ireland – where the talks would take place, and who would chair them. The second round of talks, under Brooke's successor, Patrick Mayhew, made more progress and saw notable advances, such as Molyneaux leading the first unionist delegation for talks in Dublin since 1922, and the discussions did appear to move on to substantive issues regarding the identified strands in the Mayhew sessions. However, it was not possible to secure agreement between the parties at that stage and, as discussed below, this was not necessarily a disappointment to the British government given the other changes that appeared to be taking place.

Bringing in the republicans

In parallel with the Brooke–Mayhew talks, discussions had been continuing with Sinn Féin. Hume had kept up his sporadic dialogue with Gerry Adams, Mansergh had also met key republicans for the Irish government and the British were continuing their backchannel communications via the Derry link. At times the public Brooke–Mayhew and the secret backchannel communications were not as separate as one might expect. The British used the channel to pass updates on the Brooke talks to republicans. Sinn Féin's account of the link states that 'Throughout 1992 the British government representative became very active in briefing us. The major part of these briefings was taken up by reports of the progress, or lack of it, which was being made in the inter-party talks' (Sinn Féin, 1993: 9). This may appear somewhat counter-intuitive given that the Brooke–Mayhew process was designed to achieve agreement between the constitutional parties and further isolate those that advocated violence. However, in reality, the possibility of engaging Sinn Féin was causing reflection within British policymaking circles. On occasion the British sought to portray the talks as moving in a hopeful manner (Communiqué to Sinn Féin, 22 October 1992). Such a move may well have been designed to suggest to Sinn Féin that there was the possibility that an agreement may be reached at the talks and seek to play on a fear of isolation within Sinn Féin, which had just seen Gerry Adams lose the party's only Westminster seat, West Belfast, to the SDLP's Joe Hendron. More widely, there was a clear attempt by the British to engage the republican movement in this period. As John Chilcot, head of the NIO, subsequently stated, the British passed key speeches and statements to Sinn Féin 'in advance through the backchannel because it was so important that they didn't pick up wrong messages or fail to pick up the right ones' (John Chilcot, author interview, 2001). Similarly, the British urged Sinn Féin to do the same with their key statements and speeches via the same channel. Although on occasion it appears the case that material that had not been sanctioned was given to republicans via the backchannel. David Cooke, who was at that time a senior British civil servant seconded to the NIO and involved in briefing the British contact in the backchannel, an MI5 agent known as 'Fred' (also named in other sources as Robert McLaren and Colin Ferguson), made this point. Cooke claims that on one occasion he and the NIO's political director, Quentin Thomas, were briefing Fred and gave him information on the Brooke–Mayhew talks, but it was clear this was for his own background information only. This material subsequently appeared in Sinn Féin's account as a message from the British government. Cooke argues that Sinn Féin's account tends to conflate very different messages and suggests they all had the same status (David Cooke, author interview, 2019).

The talks that were continuing between Hume and Adams were also instrumental in setting the basis for an emerging peace process. During the original Sinn Féin–SDLP talks of 1988, Hume had sought to persuade the republicans that the AIA demonstrated that the British were neutral on Northern Ireland. On occasion he made similar arguments in public. Speaking in the House of Commons on 5 July 1990, Hume asked 'Can anyone seriously say today that Britain has an economic interest in Ireland, when the British taxpayer is paying £1.5 billion a year to keep our economy going? Does anyone believe that Britain has a strategic interest in Ireland in a nuclear world, and that a military presence is necessary for strategic reasons?' (House of Commons, 5 July 1990, vol. 75, col. 1156). This was a direct challenge to Sinn Féin's assertions that the British presence was primarily motivated by strategic and economic considerations. Hume's belief that 'proof' was needed of British neutrality led him to ask Brooke to make a statement along these lines. Brooke made a major speech in November 1990 (an advance copy of which was provided to Sinn Féin via the back-channel). In the speech Brooke examined the reasons for British involvement in Northern Ireland, which he stressed were the result of the commitment to the consent principle and reflected the majority view in Northern Ireland: 'Partition is an acknowledgement of reality, not an assertion of national self-interest.' Brooke argued that the British 'presence' in Northern Ireland was not primarily the military or British politicians, 'but the reality of nearly a million people living in a part of the island of Ireland who are, and who certainly regard themselves as British'. He stressed that Britain would not 'bar the way' to a united Ireland in the future if that 'were to be the wish of the people of Northern Ireland themselves'. In a phrase designed to support the arguments Hume was making to republicans regarding British neutrality, Brooke asserted 'The British government has no selfish strategic interest in Northern Ireland; our role is to help, enable and encourage' (Hennessey, 2000: 68–69). Whilst republicans were sceptical of British claims to neutrality, Adams recorded 'his remarks did suggest possibilities worth exploring' (Adams, 2003: 98).

Indeed, republicans subsequently claimed that it was the Hume–Adams dialogue and the attempts to reach out to the Irish government and increase support in America (the creation of the so-called pan-nationalist front) that 'were more important' than the backchannel link with the British (Adams, 2003: 120). This is, however, questionable. Séan Farren, a leading member of the SDLP who had participated in the talks with Sinn Féin in 1988 and was part of the SDLP's delegation during the GFA talks, has noted in relation to the backchannel and the intergovernmental talks that led to the DSD, the 'revelation of the scale and extent of these parallel dialogues raises questions as to the value of the Hume–Adams initiative' (Farren, 2010: 296). The appeal of the Hume–Adams talks was that republicans could control these to an extent that they could not control the backchannel communication. The problem with the Hume–Adams dialogue, however, was that ultimately it could not deliver any real advances. Whilst it could seek to influence the debate regarding the advisability of engagement with Sinn Féin, and the possibility of persuading the IRA to end their violence, to achieve change they needed the support of the two governments and, ultimately, engagement with the unionist community in Northern Ireland. Talks between Sinn Féin and the SDLP could not secure these outcomes.

The backchannel between the British and Irish republicans had been in existence sporadically since the early 1970s, but few knew of its existence until the *Observer* broke the story of the link in November 1993. It was, however, a key feature in the early stages of the peace process and in the attempts by the British to persuade the IRA to end its armed campaign. In the time since its existence was exposed, more has become known about the link and journalistic investigation by Eamonn Mallie and David McKittrick, Peter Taylor, Brian Rowan and the academic work of Niall Ó Dochartaigh. Ó Dochartaigh also managed to persuade the key member of the link, Brendan Duddy, to deposit his archive at the University of Galway for researchers to examine. The Derry link was actually three people: Brendan Duddy, the Derry businessman to whose fish and chip shop Martin McGuinness had apparently delivered burgers in the late 1960s, Denis Bradley, a former Catholic priest who had officiated at McGuinness's wedding, and Noel Gallagher who had been McGuinness's best man (*Guardian*, 18 February 2008; Reiss, 2010: 49; Reynolds, 2010: 161). Duddy was the main contact and it was he who primarily met with Fred, though on occasion all three were involved in talks. On the republican side, McGuinness was the main contact who received messages from the Duddy channel. Those involved in the backchannel saw themselves as more than just message carriers. They viewed their role as not only to pass messages between the British and republicans but also to interpret events. Duddy's archive makes it clear that he saw his role as interpreting the situation for both the British and the republicans (Duddy Archive, DVD, POL35/666, 1.5).

Bradley's account also suggests that he saw their role as being more than just message carriers, arguing that 'at the specific, targeted, appropriate moment you have to go over the top otherwise, otherwise you're useless'. By going 'over the top' he meant acting in a way that those whose positions you were apparently relating had not authorised. On occasions this included constructing messages themselves, which Bradley acknowledged could be seen as 'leading policy and creating policy rather than either interpreting it or sending it on to the next person' (Bradley, LHCMA).

As noted above, the veracity of what Fred was passing onto republicans via the backchannel was also on occasion open to question. This meant that whilst the backchannel was an important part of the peace process it is not entirely clear whether the British or republicans' positions were passed on as they may have intended; it also makes analysing the role of the backchannel difficult. This arguably explains the discrepancies that exist between the accounts of the exchanges between the British and republicans subsequently published by Sinn Féin and the British government. There were several messages in the British account which Sinn Féin's 1993 account, *Setting the Record Straight,* claimed were 'bogus'. However, the Duddy archive leads to questions regarding how 'bogus' these were. If by 'bogus' the suggestion is that they had not been sent to the British via the backchannel then this is problematic. If, however, bogus means that they had not been sent at the request of republicans, then this may be the case.

The most notorious and important of these messages is the one the British claimed they had received in February 1993 which read, 'The conflict is over, but we need your advice on how to bring it to a close. We wish to have an unannounced ceasefire in order to hold a dialogue leading to peace' (Major, 2000: 431). British accounts suggest that they believed this was from McGuinness. John Chilcot, the head of the NIO at the time, argued that the fact that it had come via the backchannel 'was a matter of weighty importance' in leading them to believe that the message was genuine (Chilcot, LHCMA). McGuinness always denied that any such message was sent. There have been varying accounts of the provenance of the message. Denis Bradley was the first of the three involved in the backchannel to speak publicly of his role. In his account for the *Endgame in Ireland* documentary he suggested that the link was involved in writing the message. At that time, he claims that they were frustrated at the lack of progress and so decided to 'write something' but he suggests that it was Fred who changed the message to the one the British government received. 'We sent it, we gave it to Fred, I will swear to the day I die that Fred added the words "we need help to get out of this conflict", I think Fred knew that with those words he could turn the rest of the people in the room round to engage with each other and Fred was doing what we were doing and adding on to it to make sure that it happened' (Bradley, LHCMA). Others have suggested that Bradley did write the message and gave it to Fred, who, believing it was genuine, passed it on to the government (Bew et al., 2009: 118) or that it was 'cock-up' rather than conspiracy, as an aide-memoire written during a meeting with McGuinness was subsequently mistaken for McGuinness's words (Cochrane, 2013: 127). Peter Taylor's account suggests that Fred wrote the message based on his interpretation of what he believed Duddy felt the republicans' position to be and then passed it on to the British government, and then gave the original to Duddy. Duddy himself claimed that he did not send the message, telling Peter Taylor that once the story of the backchannel broke and the British reported the message, he was visited by 'four very senior republicans' and Duddy convinced them that he had not sent the message. 'Let me put it this way: if I'd been guilty of anything, I wouldn't have liked to have been sitting in that room' (*Guardian*, 18 March 2008). However, the fact that there is a copy of the message (which appears to be in Fred's handwriting) in Duddy's archive raises questions regarding the accuracy of his account. Given that messages from McGuinness to the British would go via Duddy to Fred and then on to the government, why would the message be in Fred's writing? If Duddy had not sent it, then why would it be in his archive? If Fred gave the message to Duddy, he would be aware that it had not come from McGuinness. This case illustrates the somewhat opaque nature of the backchannel. Whether the British were aware that the status of some of the material they were apparently receiving from republicans was questionable is impossible to know. Cooke, who was brought into working on the link shortly after the message was received, states that Chilcot has always asserted to him that they believed the message was from McGuinness (David Cooke, author interview, 2019). Similarly, it is unclear whether McGuinness and the republicans were aware of how the link was working and the nature of some of the information that was being passed to London, which was presented as originating from them. For example, when the link relayed an offer of a temporary ceasefire from the IRA to the British (which had been authorised) they decided to omit the phrase 'for a short duration' from the message as Bradley said the three of them had decided that it was 'a real liability' (Bradley, LHCMA). Again, this led to a dispute between the two sides when the accounts of the communications were subsequently published. The attempts by the link to interpret rather than simply pass messages for the two sides may well have been instrumental in advancing the peace process. There is no doubt that the 'conflict is over' message was integral in engaging the British government's interest in seeking to explore the possibility of the IRA ending their campaign and Sinn Féin entering a talks process. Ultimately, however, the republicans became exasperated with the backchannel and it was they who leaked its existence to the press in

November 1993 after the link had sent what Sinn Féin subsequently claimed was another 'bogus' message that appeared to offer the British a 'total end of hostilities'. That message does appear to have been written by Fred and Duddy who 'were angry' and believed that Sinn Féin were being sidelined. Duddy's account subsequently claimed that, as a result, whilst he and Fred were in a hotel room in London, Fred 'scribbled a number of questions on the hotel notepaper. All the questions had been asked before but the combination of the way they were written and used proved to be better'. It was this act that caused the republicans to collapse the backchannel once they learned of the message (Duddy Archive, POL35/340).

Gerry Adams later recorded his unhappiness at aspects of the actions of those that comprised the Derry link, including their role in the 'conflict is over' message, which he saw as a 'breach of the trust which the British government and we had placed in them'. He was also angered by the fact that they had revealed their activities to John Hume (Adams, 2003: 145). Duddy's diaries suggested that he had believed that Hume should be told of the link as he could put pressure on the British to act on the IRA's offer of a ceasefire. He had suggested this previously in June 1993 to McGuinness, but McGuinness had rejected the idea as he 'was most reluctant to hand the republican position over to the SDLP leader' (Duddy Archive, POL35/266). When the link did inform Hume towards the end of the enterprise, the move was criticised by Adams as 'another potentially dangerous and foolhardy decision, breaking all the rules which go-betweens must adhere to'. For Adams, the problem was that they had 'started to take decisions for us' (Adams, 2003: 145). The frustration that those in the backchannel felt at periods during 1993 is clear from the accounts of Bradley and the papers in Duddy's archive, and it does seem that the three in the link, as well as Fred himself on occasion, exceeded their briefs, but their impact on the development of the peace process was highly significant. (For a wider discussion of the backchannel, see O'Kane (2015).)

Republicans were keen to move away from a reliance on the backchannel and move to direct dialogue with the British, but the British position was that they would not meet directly with republicans whilst the violence continued. This was breached on one occasion when Fred did meet Martin McGuinness and Gerry Kelly in Derry. The status of this meeting is disputed. Sinn Féin claim that the meeting had been arranged and Fred was expected to attend along with John Deverell, then head of intelligence services in Northern Ireland. However, the British cancelled the meeting at short notice due to the IRA's bombing of Warrington. Subsequently, under pressure from the link, Fred agreed to attend the meeting on his own. When the meeting was revealed, the British stated that it was unauthorised, a point which John Chilcot subsequently stressed (Chilcot, LHCMA). However, it is far from clear that the meeting had not been previously scheduled and then cancelled due to Warrington. Duddy's and Bradley's accounts suggest that the meeting had previously been arranged. David Cooke states he was completely unaware of the meeting and did not hear about it until some time after it had happened, but he did accept that it was not inconceivable that the security services may have decided to hold an unauthorised meeting with republicans to explore their position (David Cooke, author interview, 2019). At the meeting, according to Sinn Féin's account, Fred informed McGuinness and Kelly that, 'Events on the ground will bring an enormous influence to bear. The IRA needs to provide the space to turn the possibility of meetings into a reality. A suspension is all that is being required of them.' The British believed that two or three weeks were enough to convince republicans. There would be an intensive round of talks. 'Once started, people remain until decisions were arrived at' (Sinn Féin, 1993: 18). Bradley argued that Fred stressed the necessity for an end to violence in order to allow talks to happen, but this could be a temporary and unannounced ceasefire, which could lead to talks with Deverell and Quentin Thomas in the first instance and then John Chilcot would join at a later stage (Bradley, LHCMA). This led to the offer of a ceasefire from the republicans that was delivered by the backchannel in May 1993. However, the talks never came to fruition. Sinn Féin accused the British of losing their nerve and blamed the extension of those who knew of the contacts amongst the British government, particularly the inclusion of the Home Secretary, Kenneth Clarke, who was brought into the intra-British governmental discussions on 18 May. By his own admission Clarke was 'deeply suspicious' of the contacts with the republican movement and advised John Major against pursuing the initiative (Clarke, LHCMA). However, it was not primarily scepticism within the cabinet that was the problem but the continuing IRA violence that disturbed the British. Throughout their backchannel correspondence the British had stressed the importance of 'events on the ground'. For the British, IRA actions were seen as hindering moves towards direct talks, whereas the IRA itself appeared to believe that they needed to continue their campaign in order to highlight that they were not negotiating from a position of weakness. Whilst on 10 May McGuinness sent a message to the British offering an unannounced ceasefire to facilitate direct talks, ten days later the IRA exploded a huge bomb near the Belfast Opera House causing an estimated £62 million of damage (Bew and Gillespie, 1999: 274). This was on the day that the British government were meeting to finalise their response to McGuinness's message of 10 May. It was this attack that led the British to decide to withhold their response. Instead of sending the substantive response that they had been working on, the government sent a message to Sinn Féin on 3 June stating they had been 'working out a response' to the offer of a suspension but 'before that process could be completed, renewed violence of a serious scale took place – with the inevitable consequence that the process itself had to be halted' (Sinn Féin, 1993: 26). Mayhew recalls that the mood in the government after the Opera House bomb was 'well that's it – at least for the time being that's it'. The British believed the republican movement was alternating the possibility of talks and using violence as 'hard cop/soft cop stuff', which was unacceptable to the British (Mayhew, LHCMA).

The difficulties that were evident in moving from indirect talks to direct engagement were indicative of the problematic relationship between the British government and the republican movement. Both sides had different perspectives and audiences. The British government were clearly keen to pursue the possibility of creating a process that would lead to an end to the IRA's use of violence. The indications they were getting from the various sources suggested this was a possibility. But they were deeply suspicious of the IRA in that period, mindful of the political dangers that engaging with the IRA (even indirectly) posed, and also troubled by the morality of dealing with those who used violence as a way of furthering their political ends. The British were sensitive to the fact that if contacts with the republican movement were revealed, as John Chilcot argued, they had to be able to defend their actions 'in every particle and detail' (Chilcot, LHCMA). This is why they stipulated in their most substantive message to Sinn Féin, the nine-paragraph document of 19 March 1993, that once the contacts became public the government 'would have to acknowledge and defend its entry into dialogue. It would do so by pointing out that its agreement to exploratory dialogue about the possibility of an inclusive process had been given because – and only because – it had received a private assurance that organised violence had been brought to an end' (Sinn Féin, 1993: 19). The position of the British government was that they acknowledged that they were embarking on a highly risky policy but they were seeking to limit the risks as far as possible and conduct the initiative in a way that would subsequently (they hoped) be politically defensible. David Cooke, who was the person responsible for the first draft of the nine-paragraph document, confirms that the British were conscious in their correspondence with the IRA that it must be defensible when/if it was subsequently revealed (David Cooke, author interview, 2019).

For republicans, the considerations in play were comparable, but the conclusions they came to were different and conflicting, if not contradictory. Republicans too had an audience to whom they would have to justify their position when the contacts became known. Opinion within wider republicanism was very suspicious of the British government and had been soured by the experience of the 1974–1975 truce and talks with the British government. Denis Bradley argues that McGuinness had not been involved in that round of the backchannel activity and was deeply suspicious of the link, which is the reason that he asked Bradley to get involved again in the early 1990s as McGuinness, 'wasn't the greatest lover of Brendan Duddy at that stage' (Denis Bradley, author interview, 2019). The republican perception of the 1974–1975 period was that the British had tricked republicans and used the period to weaken the IRA rather than to seriously engage with them. Indeed, Sinn Féin's account of the 1990–1993 period claims that in January 1993 'Fred' told them via the backchannel that 'the British government was not serious in 1974/75 but they were now' (Sinn Féin, 1993: 16). This scepticism towards the British and the legacy of the earlier engagement, which had weakened the IRA, seems to have led the organisation to conclude that they needed to demonstrate that, despite the engagement, they were not negotiating from a position of weakness. This would explain the level of IRA activity in the run-up to the proposed temporary cessation that would mark the beginning of direct talks. Republicans were also, like the British, conscious that they would need to justify their actions to their supporters when details of the talks were revealed. This was demonstrated by the flurry of activity on both sides once the existence of the backchannel was revealed by the *Observer* on 29 November 1993. The revelation of the link marked the end of its significance, but by November 1993 other avenues were being employed, most notably the joint declaration initiative that led to the DSD.

Unionism in the run-up to the peace process

The position of Ulster Unionism in the early 1990s was difficult. Unionism had sought to emerge from the (largely self-imposed) marginalised position it had found itself in post-AIA. The tactic of refusing to engage with British ministers and officials whilst the AIA was in place had clearly failed, and there was a need to re-enter the political debate. The Brooke–Mayhew process had enabled them to do this, and some notable significant advances had been made. However, unionists shouldered much of the blame for the failure of the talks, particularly for the end of the Brooke round in 1991. The *Independent* ran an editorial headlined 'The Shortcomings of Unionism' claiming the intransigence and incompetence of old-guard unionist politicians were largely responsible for the failure of the Northern Ireland talks (*Independent*, 4 July 1991). An article in *The Times* claimed 'future governments are likely to be even more wary of unionist intransigence and to look to increasing cooperation with Dublin' (*The Times*, 4 July 1991). The engagement with the Mayhew round of talks and the UUP's decision to go to Dublin did lead to less criticism. However, despite this engagement, unionists, within both the UUP and DUP, were concerned about the role of Dublin in Northern Ireland and opposed to power-sharing devolution.

After the Mayhew round ended without any breakthrough, the apparent increasing shift towards seeking an inclusive approach led to increased unionist unease. In February 1993 the then-editor of Fortnight magazine, Robin Wilson, identified the concerns of Unionism: 'Unionists – who recall how they were lectured at the time of the Anglo–Irish Agreement on how it would marginalise republicanism – now watch dumbfounded as not only does IRA violence continue unabated, but Sinn Féin appears more and more central to the British agenda' (*Fortnight,* February 1993: 5).

The failure to make progress during the inter-party talks and the lack of any sign that attempts to restart such a process would succeed, increased talk of closer cooperation between London and Dublin. Speculation began to emerge that the two governments might even draw up proposals and seek to bypass the political parties entirely and offer the proposals directly to the people of Northern Ireland. The Irish Tánaiste, Dick Spring, noted that this was a contentious proposal. 'Now you are reaching the Beecher's Brook of the whole issue. This could be dynamite and would have to be handled with very great care indeed. You do have to try and bring in the parties, after all they are the elected representatives and voice of the people. But ultimately an agreement might have to be put directly to the people.' Spring also seemed to suggest that a form of joint authority might be considered, arguing such proposals were 'very interesting ideas and deserve to be studied very closely' (*Guardian,* 8 July 1993). The British were quick to distance themselves from Spring's suggestions of both joint authority and bypassing the political parties. Mayhew claimed he was 'surprised' by Spring's claims which he believed 'seemed to go significantly beyond what I understood to be the position of the Irish government' (*Guardian,* 9 July 1993). But such suggestions clearly angered and worried unionist leaders, with Molyneaux claiming the 'message Mr Spring is sending is that if you don't consent, we will make you consent' (*Guardian,* 9 July 1993) and that it was 'irresponsible of Mr Spring to reveal what was obviously the game plan of the Irish government, namely unity by enforced consent' (*Irish News,* 9 July 1993).

Whilst there was political engagement with the republican movement in the early 1990s, the views and actions of loyalists were also a factor in the changing security and political context of the period. The unease that the 1985 AIA had caused within the unionist community was instrumental in a rise in activity by loyalist paramilitaries in the latter part of the 1980s and early 1990s.

The Joint Declaration

In parallel with the backchannel communication with republicans, the British were also involved in talks with the Irish government on drawing up a joint declaration. The purpose of the document would be to lay out an agreed shared position between the two governments. At the outset this was just another idea that was in the offing, alongside the backchannel and the Brooke–Mayhew talks. The idea had been first discussed by Charles Haughey in 1991 and it was reported that he had raised the approach as a possibility if the inter-party talks failed at the summit with John Major in December 1991 (*Irish Times*, 5 December 1991). There was a document passed from Dublin to London in January 1992, which was a reworking by Haughey's advisor on Northern Ireland, Martin Mansergh, the cabinet secretary, Dermot Nally and Sean Ó hUiginn of the Anglo–Irish division of the Department of Foreign Affairs, of a draft given to Dublin by John Hume (which had had input from Gerry Adams). However, this document, and one passed on to the British government by Hume the following month, were rejected by the British government given their 'presumption of a united Ireland' (Major, 2000: 447). These early drafts called for a statement that the British wished to see Ireland united and committed the British government to work to bring this unity about, positions that the British government would not, nor could not, have accepted (for the text of these drafts see Mallie and McKittrick, 1996: 371–372, for more details on the negotiations of what became the DSD see O'Kane, 2007: 104–121). As a result of the gulf between what the early drafts of a possible joint declaration seemed to be trying to achieve and what the British and unionists could accept, the initiative largely remained dormant throughout 1992. The focus of possible development for the governments and main parties in Northern Ireland remained the inter-party talks. However, by 1993 it was clear that these had not achieved the breakthrough that it was hoped they might. Whilst there were sporadic suggestions that the inter-party talks process without Sinn Féin might be restarted in 1993, in reality the two governments became increasingly focused upon the joint declaration approach.

The joint declaration was based on the possibility that a joint statement might help to entice the IRA away from violence and enable them to become involved in a new variant of all-party talks, but one that included Sinn Féin. This was different from the idea of the two governments either moving towards a form of joint sovereignty or drawing up comprehensive plans for the region that would then be put straight to the people. The reason that these two approaches, which had their advocates at times, were not seriously pursued was largely practical rather than ideological. Although the commitment to the Union that existed within certain sections of the Conservative Party meant such an approach may have been internally difficult for a Conservative prime minister, the main reason the British government would not countenance joint sovereignty was because it would have worsened the security and political situation in Northern Ireland. There is no doubt that any move towards joint sovereignty would have inflamed unionist anger, as evidenced by their reaction to the AIA, which fell notably short of joint authority. For both London and Dublin, the priority was to try and find a formula that could bring stability and peace to Northern Ireland. Whilst joint sovereignty might have theoretical appeal for Dublin, given their constitutional aspiration to unity, and for London, as it might reduce the international criticism that they sometimes faced over their handling of Northern Ireland, the practical considerations were less persuasive. Movement towards joint sovereignty would further inflame unionist suspicion (and almost certainly loyalist violence) and would not satisfy republican demands, given it would not be Irish unity.

Drawing up a comprehensive deal which would then be put to the people of Northern Ireland, bypassing the political parties, was also seen as impractical. The idea rested on the premise that the people of Northern Ireland held views that were very different from those of their political representatives, or that they were more pragmatic and accommodating than the parties that claimed to represent them. These propositions had little evidence to support them and, as we will see, arguably the electoral realignment over the next two decades would suggest that the voters were not more moderate than the parties or their leaders.

The result of these considerations was that, as the chances of negotiating a solution based on talks between the constitutional parties receded, the two governments looked to whether a joint declaration might advance the situation. A notable feature of the peace process has been the necessity for the two governments to take the lead in setting the agenda and offering documents for the parties to engage with. The joint declaration was a good and early example of this in the process.

The provenance of the text that becomes the Downing Street Declaration is debated and complicated. The reason is that the dialogue between the two governments that led to the declaration was not the only series of talks at that time. The Hume–Adams dialogue, which as previously noted, had originally been facilitated by the Belfast-based redemptorist priest, Fr Alec Reid, in 1988, had become public knowledge and a great deal of attention (and criticism) was given to it. This was both helpful and problematic for the two governments. It was helpful in that it was another way the republicans were being drawn into the political process. However, it was problematic in that it was clear that anything which was too closely linked to Gerry Adams was likely to be met with scepticism, if not outright rejection, by unionists. Hume and Adams were obviously keen to be seen to be influencing the debate and advancing their position. John Hume was clearly increasingly frustrated by what he saw as a lack of progress by the governments on a joint declaration and to act on the advances he believed he was making in his talks with Gerry Adams. In mid-1993 Hume and

Adams were passing on ideas and texts to the Irish government, and Martin Mansergh was meeting secretly with Gerry Adams (the Taoiseach, Albert Reynolds, had asked Mansergh to resume his contacts with Adams). This thinking and text did influence the wording of the first proposed joint declaration which Reynolds gave to the British cabinet secretary, Robin Butler, in June 1993. But the reality was that the text of the declaration was far too 'green' for the British government. Reynolds himself subsequently argued that he knew it would be unacceptable to the British. 'That document in June that was given to Robin Butler was basically the republican's side, the republican case. I was asked to put that forward in that shape and that form and I did but I said it's not going to run, there's no balance in it from a unionist point of view' (Albert Reynolds, author interview, 2000). But it was a way of demonstrating to republicans that they could have an influence on the political process. This influence, and access, was limited. The position of both the British and Irish government, as well as all the unionist parties, was that they would not meet directly with members of Sinn Féin whilst the violence continued.

The tension between the two governments throughout the negotiating process in the second half of June 1993 was around how 'green' the document should be, what it would suggest was on offer to republicans if they gave up violence and what it envisaged the possible outcomes of a new talks process including Sinn Féin might be. The purpose of the joint declaration was largely to try and create conditions that might persuade the IRA to end its violence and Sinn Féin to enter the political process. The declaration needed to be appealing to republicans. However, given that the wider objective of a peace process was to try and create conditions that would allow all the main parties in Northern Ireland to reach an agreement and power to be devolved to Northern Ireland, then only reaching out to republicans was insufficient. It was imperative that whilst addressing the concerns of republicans the joint declaration did not alienate the unionist parties to the extent that they would not participate in future talks. The perception of the British government was that the early drafts from Dublin were too 'green' and by the end of September 1993 the British appeared to have decided that the initiative was not worth pursuing. The British government were also frustrated by the joint statement from John Hume and Gerry Adams at the end of September which announced that they were suspending their talks which had made 'considerable progress' in order to send a report to Dublin of their proposals. Their statement claimed 'We are convinced from our discussions that a process can be designed to lead to agreement among the divided people of this island which will provide a solid basis for peace' but gave no details of what they were proposing (*Daily Telegraph*, 27 September 1993). Mallie and McKittrick claimed that Reynolds had managed to persuade

Hume to state that the report was only being sent to Dublin rather than to both governments as he was concerned that such claims would make it more difficult for the British government to pursue a joint declaration (Mallie and McKittrick, 1996: 189). It appears that Hume and Adams did not actually send a report to the Irish government. As Reynolds's press secretary, Sean Duignan, later recalled, 'Mansergh used to say to me that Hume–Adams didn't exist. It was somewhere on the back of an envelope that Hume had jotted down … You could never pin it down, they could never get their hands on the damn thing' (O'Kane, 2007: 107). Peter McLoughlin claimed that the statement from Hume and Adams that they were passing a document onto Dublin was 'disingenuous: Dublin was already well aware of the state of play between Hume and Adams. What the two were doing here was making the public aware that a serious initiative was in hand' (McLoughlin, 2010: 157). The statement, however, did cause problems for Major as 'the prospect of securing unionist agreement to anything emanating from Hume–Adams was nil' (Major, 2000: 450). Unionists were quick to register their unease about the Hume–Adams process and hard-liners in the DUP 'led by Mr Ian Paisley, are warning Sir Patrick that if he even considers proposals that "have come from the womb of the IRA", they will boycott inter-party talks' (*Daily Telegraph*, 7 October 1993).

Major was also at the time leading a Conservative Party which was deeply divided over Europe and had a majority of only seventeen. As a result, the unionist votes at Westminster were important, and the nine UUP MPs had voted for the government in a vote of confidence over the social chapter of the Maastricht Treaty just two months earlier. Unlike the negotiations which led to the AIA, the British government did consult the unionists over the drafts of the joint declaration, and Molyneaux's concerns over the document were also instrumental in leading the British to decide in October that, as the British cabinet secretary, Robin Butler, recalled, the 'joint declaration had no future' (O'Kane, 2007: 109) and he was sent to deliver this message to Albert Reynolds.

There were several reasons why the joint declaration idea was not abandoned. At one level there was little to replace it as an initiative. Despite the concern that the process and possible outcome was becoming too closely associated with Adams, the two governments were increasingly of the opinion that there was the chance of persuading the IRA to stop their armed campaign. Second, the chances of reconvening the inter-party talks were slim. Unionists were suspicious of the joint declaration process and Hume–Adams, and the SDLP were clearly prioritising the Hume–Adams process, which both reduced their interest in an inter-party talks process of the Brooke–Mayhew variant, and reduced the likelihood that the unionist parties would engage whilst the SDLP and Sinn Féin leadership were in talks.

Despite the frequent suggestions by the two governments that they were looking into restarting the talks, indeed as late as 21 October 1993 Mayhew seemed to be suggesting that was the government's plan, by 4 November Mayhew and Spring acknowledged that such an approach was not realistic, and indeed could be 'counterproductive' as 'the groundwork to get around the table does not exist' (*Daily Telegraph*, 4 November 1993).

This period saw a notable and deeply concerning increase in violence in Northern Ireland. On 23 October the IRA had detonated a bomb in a fish bar on the Shankill Road in Belfast, killing ten people, including the bomber. The IRA claimed they were targeting a meeting of the UFF which they believed was being held above the shop, but the only people killed were Saturday morning shoppers. The attack not only caused outrage and condemnation but also led to reprisal attacks by loyalist groups. The following week the UDA attacked a Halloween party in a pub in Greysteel, killing eight people. It seemed that Northern Ireland was in the grip of a spiralling sectarian conflict. The violence led to calls for any process that was linked to trying to entice in those who used violence to be dropped. The *Daily Telegraph*, which had never been supportive of such an approach, argued after the Greysteel attack, 'there never was and never will be any point in peace talks which require the participation of Sinn Féin or the Protestant UVF/UFF – the terrorists have too much invested in sustaining the violence (not least to keep the protection rackets going) to be interested in a negotiated peace' (*Daily Telegraph*, 1 November 1993).

Despite such sentiments, the British government did not abandon the joint declaration initiative. Although they had indicated to Dublin that they were not pursuing the initiative, a few weeks later, at the end of November, Robin Butler contacted his Irish counterpart, Dermot Nally, to say that they did wish to continue with talks on a possible joint declaration. Around this time the existence of the Derry backchannel had been revealed, which had caused surprise and anger in the Irish government who were unaware of its use. The returning to the joint declaration initiative by the British was not, however, simply a result of the end of the backchannel. By late November that process had probably served its purpose and it would not have been able to secure a ceasefire and begin an inclusive process via exclusively secret communication with the republican movement. It was clear that the only avenue that might fruitfully lead to progress was that of the joint declaration, and what became known as the peace process. The exclusion-based inter-party talks were looking less like a realistic objective, the backchannel communication was coming to an end and in Northern Ireland violence was increasing, and increasingly sectarian and indiscriminate. However, there remained the problem of how a joint declaration could be 'sold' if it was associated with Gerry Adams, whether the unionists would be willing to enter into talks with republicans even in the event of a ceasefire, and what the likely reaction of loyalists would be to such moves.

The chances that unionists might be amenable to a more inclusive process, including Sinn Féin soon after a ceasefire, did not appear good. David McKittrick had reported that the UUP leader, James Molyneaux, told his party conference in mid-October, 'Sinn Féin could only be considered for access to the democratic process when the IRA had been extirpated, when there was a cessation of terrorism and when all arms and explosives had been surrendered.' They would then have to go through a five year 'quarantine period' (*Independent*, 18 October 1993). Despite what some might subsequently claim, there was little to suggest at the time that the plans were to extirpate the IRA. A five-year gap between the end of violence and engagement with Sinn Féin would not have led to a ceasefire and, as was to become apparent over the next decade, the issue of how to deal with arms and explosives was far from simple.

The British, however, sought to distance themselves from Hume–Adams by introducing an entirely new draft to the process, a move which infuriated the Irish government. John Major claimed that he knew that the Irish 'would not, and indeed probably could not accept an entirely new British draft' but suggested that it was done in order to 'demonstrate the width of the gap between us and would help us to seek the middle ground between the two positions' (Major, 2000: 451). Robin Butler suggested, however, that the new draft was one to be engaged with and they 'genuinely thought that this put what the essence of the document was that we had before us in a more digestible form' (O'Kane, 2007: 115). Whatever its purpose, Major was right in his suggestion that it would be unacceptable to Dublin, and it was greeted with anger by the Irish government. Dermot Nally apparently fumed to Reynolds that it was 'unforgivable' and asked if the British 'thought he was the Prime Minister of Tonga' (Finlay, 1998: 201). Nally's explanation for the anger that was felt by the British attempt to enter a new draft at that late stage was because the draft they had been working on had been communicated via secret channels to unionists and Sinn Féin. Indeed, the Irish government had also solicited an input from loyalist paramilitary groups via the Presbyterian minister, Roy Magee. Nally argued that it would be unacceptable at that stage to adopt a new draft. The issue came to a head at an Anglo–Irish meeting in Dublin on 3 December, a stormy event which Major described as 'the frankest and fiercest exchanges that I had with any fellow leader in my six and a half years as Prime Minister', and Reynolds recalled that Major 'chewed the bollix off me but I took a few lumps out of him!' (Finlay, 1998: 203). The two leaders were divided over issues around Britain's belief that the Irish had prevented progress on restarting inter-party talks, the Irish anger over the existence of the backchannel, and the attempts to introduce a completely new draft. The exchanges did not, however, damage the process and, indeed, during the exchanges, Butler acknowledged that the British had allowed their draft to be sidelined and re-engaged in negotiations with the Irish on the original drafts (O'Kane, 2007: 116). These negotiations were ultimately successful and the joint declaration, now known as the Downing Street Declaration (DSD) was signed two weeks later in London.

The importance of the DSD

The DSD played an important role in the peace process. It was, as noted earlier, the first of many joint governmental documents which were to provide a focus for the parties in Northern Ireland. It was generally welcomed by commentators and the press upon its publication. It was clear that its aim was to try and create conditions under which the IRA would be willing to end its armed campaign. Major made clear the conditions under which the government would enter talks with Sinn Féin when he made a statement about the DSD in the House of Commons. 'If there is a permanent end to violence, and if Sinn Féin commits itself to the democratic process, then we will be ready to enter into preliminary exploratory dialogue with it within three months.' Major noted that the prospect of the government talking to Sinn Féin would be concerning to unionists but sought to reassure them that the DSD was based on the consent principle (as consent for any change in Northern Ireland's constitutional status had to be given in concurrent referenda North and South). He also stressed that this was acknowledged in the DSD by the Irish government. 'The Taoiseach fully accepts the principle that any constitutional change could come about only with the consent of a majority in Northern Ireland' (*Hansard*, 15 December 1993, cols 1072–1073).

The reaction of the UUP to the DSD was somewhat muted. Molyneaux neither endorsed nor condemned the declaration, but sought further reassurance on the issue of consent, asking that it would not be a move towards joint authority and that Sinn Féin would not be given 'an immediate place at the talks table'. It is interesting that he did not take issue with Major's assertion that Sinn Féin could enter exploratory dialogue within three months of an end to violence, given that he had appeared to state a five-year period was necessary several weeks before. Molyneaux's fellow UUP MP (and subsequent leader), David Trimble, suggested that his party were 'suspending judgement' at that stage on the DSD (*Hansard*, 15 December 1993, col. 1087). However, the DUP's MPs did not feel the need to suspend judgement. The party's leader, Ian Paisley, claimed the people of Northern Ireland looked at the DSD as 'a sell-out act of treachery' (*Hansard*, 15 December

1993, col. 1076), whilst his deputy, Peter Robinson, asked the Prime Minister, 'what loyal Ulster has done wrong to have this further betrayal visited on it' (*Hansard*, 15 December 1993, col. 1085).

In many respects the DSD was not an original document; many of the assertions it made and positions it outlined had been stated before. The British reiterated their stance that they had no 'selfish strategic or economic interest' in Northern Ireland. The two governments' acknowledgement that the status of Northern Ireland could not be changed without the agreement of the majority of the people in Northern Ireland had been a stated British government position since the 1970s and had been included in the AIA. But where the DSD did mark something of a departure was that it was phrased in such a way as to try and address the demands of republicans whilst seeking not to raise the fears of unionists. Or, as Albert Reynolds had told the Irish Parliament, 'In paragraph 4, I believe, there is full respect shown for the basic principles of republican philosophy, but in a manner that is consistent with safeguarding the democratic rights of unionists' (Dáil Éireann, *Debates*, 15 December 1993, vol. 437, no. 3). Paragraph 4 did acknowledge the right of the people of Ireland to self-determination. It stated the 'British government agree that it is for the people of the island of Ireland alone, by agreement between the two parts respectively, to exercise their right of self-determination on the basis of consent, freely and concurrently given, North and South, to bring about a united Ireland, if that is their wish'. This phrasing did two things; it seemed to address Sinn Féin's long-standing demand that the Irish had a right to self-determination, whilst at the same time, by stating that there was the necessity for 'concurrent' consent, it preserved the necessity for a majority of people in Northern Ireland to agree to a united Ireland. The British also addressed the long-standing demand by republicans that they should become 'persuaders for unity', a position that they were unwilling to adopt. They noted their desire 'to enable the people of Ireland to reach agreement on how they may live together in harmony and partnership'; the word 'unity' had been removed from the earlier drafts. The declaration was also clear in its appeal for those groups using violence to see that the political process was open to them once they ceased their violence. Although not specifically named in the document, it was clear that one of its primary purposes was to try and entice the IRA to end its campaign. To this end it was noted that,

> The British and Irish Governments reiterate that the achievement of peace must involve a permanent end to the use of, or support for, paramilitary violence. They confirm that, in these circumstances, democratically mandated parties which establish a commitment to exclusively peaceful methods and which have shown that they abide by the democratic process, are free to participate fully in democratic politics and to join in dialogue in due course between the Governments and the political parties on the way ahead. (DSD, paragraph 10)

In addition to the clauses specifically designed to appeal to republicans, many of which took the form of commitments by the British government, there was an attempt to balance the declaration by the clauses in which the Irish government sought to address unionist concerns. In paragraph 5 'The Taoiseach, on behalf of the Irish government' underlined the commitment to consent as, 'it would be wrong to attempt to impose a united Ireland, in the absence of the freely given consent of the majority of the people of Northern Ireland'. It also included the six 'rights' which the loyalist paramilitaries had passed to Reynolds via the Rev. Roy Magee. These were the rights of free political thought; of freedom and expression of religion; to pursue democratically national and political aspirations; to seek constitutional change by peaceful and legitimate means; to live wherever one chooses without hindrance; and to equal opportunity in all social and economic activity, regardless of class, creed, sex or colour. The Irish government also undertook to examine for unionists

> any elements in the democratic life and organisation of the Irish State that can be represented to the Irish overnment in the course of political dialogue as a real and substantial threat to their way of life and ethos, or that can be represented as not being fully consistent with a modern democratic and pluralist society, and undertakes to examine any possible ways of removing such obstacles. (DSD, paragraph 6)

Finally, the Irish government suggested that they would put forward and support proposals to change the claim in the Irish constitution to Northern Ireland, which had long been a bête noire for unionists, 'in the event of an overall settlement' (DSD, paragraph 7).

Towards a ceasefire

Although the DSD was an important development in the peace process, its impact was not instantaneously transformative. Despite not being rejected by the main unionist party, and being welcomed by the SDLP, it was unclear whether it would have the desired impact on what was arguably its primary audience: the republican movement. On the day it was released, Sinn Féin's, Mitchell McLaughlin stated that 'the general reaction among many nationalists is one of disappointment. This is especially so because of the heightening of expectations in the lead up to the meeting between Mr Reynolds and Mr Major' (*Guardian*, 16 September 1993). Republicans called for clarification from the two governments, a request which the British government originally rejected, arguing that Sinn Féin was just seeking to renegotiate the document. They eventually reversed this decision five months later and responded to questions that Sinn Féin had sent via the Irish government (NIO Statement, 19 May 1994, CAIN). Their original refusal to address Sinn Féin's questions was an unnecessary mistake as it had enabled Sinn Féin to portray the British as intransigent and not serious about the peace process.

In the months after the DSD, the two governments sought to continue to put pressure on republicans but also entice them. Albert Reynolds noted a few days after the DSD that the governments, 'would be expected to respond' if republicans and loyalists did not end their violence. Reynolds made the case that people now wanted the armed groups to end their campaigns. 'After a period in which such strong support has been expressed by the people in both communities for peace, I think there would be revulsion over a resumption of full-scale violence' (*Financial Times*, 20 December 1993).

Post-DSD there was a division between the British and Irish governments over whether Gerry Adams should be granted a visa to visit the US in February 1994. The Major government strongly opposed the move, and it was clear that the US State Department and the US ambassador to London, Raymond Seitz, were also against a visa for Adams (*Independent*, 6 February 1994). In deciding to grant the visa, press reports suggested that Clinton's administration was taking a step that previous administrations would not have. 'It is almost inconceivable that the Bush or Reagan administrations would have delivered such a public slap in the face to America's closest ally' (*The Times*, 31 January 1994). Indeed, it was also claimed that the visa was granted against the advice of the US diplomat who interviewed Adams in Belfast after the application was received (*The Times*, 5 February 1994). It was the case that the Reagan and Bush administrations had not granted Adams a visa to travel to the US, but they were not in office at the beginning of the peace process. Although Bill Clinton had suggested during his election campaign in April 1992 that he would consider a visa for Adams if elected, applications for visas for Adams were refused by the Clinton administration during his first year in office. Indeed, once in the US, Adams claimed over the years he had had eight previous visa requests refused (*Guardian*, 3 February 1994). The context by January 1994 was seen to be different; not only had there been the DSD, but the IRA had maintained a week-long ceasefire in September 1993 during a visit by a high profile Irish-American delegation, led by former congressman and friend of Clinton's, Bill Morrison. Clinton was willing to take a risk and grant a 48-hour visa for Adams to attend a 'peace conference' in Washington. Nancy Soderberg, Clinton's deputy national security adviser, who had previously worked in Edward Kennedy's office, argued that there was a belief in the White House that things were changing in Northern Ireland and this was, to a significant degree, a result of the information they were getting from John Hume. Soderberg recalled that Hume had, six months previously, opposed a visa application from Adams as 'it's not ripe yet', but had advised that it should be supported in January 1994 and the Clinton White House allowed Adams into New York (Soderberg, LHCMA).

The visa issue, and the subsequent one issued in 1995, raises some interesting points in relation to the early stages of the peace process. Both governments, the US and the SDLP believed that there were reasons to believe that the IRA might be amenable to overtures to abandon the armed struggle. Ulster Unionists were obviously also in favour of an end to the IRA's use of violence but were more cynical about whether this was likely and, importantly, what incentives should be offered to them to do so. It was on this issue of what incentives should be offered to republicans, and when, that the parties differed. There were related power disparities between these actors. The British government, given their sovereignty over Northern Ireland, had most 'power'. The other actors were, however, powerful in some respects. Since 1985, the British had largely accepted that an intergovernmental approach was necessary towards Northern Ireland, so they were keen to act in concert with Dublin where possible (though this did not extend to not taking actions that Dublin did not support on occasion). This intergovernmental focus gave Dublin leverage and influence, as did the Irish government's close relationship with the SDLP. The SDLP's power stemmed in part from Hume's talks with Adams, which were important in persuading others that the republicans might be considering a change in approach. Hume's personal standing in both the Republic of Ireland and Washington also meant that the party and its preferences were key to the peace process. Reynolds was reportedly shocked by the reaction within his party when he sought to distance himself from Hume in the run-up to the DSD (*Independent on Sunday*, 7 November 1993) and Soderberg cites the support of Hume for the visa as a key factor in Clinton's decision (Soderberg, LHCMA). The US's position was slightly different from that of London, Dublin and the SDLP. America's 'power' came from their support for the actions of the governments and the parties during the peace process, which, as will be seen, at times was critical. The British, given considerations related to the 'special relationship' and the desire to limit negative publicity internationally over their role in Northern Ireland, were keen that the US government was supportive of their handling of the peace process. Ireland, given the large Irish diaspora in the US and the work of influential Irish-Americans and the government itself, had long had a level of access in the US that was disproportionate to the state's size and geostrategic importance. However, America's role was, as nicely summarised by Will Hazelton, 'encouragement from the sidelines' (Hazelton, 2000). American policy preferences and actions were rarely notably different from those of the UK. Indeed, American governments had largely resisted pressure from other actors to criticise British governments and seek to change British policy regarding Northern Ireland. As a former ambassador to London, Raymond Seitz, noted 'so long as relations between Dublin and London remained civil, and so long as the British government continued to put forward negotiable options for the constitutional leaders of the North to discuss, genuine American interests were not affected' (Seitz, 1998: 285). However, the difference in relation to the visa was that this was one issue over which the US did have 'power' given that it related to who they chose to allow into their country and under which conditions. On this occasion they decided to side with the Irish government and the SDLP against the wishes of the British government.

The trip itself was something of a triumph for Sinn Féin. Adams received a huge amount of media attention during his two-day visit. He gave seven major press interviews, including high-profile shows such as Larry King Live and Good Morning America, as well as four press conferences, a speech at the National Committee on American Foreign Policy's Conference and several meetings with supporters and various groups. Ulster Unionist leaders had been invited to the conference but refused, believing it was simply a vehicle to get Adams into the US. John Hume and the Alliance Party leader, John Alderdice, did attend the conference and Alderdice appeared on the Larry King show via telephone whilst Adams was being interviewed in the studio. As Sharrock and Devenport noted in their biography of Adams, 'As Larry King warmed to Adams' words of peace, he asked Alderdice, "Can't we both agree to stop the killing?" As the leader of the party with unimpeachable anti-violence credentials, Alderdice didn't know how to answer this point. Spluttering on the other end of the phone line, he came over as apparently more intransigent than Adams, the man of peace' (Sharrock and Devenport, 1997: 328). The British strategy of refusing to debate with him meant he had a free ride. The reason for not engaging with Adams in the US was explained by an embassy official, 'I just don't think we can dignify Adams or enhance his status by putting up government officials to debate him.' It was only after he had returned to Belfast that the British embassy in Washington sought to challenge the narrative he had offered. The British ambassador, Sir Robin Renwick, was interviewed on CNN to, as an aide put it, 'rebut the kind of garbage coming out Adams's mouth'. Renwick claimed, 'When I listen to Gerry Adams, I think, as we all do, it's reminiscent of Dr Goebbels' (*Independent*, 6 February 1994).

Despite the successful coverage generated by the American trip and the hopes that a ceasefire was close, the first half of 1994 was marked by uncertainty and disappointment. The months after the DSD and Adams's visit to the US saw continued violence in Northern Ireland. A relentless, often daily, series of shootings and bombings, by both republicans and loyalists, led many to question the optimism that had followed the DSD. The attacks were often sectarian in nature, and shootings led to reprisal shootings. Some, such as the killing by the UVF of six men watching the Republic of Ireland's world cup match in a bar in Loughinisland in June, attracted widespread debate and condemnation. But most received little coverage. Similarly, some actions, such as the IRA's three mortar attacks (none of which detonated) on Heathrow airport over a five-day period in March 1994 garnered international attention, particularly given that it came just weeks after Adams's US trip. Indeed, Adams came under some criticism for his comments after the attacks that 'the conflict is ongoing; every so often there will be something spectacular to remind the outside world' (*Independent*, 11 March 1994), which seemed somewhat at odds with the image he had sought to present in America. After the third Heathrow attack, Dick Spring noted, 'The people on the two islands must view with growing dismay the prospects now for an early cessation of violence' (*Guardian*, 14 March 1994). The announcement of a three-day ceasefire over the Easter weekend by the IRA was not taken as a positive step but was highly criticised by the two governments and the media. Albert Reynolds's press secretary, Sean Duignan, claimed he 'subsequently learned that the widely dismissive response to the three-day ceasefire had a salutary effect on Sinn Féin. They freely admitted afterwards that they had anticipated favourable political and public reaction and were shocked at the wave of derision provoked by the announcement' (Duignan, 1995: 140).

There were also signs that loyalism believed that the IRA might be considering a ceasefire. In July, the umbrella group for loyalist paramilitary groups, The Combined Loyalist Military Command (CLMC) issued a statement that they would take part in 'civilised and productive' dialogue if there was an IRA ceasefire, but also stated that there must be no diminution of Northern Ireland's position in the UK (*Guardian*, 16 July 1994). However, the clarification did not lead to an immediate ceasefire. IRA and loyalist violence continued apace and there was general disappointment when Sinn Féin refused to endorse the DSD after a special conference in Letterkenny to consider the document. Adams said afterwards that, 'The declaration does not deal adequately with some of the core issues and this is crucial', though he did note it had some 'positive elements' (*The Times*, 25 July 1994). Their stance was widely criticised and led almost all the key personnel in the Irish government to believe that the move towards a ceasefire was over. Reynolds's press secretary recorded in his diary that Reynolds said to him, '"You think it's over too Diggy". I say nothing, shrug. He says, "So, I am in a minority of one"' (Duignan, 1995: 145). However, in his memoirs, Reynolds suggests that he himself began to have doubts as a result of the Letterkenny conference's failure to endorse the DSD, noting, 'even I began to wonder if maybe

Adams and McGuinness had lost their influence with the [IRA] Army Council' (Reynolds, 2010: 396). The journalist Andrew Marr summed up the mood of many when he wrote, 'The republicans had their moment of history, and they blew it. The failure of Sinn Féin to grasp the opportunity given by the Downing Street Declaration sends the province back to the mire of murder and hopelessness' (*Independent*, 26 July 1994).

Yet, just five weeks later, on 31 August, the long hoped-for ceasefire was declared by the IRA. The statement said 'Recognising the potential of the current situation and in order to enhance the democratic process and underlying our definitive commitment to its success, the leadership of the IRA have decided that as of midnight, August 31, there will be a complete cessation of military operations. All our units have been instructed accordingly' (CAIN). The Irish government, SDLP, nationalist community in Ireland, and international opinion, were enthusiastic and saw the announcement as a major achievement. The British and unionists, whilst welcoming the end of the violence, were more reserved in their response. For the British government the absence of the word 'permanent' from the announcement was unacceptable. John Major argued that the announcement represented a 'very great chance for peace'. However, he claimed the government needed, 'to be sure that the cessation of violence is not temporary that it is not one week or one month but permanent. Once we have that we can move forward. I do not mind how it is expressed. I don't mind if it is said that the armed conflict is over, that the days of violence are gone for good. But I do need to know that violence is ended for good and that it is not a temporary ceasefire' (*The Times*, 1 September 1994). The Irish government was unhappy about London's position. Reynolds asked, 'Why get hung up on a word? It does not worry me in the least. It is a total end to violence. That's enough for me.'

Why did the IRA end their campaign?

Although it is obviously easy to identify when the IRA announced the end to the campaign of violence, it is obviously harder to categorically identify *why* they did so. The Provisional IRA had used violence for almost a quarter of a century with very few exceptions. Indeed, the experience of their previous ceasefires in the early 1970s, when they believed that they had been 'duped' by the British government and their movement weakened, was often taken as meaning that they would not end or suspend their campaign before the British announced their intention to leave Ireland. Commentators have offered various reasons for the decision of the IRA to end their violence. As discussed in the previous chapter, the debate regarding whether stalemate or

defeat explain the shifts in republican tactics has been interesting, but this
was not the debate in play at the time of the announcement. Most commentators did not believe that the IRA had been forced to end their campaign at
this time, so explanations as to why they chose to do so are important.
Richard English, in his informed study of the IRA, which drew heavily on
interviews with key figures in the republican movement, noted three important internal considerations for the IRA. He argues that explanations which
stress the role of external actors and the international dimension are less
persuasive (English, 2003: 305–307). For English, the main points were,
first, the realisation that there was a military stalemate with the British government, and as a result continuing fighting 'was not going to better the
bargaining position that republicans possessed', and indeed might reduce it.
Second, there would be political rewards if the violence stopped; there was
the 'prospect of ending the political ghettoization' and to open new avenues
and opportunities for republicans to pursue their policy preferences. Third,
'militant republicans recognized some of the key realities about the broader
politics and economics of the north that had earlier been eclipsed from their
vision', notably they factored unionists and Unionism into their thinking to
a greater extent (English, 2003: 307–315). In another influential account of
the IRA, the journalist Ed Moloney charted what he saw as the struggle
within the IRA between the 'politicos', centred around Gerry Adams and
Martin McGuinness, and the more traditional militarists. For Moloney this
battle was key, and he argues that there 'were really two peace processes
running in the years leading up to the 1994 IRA ceasefire'. The one, which
the IRA's Army Council (which included both the 'politicos' and militarists)
believed they were engaged in, was about trying to secure a commitment
from the British government of an intent to withdraw, and the one which the
politicos alone were engaged in. This was 'founded on a fundamental redef-
inition of British withdrawal, one that would allow Sinn Féin to accept the
principle of consent and to negotiate a deal with unionists that fell short of
what most republicans would traditionally regard as Irish unity' (Moloney,
2002: 395). Moloney's distinction between these two positions highlights
some of the challenges of evaluating the IRA's decision. Given its clandestine
nature and structures, it is very difficult to ascertain what was being debated
and decided within the movement. Moloney's account is a fascinating analysis of the intra-IRA power struggles, focusing primarily on Gerry Adams
and his attempts, according to Moloney, to steer the movement away from
armed struggle towards an unarmed strategy, a process that the author suggests Adams and his close confidants were involved in since the mid to late
1980s.

Other commentators have questioned elements of Moloney's account,
suggesting that he accords too much control, and foresight, to Adams.

Tonge et al. have questioned the stalemate thesis (and Moloney's explanation) on the grounds that such accounts place too much emphasis on the military aspects of the IRA campaign and pay insufficient attention to the ideological and political aspects of republicanism. They also argue that existing accounts are too focused on the elites of the republican movement and the claims of authors, such as Moloney, 'that such leaders were imbued with such extraordinary Machiavellian powers of cunning and duplicity that the "foot soldiers" were simply tricked into a peace process and political compromises that they did not desire' (Tonge et al., 2011: 15). For them it was the interplay of the political and military aspects of the conflict that explain the end of the violence in Northern Ireland. The wider focus that Tonge et al. encourage commentators to consider when seeking to explain the end of the armed campaigns in 1994 is welcome, but their own accounts beg some questions. Although they do argue that the views of the 'foot soldiers' need to be given greater consideration, their own work does not really demonstrate how the rank and file of these organisations were instrumental in bringing about the changes that occurred in the period. Also, their suggestion that the decision by the IRA to end its campaign in 1994 represented something of a tactical change is open to question. They note that the IRA had a history of tactical adjustment and seek to portray the decision-taking in 1994 in a similar vein, arguing that the republicanism of the Provisionals 'was based upon tactical flexibility as much as ideological dogmatism or diehard militarism' (Tonge et al., 2011: 8). However, this arguably underplays the shift that the end of the campaign in 1994 represented. The Provisional IRA's stated *raison d'être* was a united Ireland and its methodology centred upon the use of the armed struggle. Its experience of the previous 'indefinite ceasefire' of 1975 had greatly coloured its view of ending violence short of securing their aim. Their position had been frequently stated that they would not end their campaign short of a British declaration of intent to withdraw and, indeed Adams himself had stated in 1982 that if they did, he would not remain a member of the republican movement. Whilst it is true that by the early 1990s there were attempts to suggest that they were always more concerned with issues related to equality rather than liberty, this was a departure from the narrative and justification that they had previously offered during the Troubles period. Tonge et al. are correct in arguing that when seeking to establish why the 'guns fell silent' in 1994, we should not just focus on the narrow terrain of military factors, but if you widen the issues related to stalemate to include the political factors as well as the military ones, the explanation retains merit.

It is impossible to identify definitively why the IRA ended their campaign in 1994. It is likely that several factors were in play. As Richard English noted, the belief that there was a stalemate (politically as well as militarily given Sinn Féin's failure to progress electorally) was likely to be influential. Other factors such as the pressure they were under as a result of British surveillance and infiltration, increasing loyalist targeting and intra-communal pressure may well have played their part. But ultimately, whatever the individual factors that led to the decision, the IRA seems to have concluded that they stood to potentially gain more from ending their armed campaign than from continuing it. This was an important and seismic departure from their previous position, however it was subsequently portrayed. It is the case that the republican movement did not give up on the aim of securing a united Ireland in August 1994, but they did appear to accept that this was not going to be achieved by their armed campaign, a view they had rejected for most of the previous quarter of a century. What is also clear is that the end of the IRA's armed campaign was the single most important development that enabled the fledgling peace process to develop and, as will be discussed, most of the advances in Northern Ireland's political situation over the next few years were contingent upon it, and on its continuation.

Loyalism's response

As noted, by the early 1990s loyalists were killing more people than republicans. Yet their actions were often seen as reactive to republican violence, which is one of the reasons that the ending of the IRA's violence seemed to be a greater priority than the actions of loyalists. The reaction of loyalists to the IRA's ceasefire was, initially, one of concern. There was widespread speculation that a secret deal had been done by the British with the IRA; a deal that would be to the detriment of the Union. The leader of the Progressive Unionist Party, which had close links to the UVF, noted that when the IRA announced its ceasefire, 'my community were dismayed – absolutely dismayed … They were dismayed because they believed that some secret surreptitious deal had been done with a betraying British government' (Ervine, LHCMA). Loyalists tasked Archbishop Robin Eames to directly ask John Major if a deal had been done with the IRA, and he took the Prime Minister's assurances back to the CLMC (Eames, LHCMA). Eames, and a fellow clergyman, Roy Magee, were instrumental in acting as intermediaries between loyalists and the British and Irish governments and had been a main point of contact for both governments during the negotiations of the DSD. Loyalists were concerned in the early 1990s that they did not have any channels to the governments and Eames was persuaded by Magee to meet with the CLMC and raise their concerns with the two governments. The role of the clergy was a notable aspect of the development of the peace process in Northern Ireland. Indeed, Fr Alec Reid also held meetings with loyalists.

Ervine notes that although Reid was a 'decent man' he was unpersuaded by Reid's claims that the IRA's quarrel was not with loyalists (Ervine, LHCMA).

Loyalists were reassured by Eames's reports of his discussions with John Major, and six weeks after the IRA announced the end of their campaign, in the CLMC's statement on 13 October, reference was made to 'having received confirmation and guarantees in relation to Northern Ireland's constitutional position within the United Kingdom'. The statement also asserted that 'The Union is safe.' Their statement did suggest that the ceasefire was permanent, but had a proviso noting that the 'permanence of our ceasefire will be completely dependent upon the continued cessation of all national-ist/republican violence; the sole responsibility for a return to war lies with them'. There was another notable difference to the IRA's statement in August in that the CLMC statement offered 'to the loved ones of all innocent victims over the past 25 years, abject and true remorse' (Bew and Gillespie, 1996: 71–72). Robin Eames subsequently claimed that a condition of him agreeing to interact with the loyalist leadership was that if they stopped, they must express regret (Eames, LHMCA).

Although the reasons for the loyalist ceasefire have received less attention than those of the IRA, there has been some informative scholarship on loy-alism in recent years (see the work of authors such as McAuley, Edwards, Shirlow and Spencer). Some of the suggested reasons for the IRA's ceasefire, such as stalemate, war-weariness, generational considerations, are also in part persuasive for loyalists. But their violence had also been seen as reactive to that of republicans and, of course, their objective was different to that of republicans. They were effectively seeking to maintain the status quo, the Union, whereas republicans were seeking to overthrow it. Therefore, for loyalists, any outcome which appeared to result in an end of the IRA's campaign that did not imperil the Union could be seen, and portrayed, as a victory (Tonge et al., 2011). Once their fears that a deal had been done with republicans were assuaged, this is the narrative that they offered. Shortly after the IRA's announcement, graffiti appeared which stated, 'on behalf of the loyalist people of the Shankill Road we accept the unconditional surrender of the IRA'.

From ceasefire to violence

With the ceasefires of the main armed groups in Northern Ireland the peace process was, potentially, put on a trajectory to transform the conflict in, and governance of, Northern Ireland. But the peace process was not simply about ending the violence, which was a symptom of wider problems. The period running up to the ceasefires had illustrated that without an end to the violence there could not be a meaningful peace process. However, the period immediately after the ceasefires was to illustrate that even with the ending of violence there might not be a meaningful peace process. The main problems centred on the issues of whether the IRA's ceasefire was permanent, how long should the 'quarantine' period be before substantive talks could take place and what to do about the illegally held weapons of armed groups. As noted earlier, it had been made clear to republicans before the ceasefire that any end of violence needed to be permanent rather than temporary. The absence of this word in the IRA's statement caused problems for both the process and relations between the British government and republicans, the Irish government and nationalists in Northern Ireland. The Irish government soon announced that they were accepting the IRA's ceasefire as permanent and Sinn Féin's leadership appeared to move quickly to address British concerns. Adams stated in an interview that the Irish government's assumption that the peace process was permanent was correct, and McGuinness stated that the ceasefire would apply 'under all circumstances' (*The Times*, 2 September 1994). Britain was not reassured at that stage. Major's explanation for his government's stance on this point was that the situation was more complicated than Dublin or republicans made out, given the competing interests and concerns of others he was trying to balance. Major noted that he was under pressure from the Irish government to accept the permanence of the ceasefires

> but this just wasn't practical politics. They had no conception I don't think of the disquiet that there was in the cabinet, in parliament, amongst unionist opinion about whether this ceasefire was going to be permanent or not. Now I was very happy to make progress, very happy to move forward, but I could not have done so, I could not have commanded a majority within the government, within Parliament, until we were certain this was genuine, and that certainly needed a period of time to elapse. (Major, LHCMA)

Major's perspective is understandable and not without rationale. It was a constant British refrain throughout the early days of the peace process that the Irish (and nationalists and republicans) presumed that the government had a level of influence over unionists and within the Conservative Party and Parliament, which they did not believe they had. There was undoubtedly unease not only within the British government and Parliament, which in truth was not particularly pronounced but given Major's slender majority within the House of Commons was a consideration, but, more problematically, within Unionism. Major needed to keep the main unionist parties onside, not only because of Westminster arithmetic, but, more importantly, because without them there could be no peace process. It would not do to alienate Ulster Unionism to the extent that they were unwilling to participate in all-party talks with nationalists and republicans. But over the two issues that caused the main problems in the immediate post-ceasefire period – whether the ceasefires were permanent, and the issue of decommissioning – the Major government did not manage the situation well. Quentin Thomas, who was number two in the NIO in this period, was critical of the government on this point. Speaking in 2005 he noted,

> When they announced they were having a ceasefire, there was a strange psychological flip and ministers, I'm talking specifically about the Prime Minister, John Major, wanted to show that he was not a patsy and that he couldn't be conned that easily, so he started to say, 'well you haven't said permanent, have you?' Now, you couldn't say that any of that was wrong, but it may, if I may respectfully suggest, it may have been tactically inept, because what it amounted to was looking at a gift horse in the mouth, and of course they couldn't then say permanent because they don't do things like that, if you ask for it that's the last thing they'll say. So, we were then slightly stuck, and they were slightly stuck. (O'Kane, 2007: 127)

Thomas is suggesting that strategic 'bigger picture' considerations were not necessarily the main driving factor for Major in this period. Thomas made the interesting observation that Britain had the 'bad tendency to declare something an issue of principle and then act in a way that shows that it can't really have been because we fudged it' (O'Kane, 2007: 137). This was the case over the insistence that the IRA declare their ceasefire permanent. Despite their failure to do this, the British government announced on 21 October that they would make a 'working assumption' that the ceasefire was permanent. This was a welcome development given that it broke a log-jam in the process and enabled meetings between Sinn Féin and the government to be scheduled. However, as Thomas noted, such action demonstrated that the demands made by the government were not matters of principle. As will be seen, the issue of what were 'red lines' and what merely aspirations was to dog the peace process over the coming years.

Having overcome the permanence hurdle, the other major barrier to progress was the issue of decommissioning. The question of when decommissioning was raised, and by whom, caused division between the two governments and between the British and republicans. Sinn Féin claimed that the issue was not in play until the British introduced it post-ceasefire. Gerry Adams claimed, 'The demand for the surrender of IRA weapons as a pre-condition to negotiations was never mentioned by the London government before 31 August (1994). In fact, the British were engaged in intensive contact and dialogue with Sinn Féin for two years prior to the IRA cessation and never at any time was the issue of decommissioning raised.' He went on to claim that if it had been raised as a precondition by the British before the ceasefire, 'it is possible that there would have been no IRA cessation' (*Irish Times*, 15 June 1995). The Irish government also became frustrated by Britain's insistence that there needed to be decommissioning before Sinn Féin could enter all-party negotiations. Spring seemed to endorse Adams's unease about the focus on decommissioning when he argued in June 1995 'If we take the attitude that nothing will happen unless there's a surrender or decommissioning of arms, then I think that's a formula for disaster' (*Irish Times*, 15 June 1995). However, it is clear that the issue of guns had been raised before the ceasefire. Indeed, Dick Spring was one of the people who suggested it was an essential part of the peace process. On the day the DSD was signed, Spring told the Dáil, 'Questions were raised on how to determine a permanent cessation of violence. We are talking about the handing up of arms and are insisting that it would not be simply a temporary cessation of violence to see what the political process offers. There can be no equivocation in relation to the determination of both governments in that regard' (Dáil Éireann, *Debates*, 15 December 1993, vol. 437, col. 77). Spring seemed to repeat this position two months before the ceasefires when he was asked in the Dáil, 'Is it possible for Sinn Féin to participate in talks with the constitutional parties and in the proposed Forum for Peace and Reconciliation without clear, unequivocal and demonstrated disarmament by the IRA? That deserves a simple answer.' Spring replied, 'It is not possible' (Dáil Éireann, *Debates*, 1 June 1994, vol. 443, cols 1021–1023). Evidence is also available that republicans themselves indicated an awareness that decommissioning would have to be addressed. Sean Duignan recorded in his memoirs of his period as Reynolds's press secretary that two weeks after the ceasefire was declared, Adams and McGuinness met Reynolds and Spring in Dublin. He was told immediately after the meeting (which he did not attend) that McGuinness said, 'We know the guns will have to be banjaxed' (Duignan, 1995: 151). When interviewed a few years later about this, Duignan stated it was Spring who told him of the comment by McGuinness. 'Now "banjaxed" is not, I think, a Northern word. I've heard subsequently that McGuinness denies he said it, but when he was asked "well did Adams say it?" he remained mute. And perhaps, because you don't make up that kind of a quote, perhaps Spring is wrong about which of them said it' but he recalled that, 'I remember the quote because I took it down straight away'; and he remained convinced 'it was said in the room' (O'Kane, 2007: 134). This suggestion that republicans were aware that the guns would be an issue is also supported by some comments that they made pre-ceasefire. In January 1994, eight months before the ceasefire, whilst pressing for British clarification of the DSD, Adams said he could not be expected to go to the IRA, 'to ask them to stop their campaign so that we can be engaged in talks after twelve weeks of "decontamination" where we can have exploratory talks with senior British civil servants about how the IRA can hand over its weapons' (*Irish News*, 8 January 1994). Although the tone is flippant, the fact that he raises the issue of arms suggests he was aware that they were, at least potentially, likely to be an issue. However, once republican resistance to decommissioning before all-party talks became apparent, the Irish government moved away from Spring's earlier demands for decommissioning before Sinn Féin joined a talks process. Albert Reynolds argued that Spring's earlier comments did not reflect Irish government policy and Spring's own stance changed. In November 1994 he told the Dáil,

> We are all very conscious, and those leading the Sinn Féin organization to the negotiation table are very conscious also, of the history of that organization and of the numerous splits that have taken place this century. They are conscious of doing everything possible to avoid that. I think it would be unrealistic … to expect that the arms be handed over right now, but I hope that it can be done in due course. (Dáil Éireann, *Debates*, 18 November 1994, vol. 445, cols 2067–2069)

This Irish government's position was a result of concerns over the stability of the peace process and fears that the IRA may return to violence, or split, if it appeared that there were to be barriers erected to their participation in the political process (Duignan, 1995: 136).

For the Major government, however, decommissioning became seen as a marker of the IRA's commitment to the peace process. The British refused to arrange for the all-party talks, which Sinn Féin were demanding, before decommissioning. This could, in part, be explained by the British government seeking to ensure that they did not create a situation whereby inviting Sinn Féin into the talks would result in unionist parties leaving them. Mayhew had written to Gerry Adams in June 1995 refusing a request for Sinn Féin's participation in wider talks, claiming, 'The plain fact is that there will be no substantive political talks which would include Sinn Féin without progress on the [decommissioning] issue not least because other parties will not take part in them' (*Irish Times*, 15 June 1995). However, Britain's early insistence on the importance of decommissioning before all-party talks was not simply a response to a fear regarding the likely demands of Unionism. Indeed, Trimble's biographer, Dean Godson, records that John Major was annoyed with the apparent lack of attention the issue was getting from the recently appointed leader of the UUP, at their first meeting in September 1995 (Godson, 2004: 162).

The British sought to moderate the position in November 1995. Patrick Mayhew spelt out in a speech in Washington the three conditions which had to be met before Sinn Féin could enter talks.

> We will be pressing to achieve three things: a willingness in principle to disarm progressively; a common practical understanding of the modalities, that is to say, decommissioning – what it would actually entail; and in order to test the practical arrangements and to demonstrate good faith, the actual decommissioning of some arms as a tangible confidence-building measure and to signal the start of a process. (*Guardian*, 8 March 1995)

This was seen as a watering down of Britain's previous position which had suggested that the IRA had to fully decommission before they were admitted to the talks. Mayhew seemed to suggest that an undertaking to disarm and the decommissioning of some weapons would be enough. This softening of position did attract some criticism from unionists; the UUP MP, Ken Maginnis claimed, 'The man must be stark raving mad to suggest that those with a hundred tons of the most sophisticated weapons can only get away with a token gesture' (*Guardian*, 8 March 1995). But the softening was not sufficient to break the logjam. Adams portrayed the demands over decommissioning as 'bad faith' and accused the British of 'reneging on its commitments to all-party negotiations given publicly prior to 31 August' (*Irish Times*, 15 June 1995).

The issue of decommissioning continued to undermine the process throughout the Major premiership. Attempts were made to reduce its importance by the creation of the International Body on Decommissioning which was led by the former American senator George Mitchell, the Canadian, General John de Chastelain and the former Finnish Prime Minister Harri Holkeri. The idea had come from the Irish government at a summit in June 1995. Mitchell later recalled that the purpose of the Commission was to get the British off 'the hook of prior decommissioning' that it 'had gotten itself on' (Mitchell, 1999: 29–30). However, although the British agreed to the Commission they publicly asserted that they were not willing to abandon the Washington three demands for some decommissioning before talks began. When it became apparent that this was not what the Mitchell Commission was going to recommend, Major told Mitchell that if the Report did not call for prior decommissioning, he would have to reject it. Mitchell and his colleagues were unwilling to endorse the British preference for prior decommissioning. Mitchell told Major that the Chief Constable of the RUC had informed them that Adams could not have secured prior decommissioning by the IRA even if he had asked them for it. Mitchell later noted 'I don't think he [Major] or his top officials cared to hear that' (Mitchell, LHCMA). When the Report was published in January 1996, it stated that 'we have concluded that the paramilitary organisations will not decommission any arms prior to all-party negotiations' but suggested instead that 'some decommission should take place during the process of all-party negotiations, rather than before or after, as the parties now urge'. The Report also set out six principles, which all participants in the talks should sign up to. These were that all parties:

> affirm their total and absolute commitment: a. To democratic and exclusively peaceful means of resolving political issues; b. To the total disarmament of all paramilitary organisations; c. To agree that such disarmament must be verifiable to the satisfaction of an independent commission; d. To renounce for themselves, and to oppose any effort by others, to use force, or threaten to use force, to influence the course or the outcome of all-party negotiations; e. To agree to abide by the terms of any agreement reached in all-party negotiations and to resort to democratic and exclusively peaceful methods in trying to alter any aspect of that outcome with which they may disagree; and, f. To urge that 'punishment' killings and beatings stop and to take effective steps to prevent such actions. (Mitchell Report, 1996)

This unwillingness of the Mitchell Commission to endorse prior decommissioning was problematic for the British government, given it had made it clear it was committed to this course. Mayhew circulated a document to cabinet colleagues examining the government's options. He argued they could reject the Report, which would be 'highly damaging' as the government would face criticism for the continuing impasse. They could accept the Report's recommendations, which Mayhew advised against, as he did not believe it was the correct course, or take, 'a positive line in response to the Report, in no way abandoning Washington 3, but promote a modified way ahead involving an elective process, as identified by the Report albeit rather faintly ... ' (Godson, 2004: 196–197). This was a reference to the one paragraph towards the end of the Report (Article 56, of 62), which had stated if 'it were broadly acceptable, with an appropriate mandate, and within the three-strand structure, an elective process could contribute to the building of confidence'. This had been something which the unionist leader David Trimble had apparently favoured and the NIO minister, Michael Ancram, had requested to Mitchell to be included in the Report (Mitchell, LHCMA). This then became the route that the British government advocated to move to all-party talks. In response to the publication of the Mitchell Report, Major noted that the Report had stated that paramilitaries would not decommission before the talks, but observed, 'The House will note that the body did not conclude that they cannot decommission; the body concluded that they will not, and the House will draw its own conclusions.' He then offered two possible ways that Sinn Féin could join the talks, 'The first is for the paramilitaries to make a start to decommissioning before all-party negotiations. They can – if they will. If not, the second is to secure a democratic mandate for all-party negotiations through elections especially for that purpose. Those are two routes to all-party negotiations and to decommissioning' (House of Commons, *Debates*, 24 January 1996, vol. 270, col. 355).

Major's stance was supported by the UUP with their leader, David Trimble, stating of an elected body, 'in view of the refusal of Sinn Féin-IRA to make the necessary moves in relation to weapons, we regard [it] as the only way forward'. This was a sentiment echoed by the DUP's Peter Robinson who agreed that, given the unwillingness of the IRA to decommission before talks, 'the only real way forward is through an election' (House of Commons, *Debates*, 24 January 1996, vol. 270, cols 358 and 360). However, the proposal angered Dublin and some in Northern Ireland. The Irish government believed that they had not been sufficiently consulted on the approach and the fact that the ceasefire had held since August 1994 should be sufficient to reassure those sceptical of the IRA and Sinn Féin's intentions. The Irish Taoiseach, John Bruton, asked 'Why not sit down and talk to Sinn Féin? After 16 months without violence, surely unionists have now become confident enough to take the risk of talking to Sinn Féin? You do not have to agree but you can start talking and that can be done directly by the two parties themselves even without any government structure or format – and it can be done straight away' (*Guardian*, 26 January 1996). The Irish government's position was that an 'elective process in Northern Ireland should flow from all-party talks, not *vice versa*' (Dáil Éireann, *Debates*, 31 January 1996, vol. 460, col. 1847). Behind the scenes in Dublin, 'senior government sources' were suggesting a greater annoyance with the British government, telling journalists, 'Major's just told the Provos: "Right, you've just completed the hurdle race lads, now please can you do it again, only backwards this time"' (*Guardian*, 26 January 1996). John Hume responded angrily in the House of Commons. Alluding to Major's slim majority in parliament he stated, it 'would be particularly irresponsible for a government to try to buy votes to keep themselves in power', and called on the government to fix a date for all-party talks 'rather than waste time as he has for the past 17 months' (House of Commons, *Debates*, 24 January 1996, vol. 270, col. 360). This was a view held by Gerry Adams who accused the British of 'dumping' the Mitchell Report and claimed, 'Mr Major has now adopted an entirely unionist agenda in an attempt to buy unionist votes in Westminster' (*Irish Times*, 25 January 1996).

The question of to what extent the Report had been 'dumped' was debated for a period after its release. In his analysis of the government's actions Thomas Hennessey argued that it was subsequently 'virtually forgotten that the British government had accepted, not rejected, the Mitchell Report', but this is highly questionable (Hennessey, 2000: 101). Whilst Britain asserted their acceptance of the Report – which Major repeated in his autobiography (Major, 2000: 486) – by basing their subsequent policy on what was effectively a relatively minor passing reference to an elected body rather than the call for decommissioning during all-party talks, the approach was clearly not an endorsement of the recommendations of the Mitchell body. Mitchell himself was subsequently less exercised by the British government's approach and less critical of it than many had been at the time. He recorded in his memoirs that Major 'reviewed our report, heaped praise on it, then proceeded to suggest an alternative route to negotiations' (Mitchell, 1999: 39). But, interviewed in 2000, he noted that he was fully aware from the start that the government were not obliged to accept the report, but could reject it, or take parts of it. Indeed, he went so far as to claim of Major's decision 'in retrospect it was an astute political manoeuvre to enable the negotiations to begin by another route' (Mitchell, LHCMA).

The divisions over decommissioning and the path chosen by the British government was illustrative of many aspects of the early stages of the peace process. It again demonstrates the importance of context and highlights the difficulties of making decisions based upon imperfect knowledge and uncertainty of outcomes. By 2000 it may have been possible to argue that the decision to use an electoral route to all-party talks was an astute political manoeuvre by Major, but this was far from universally believed in 1996. The issue over decommissioning also highlighted something of a power disparity between the parties involved. The British were able to select a course that was unpopular with their Irish counterparts in Dublin, and with the main parties of the minority community in Northern Ireland, due to the fact that as the sovereign government they could set the agenda and, to an extent, the mechanisms of any talks process. It also illustrated that there were different considerations in play. Britain was concerned that a move to all-party talks before decommissioning might alienate unionists and so be detrimental to the wider objectives of a peace process. However, as Quentin Thomas suggests, this was not the sole explanatory factor in Britain's decision. There were also sectors of the wider Conservative Party, and indeed the British cabinet, that were uneasy with treating Sinn Féin as a political party like any other. Suspicion over whether the IRA were genuinely committed to permanently ending the violence meant that decommissioning became something of a litmus test for the IRA. Dublin's position was different from London's. Although Dublin also desired decommissioning they believed that if republicans were pushed too hard on this before all-party talks then the ceasefire may collapse and the 'hard men' would push the IRA back to the armed struggle. Therefore, for Dublin, the key became movement towards all-party talks during which decommissioning could be dealt with, a position they believed that the Mitchell Report had endorsed. Republicans throughout this period suggested that the concerns of Dublin were correct and increasingly argued that they had been assured by the British government that if the IRA ended their armed campaign, they would be swiftly included in a wider inclusive talks process. Their narrative throughout the decommissioning debate was that the British had introduced it as a subsequent precondition. For their part, nationalists, and in particular John Hume, also felt that the insistence on decommissioning before all-party talks was an ill-advised tactic that threatened the peace process. Although differences were to emerge over the issue of decommissioning within nationalism over the coming years, at that stage there was little pressure from within the SDLP for the IRA to decommission before all-party talks. Unionism, as noted above, did periodically suggest that decommissioning was necessary before they would enter all-party talks, but it was the British government, rather than the main unionist leaders, who took the lead on the issue.

The difficulty in analysing this period, and why it can be argued that it is illustrative of many aspects of the peace process, is that there is a logic to, and evidence for, all the strands of the debate. It is important to bear in mind when analysing the peace process that there was, for no party, a strategic masterplan being followed, and no party had the ability to force their policy preferences on the other main players. Whilst it was noted above that there was something of a power imbalance in favour of Britain in terms of setting an agenda and creating the mechanisms of the process, this should not be overstated. Britain could set the agenda and create mechanisms for talks, or refuse to do so, but as events demonstrated, if the other players rejected their proposals, progress could not be made. The 'astute political manoeuvre' by Major on 24 January 1996 in insisting that the move to all-party talks was dependent upon successfully participating in an electoral process, appeared less astute on 9 February when the IRA announced the end of its ceasefire and detonated a huge bomb near Canary Wharf, East London, killing two people, injuring over a hundred and causing £85 million of damage.

The resumption of IRA violence had several results in relation to the peace process. Inevitably, it sidelined the issue of decommissioning in the immediate term. Given that the IRA had resumed the use of weapons, whether they were about to give them up was no longer a relevant question. The end of the ceasefire can also be seen as validating the position of both those who argued that the ceasefire was being put under unwarranted pressure by the British approach and those who argued that it was only ever simply a tactic. John Major linked the violence to the previous demands for the ceasefire to be declared permanent, 'we never lost sight that the IRA commitment had not been made for good … I regret to say that the events of last Friday showed that our caution about the IRA was only too justified' (Bew and Gillespie, 1999: 324). The IRA's statement announcing the end of its ceasefire claimed, 'the blame for the failure thus far of the Irish peace process lies squarely with John Major and his government'. According to the IRA 'the British government acted in bad faith, with Mr Major and the unionist leaders squandering this unprecedented opportunity to resolve the conflict' (Bew and Gillespie, 1996: 160). This was not a position that was widely shared, and the IRA's action was condemned domestically and internationally. The decommissioning issue and the reaction to the Mitchell Report had angered the Irish government. Indeed, in his memoirs, Fergus Finlay, the advisor to the then Irish Tánaiste, Dick Spring, called Major's handling of the Mitchell Report 'the biggest own goal of the entire peace process' claiming it drove 'a wedge of solid mahogany into the peace process'. Finlay's observation on the ending of the ceasefire was that the 'Provos' patience had run out' (Finlay, 1998: 300–301). This was in line with the suggestion before the ceasefire that the British were pushing too hard on decommissioning. However, the resumption of the violence also forced the two governments to shelve their differences (which was 'aided' by the fact that the difference over how to deal with decommissioning was no longer the pressing issue it had been). The Irish government had no desire to be seen to be taking a stance that might in any way suggest that the IRA's resumption of violence was excusable or even understandable. As a result, Dublin dropped their objections to the electoral process and the two governments announced after a summit on 28 February that they were consulting on the form that the electoral process would take but inclusive all-party talks would begin on 10 June. Sinn Féin could join the talks if the IRA's ceasefire had been restored.

It is notable that the resumption of violence did not result in the main parties deciding the peace process was over. It might have been expected that the resumption of the IRA's armed campaign would have led to the conclusion that the IRA's ceasefire had been purely a temporary tactic and that they had proven themselves unreliable and unworthy partners with whom to embark upon a peace process. Yet, as Major noted in his memoirs, whilst the Canary Wharf attack was a huge setback, he refused to accept it was 'the end of the road' (Major, 2000: 489). Similarly, the Irish diplomat, Sean Ó hUiginn, argued that the Irish government did not see the resumption of violence as the end of the road as the republican leadership had not embarked upon the peace process lightly and 'wanted this project to succeed' (Spencer, 2015: 176). This, however, begs the question as to why the IRA would take such a risky step as to return to violence. An interesting observation is made by former IRA member Seanna Walsh. Walsh was in prison in 1996 but was the person in 2005 that would read out the statement that the IRA's war was over. He argued that the resumption of violence 'was part of the negotiations and not designed to take us back to the situation that existed prior to 1994. I know it sounds very callous now, but

Canary Wharf looked like negotiations by other means' (Spencer, 2015: 173). Indeed, even in the immediate aftermath of the Canary Wharf attacks, the major players did not seek to completely isolate Sinn Féin. British officials, though not politicians, continued to meet them and Adams was allowed a visa to enter the US in early March.

In the elections, which were held on 30 May, Sinn Féin polled their largest ever vote in Northern Ireland to date (15 per cent) and secured seventeen seats in the 110-seat Forum from which the parties would draw their delegates for the proposed all party talks. This could be interpreted either as encouragement for the peace process and an incentive for the IRA to restore its ceasefire so Sinn Féin could participate in the forthcoming talks, or as an endorsement for the return to violence by the IRA. However, given the purpose of the elections, it was more convincingly perceived as a vote in favour of a peace process. The system that was used in the elections was a complicated one, which had a regional top-up aspect. This successfully achieved its aims in that the two emerging parties associated with loyalist paramilitary groups, the Progressive Unionist Party, which had links with the UVF, and the Ulster Democratic Party (UDP), linked to the UDA, secured sufficient votes to achieve two seats each. This ensured that the voice of loyalism would be represented at the talks, an important consideration given the aspirations of the peace process. The newly formed Women's Coalition also polled sufficiently to gain representation at the talks – a welcome development for many in Northern Ireland's politics, as did a Labour coalition. The SDLP retained their position as the largest nationalist party, securing 21.4 per cent of the vote and gaining twenty-one seats. The picture within Unionism was more nuanced, however, and was an early harbinger of the divisions that were to come into sharper focus after the signing of the GFA. David Trimble's UUP, the party which since the formation of the state had been the main electoral champion of Ulster Unionism, again topped the poll with 24.2 per cent and thirty seats against the DUP's 18.8 per cent and twenty-four seats. However, as the journalist David McKittrick noted in his analysis of the results, this was the UUP's lowest ever tally in a Northern Ireland election, excluding those to the European Parliament. In the previous six elections in Northern Ireland, the party had never achieved less than 29 per cent of the vote (*Independent*, 5 June 1996). The party which was most adversely impacted in the election was the non-sectarian Alliance Party which saw its vote slump to 6.5 per cent.

The 'all-party talks' convened on 10 June 1996 but the failure of the IRA to restore its ceasefire meant that Sinn Féin were excluded from the sessions. As a result of this exclusion the talks inevitably made little progress. Given that the peace process was premised on an inclusive approach focused on ending the violence, a process without Sinn Féin was, as Fergus Finlay had observed a couple of months earlier, 'not worth a penny candle' (*Daily Mirror*, 26 April 1996). The IRA underlined their alienation from the process five days after the talks began by detonating a huge bomb near the Arndale Centre in Manchester, injuring 220 people (*Sunday Times*, 16 June 1996). They continued the tactic of large bombs in England and Northern Ireland throughout the rest of Major's premiership, and attempts to persuade them back into the peace process failed, until the election of Tony Blair's New Labour government in May 1997.

Conclusion

To what extent was the 1994–1996 ceasefire a missed opportunity and who was to blame for the resumption of the violence? The emergence and development of the peace process in the early 1990s was complicated. Inevitably all sides had different objectives and different expectations as to what should, and would, happen. The republicans retained the aspiration of a united Ireland but had come to believe that the armed struggle was of deteriorating effectiveness. As a result, they were open to exploring the possibilities of whether their position could be improved by ending the violence and participating in a political process. This was clearly a major shift in their position. Twenty-five years of violence had clearly not forced the 'Brits' from Ireland and there was little to suggest that continuing the struggle would lead to a different outcome. There was also the problem of escalating loyalist violence, which was taking its toll on the wider nationalist community and on republicans. The leadership at the top of the movement was largely made up of people who had been involved for most of that period, and it may well have been the case that they were looking for ways to avoid another generation having to live through the violence. The emerging peace process and the interaction the leadership had with the British government, albeit not directly, led them to believe that, if the violence ended, they would be allowed to participate in wider negotiations. Their hope was that they could use these talks to advance their position, though it must have been clear to them that they were not ending the violence to enter talks to bring about Irish unity, in the short term.

The British government, which for over twenty-five years had to deal with the violence in Northern Ireland, found themselves faced with the possibility of securing the agreement of the main armed group to end its campaign. Although the violence in Northern Ireland was not likely to cause an existential crisis for either the British security forces or the governing of Northern Ireland, it was a serious problem and one which governments for many years had wished to end. There was little sign that the British were close to defeating the IRA, so a negotiated process that saw them agree to end their campaign had obvious appeal.

Although the IRA and the British government were not the only actors involved in the conflict, in many respects at that outset of the peace process, they were the key ones. Obviously, a peace process could not develop unless the other actors, including the political parties associated with Unionism, the SDLP, loyalists, and the Irish government, agreed to participate. However, it could not begin at all unless the IRA ended their violence and they would not do this without reassurances from the British government regarding what would happen if they did. Events after the ceasefire was called in August 1994 were both frustrating and explicable. They were frustrating as, once the IRA had decided to end their violence and the loyalists followed suit, it might have been expected that more progress would have been made. It is explicable, however, given the wider tensions and competing expectations that were in play. Republicans believed that the British had failed to move to the all-party talks within the three-month period mentioned during the backchannel talks. As a result, the IRA re-evaluated whether more could be achieved by non-violent methods, at least in the short term, and resumed their campaign. As noted, this led to questions over whether they had been serious about the peace process and if their ending of violence had been anything other than a temporary tactic. It is clearly the case that the IRA were responsible for the resumption of violence, given that they chose to end their ceasefire, but to understand that decision it needs to be placed in context.

By February 1996, there was a perception, beyond the IRA, that the move to all-party talks had taken too long. The SDLP and the Irish government were openly critical of the delays and the decision of the British to create an electoral process to try and overcome the decommissioning impasse, an issue that both the Irish government and the SDLP believed had been allowed to take on too much significance by the British. The Major government was undoubtedly in a difficult position regarding IRA intentions, and how they could be demonstrated, during the 1994–1996 ceasefire. London was conscious of needing to keep Unionism on board; there could be no wider negotiations without unionist parties. Unionism, and loyalism, were highly sceptical of republican intentions (and concerned over British ones) at the outset of the peace process and Major's government was correct to seek to reassure them. However, it remains unclear whether Unionism could have been reassured and progress made by methods that would not have resulted in a twenty-month gap between the calling of the ceasefire and the firm date for all-party talks, by which time the IRA ceasefire no longer existed. It would certainly have been difficult, but the situation was not helped by the Major government acting in ways that were, as Thomas noted, 'tactically inept'. Despite this tactical ineptitude it should also be noted that the Major government, along with their Irish counterparts, took significant risks for peace in Northern Ireland. Their actions in trying to create conditions that would persuade the IRA to examine its commitment to the use of violence and agree to call a ceasefire were impressive. Similarly, the willingness of the other key players in Northern Ireland politics, and wider civil and religious society, to seek to challenge and change the politics of Northern Ireland in the early 1990s was remarkable. That it did not fully succeed at that stage should not lead to the conclusion that it 'failed'. Bringing the region out of a violent conflict that had lasted over a quarter of a century was never going to be straightforward or lineal. By the time the ceasefire was broken in 1996, relations between the key actors of the British government and republican movement had deteriorated to such an extent that it was impossible to put the peace process back on course until after the British general election of 1997. When the electoral landslide swept Tony Blair and New Labour into power, the process restarted but, as will be shown, it was a continuation of the peace process that was being explored under Major, rather than a departure from it.

3

New Labour's new peace process? Negotiating the Agreement, 1997–1998

The period between the resumption of the IRA campaign in February 1996 and the entry of Sinn Féin into all-party talks in September 1997 was a rather bleak and unproductive one. On the political level, although the all-party talks did begin in June 1996, given Sinn Féin's absence, they made little progress. Whilst there was no real interest in either governments or in the SDLP in abandoning the inclusive aspirations of the peace process and returning to an exclusion-based approach, neither was there any willingness to allow Sinn Féin into the talks whilst the IRA's violence continued. Politically, the focus became how to create conditions that would lead to the IRA restoring their ceasefire and enabling Sinn Féin to enter talks. However, the IRA showed little inclination to restore their ceasefire during the period. Although the ceasefires of the main loyalist groups, the UDA and UVF were not called off in response to the IRA's resumption of their campaign, loyalist violence was also a feature in this period. A new group, the Loyalist Volunteer Force (LVF) emerged from a splinter within the UVF. The LVF was led by Billy Wright, who was reported to have been the UVF's Commander in Mid Ulster, and unhappy with the UVF's ceasefire.

The period between IRA ceasefires can be seen as something of a brief 'hiatus' in the peace process, but it does illustrate important wider points in relation to the peace process itself and the situation in Northern Ireland in this period. The fact that the end of the IRA ceasefire in February 1996 was not taken to be the end of the peace process illustrates how central the idea of inclusion and all-party talks had become to the approach of the British and Irish governments, as well as to nationalism in Northern Ireland, and to international actors such as the government of Bill Clinton in the US. This is more notable given that there was no immediate suggestion that the ending of the ceasefire was believed to be a temporary tactic or negotiating signal by the IRA. Indeed when Bertie Ahern, who was leader of the main opposition at that time, was asked many years later whether he had the impression that the end of the ceasefire was temporary or tactical he stated, 'No, definitely not … There was lots of intelligence available to us that the whole movement was back on a war footing, and there was no indication right through 1996 that we would be able to get back into a ceasefire position' (Spencer, 2020: 241–242). Rather than categorically state that the resumption of violence marked the end of the peace process, both governments looked for ways to create conditions which would enable the ceasefire to be restored.

Undoubtedly the election of Blair's New Labour government in May 1997 was instrumental in restoring the peace process. The event changed the electoral landscape at Westminster. By the time of the election John Major was leading a minority government in Parliament, whereas Tony Blair had a majority of 179 seats. This meant that there could be no suggestion of his being dependent upon unionist votes to retain power. However, it is questionable whether Blair's approach was significantly different in substance to that which Major had proposed towards the latter period of his time in office. Blair's first major speech on Northern Ireland as Prime Minister, and indeed his first major speech outside London as Prime Minister, was to the Royal Ulster Agricultural Show on 16 May. The speech was designed to reassure unionists, perhaps not least because historically Labour's official policy was in favour of Irish unity, by consent, which had been dropped from their 1997 election manifesto (*Irish Times*, 3 March 1997). His NISS, Mo Mowlam, subsequently described it as 'a speech of seminal importance in our bid to build an inclusive talks process' (Mowlam, 2003: 77). In the speech the Prime Minister stated he was 'committed to the principle of consent'. He also asserted his agenda 'is not a united Ireland … unionists have nothing to fear from a New Labour government. A political settlement is not a slippery slope to a united Ireland. The government will not be persuaders for unity.' In doing so he was seeking to distance himself from what Labour's policy had previously been, but this also served to underline to republicans that his government was not offering anything notably different from that of his predecessors. This emphasised the continuation of traditional bipartisan approaches to the issue of Northern Ireland in British government. In the speech, Blair went even further by claiming 'none of us in this hall today, even the youngest, is likely to see Northern Ireland as anything but a part of the United Kingdom'. However, the speech was not simply designed to reassure unionists, it also had the aspiration of encouraging the IRA to end its violence to allow Sinn Féin to enter the talks process. To this end he asserted his government's view that the 1995 Framework Documents (FWD), which the previous British and Irish governments had published as a possible outline of a solution, but the unionists had rejected, was 'a reasonable basis for future negotiation'. He also stressed the need for an Irish dimension to a solution and announced that British officials could meet Sinn Féin to discuss the situation, even though the IRA had not restored their ceasefire. But a key aspect of the speech, which was a tactic that the Blair government would seek to use frequently during the coming years, was to create an impression of dynamism, a sense of an opportunity that could be missed, and a risk of marginalisation. Blair pointedly announced, 'My message to Sinn Féin is clear. The settlement train is leaving. I want you on that train. But it is leaving anyway, and I will not allow it to wait for you.' This suggestion of deadlines and exclusions was one which would lose some of its impact over the coming years, but in 1997 the newly elected Prime Minister appeared to bring political stability, urgency and hope to the process. Blair did appear to believe he could bring about a breakthrough on Northern Ireland. His press secretary, Alastair Campbell, recorded in his diary after his first meetings as Prime Minister with David Trimble and John Hume, 'TB said he reckoned he could see a way of sorting the Northern Ireland problem. I loved the way he said it, like nobody had thought of it before' (Campbell, 2011: 16).

Behind the dynamic rhetoric there were, however, continuities with the approach that John Major had outlined in Parliament six months earlier. In November 1996 the IRA had apparently outlined their conditions for a reinstated ceasefire. These had been passed on to Major by John Hume, after his talks with Gerry Adams. The reported conditions were 'Sinn Féin's immediate entry to talks; an agreed timetable for the talks to be completed, perhaps six months; renewed confidence-building measures by the government on issues such as the release of prisoners; and no insistence on prior decommissioning of IRA weapons' (*Observer*, 24 November 1997). In the House of Commons the following week, Major outlined the conditions that were necessary for Sinn Féin to enter talks.

> When Sinn Féin could join the talks depends on its own actions. We need to see an unequivocal restoration of the ceasefire, we need to be able to make a credible judgment that it is lasting, and we need to know that Sinn Féin will sign up to the Mitchell principles. Those matters are in Sinn Féin's hands. We are not seeking delay; we wish to see inclusive talks involving all parties as soon as possible, but if Sinn Féin continues to exclude itself, the talks must and will go on without it. (*Hansard*, 28 November 1996, vol. 286, col. 461)

The government also published a more detailed response, which it had passed on to Hume on 23 November (CAIN). The government's position sought to address some of the conditions that the IRA seemed to be raising, though it did so in a way that was likely to be too vague for them. Despite this vagueness the document did suggest that the envisaged process was British talks with Sinn Féin 'at various levels', joint discussions between the British and Irish governments and Sinn Féin, consultations with all parties regarding how to move the process forward, then the move to plenary all-party talks including Sinn Féin. It was also clear that there would not need to be prior decommissioning by the IRA; the government stated that it supported the Mitchell plan of decommissioning during the talks. There was no firm deadline for when the talks would be concluded but the document noted that a plenary session was scheduled for December and that progress would be reviewed by the end of May 1997. The lack of certainty in the document made it difficult to state exactly what was being offered to the republican movement in November 1996, but the journalist John Kampfner interpreted the message as, 'you get a move on and issue your statement before Christmas; follow that up with the necessary demilitarisation steps such as an end to targeting, training and small-scale intimidation, and we will get you into the talks by the time they resume in the New Year' (*Financial Times*, 29 November 1996). The lack of specific details in the British statement in November 1996, along with the mistrust between republicans and the British government and the awareness of the imminence of a British election, meant that no progress was made. But it is interesting to note the similarity between what Major's government suggested the 'cost' of Sinn Féin entry into talks would be and the conditions that the Blair government suggested needed to be met, once it came to power. In the weeks after Blair's 16 May speech, the new government fleshed out its approach. The government announced that decommissioning would be dealt with by an international commission during all-party talks, with a special committee created under the talks process to monitor progress. Blair also revealed that Sinn Féin had been informed that a judgement would be made on whether they could enter talks six weeks after a ceasefire was called, that talks were expected to begin in September 1997 and to be concluded by May 1998 (*The Times*, 26 June 1997). In many respects this was like Major's plan, but with the advantage of more specifics on the timescales involved, and the government's sizeable majority, which impacted on the perception of whether it could be delivered or not. It should also be noted, however, that it was not the case that the situation improved instantly once Blair replaced Major. The IRA's continuing activities in this period, notably the killing of two policemen in Lurgan, Northern Ireland on 16 June, both infuriated and confused the new Prime Minister. The killings led Blair to say privately 'What on earth do you do? We do everything we can. Clearly, they don't want to know' (Campbell, 2011: 60). Despite the fears and continuing violence, the IRA were moving towards a new ceasefire and politically they appeared to be continuing their upward trajectory. In the general election in Northern Ireland on 21 May, Sinn Féin secured almost 17 per cent of the vote (compared with 12.4 per cent four years earlier) and in the Irish Republic's general election on 6 June (which saw Fianna Fáil's Bertie Ahern emerge as Taoiseach) Sinn Féin secured its first Irish parliamentary seat since the start of the Troubles.

On 19 July 1997, an announcement was made that 'having assessed the current political situation, the leadership of Oglaigh na hEireann are announcing a complete cessation of military operations from midday Sunday 20 July 1997. We have ordered the unequivocal restoration of the ceasefire of August 1994. All IRA units have been instructed accordingly.' The statement claimed the previous British government and Ulster Unionists had 'blocked any possibility of real or inclusive negotiations' which was why the previous ceasefire had been 'reluctantly abandoned' (*An Phoblacht/Republican News* (*AP/RN*) 24 July 1997). The implication was clear, it was the perception that Sinn Féin would be included in inclusive talks which led to the announcement in July. This was confirmed by the Secretary of State, Mo Mowlam, a few weeks later when she announced that, on the basis of the ceasefire, Sinn Féin would be invited to join the all-party talks on 15 September. However, Mowlam caused fury amongst unionists in her comments on consent, when she stated, 'consent means a willing accommodation … I don't define it by numbers necessarily. I don't necessarily define it in a functional geographical sense.' The PUP's David Ervine, who had strong links to the loyalist UVF argued, 'The very plinth on which we base our approach to the negotiations, and on which the loyalist ceasefire is based, has been snatched from under our feet' (*Guardian*, 30 August 1997). In her memoirs Mowlam played down the comment and attributed its impact, in part, to the 'silly season' of August when there is 'not much news about'. Whilst she did not record the actual comment in her book, she stated that she had given 'an honest answer' to a question on consent, 'but it only made matters worse' (Mowlam, 2003: 125–127). The statement was ill-advised and was, silly season or not, inevitably going to concern unionists. It increased unionists' suspicions of Mowlam; Trimble in particular had a difficult relationship with her (Powell, 2009: 26). According to his biographer, Dean Godson, after this event 'as far as Trimble was concerned, she never recovered and thereafter Trimble's important dealings with the government were exclusively with No.10' (Godson, 2004: 290). This might be something of an overstatement, as Mowlam was to remain an important actor in the talks to come, but what is clear is that the episode did damage her and her relationship with unionists.

After Sinn Féin signed up to the Mitchell Principles on 9 September things were in place for the beginning of all-party talks, chaired by Senator George Mitchell. However, just two days later an IRA spokesperson was interviewed in *An Phoblacht/Republican News*. The interview offered a fuller explanation of why the IRA had decided to restore its ceasefire. As the brief statement had hinted in July, it suggested that it saw fundamental differences between the Blair government and its predecessor, and welcomed the election of the Fianna Fáil-led government in the Republic. Whereas, according to the IRA,

Major's government 'had imposed a number of blocking mechanisms or obstacles to prevent inclusive and meaningful peace talks taking place', Blair's government had sought to address the IRA's 'four key issues'. These were 'the removal of the precondition of decommissioning; setting a time frame for any talks; immediate entry into talks for Sinn Féin on the basis of its democratic mandate'; and 'confidence-building measures by the British government'. The spokesperson claimed the new British government had moved publicly and speedily to address these issues (*AP/RN*, 11 September 1997).

Whether the stance of the Blair government differed, to the extent that the spokesperson seemed to be suggesting, from Major's approach is open to question, but there was clearly a firmer time frame offered under the new government. Whilst there was nothing especially contentious regarding the explanation of why the ceasefire was called, the interview did contain a couple of problematic assertions. When asked about decommissioning, the IRA's position seemed to suggest that they were not contemplating abiding by the Mitchell plan of parallel decommissioning during the talks process. Asked whether the IRA's previous position that there would be no decommissioning had changed, the reply was, 'No, our position on decommissioning has not changed in any way at all. I don't think anyone has ever realistically expected us to agree to decommissioning this side of a political settlement. There is no historical precedent in Ireland for such a demand ... Decommissioning on our part would be tantamount to surrender' (*AP/RN*, 11 September 1997). Even more contentiously, the IRA clearly did not see themselves as bound by the Mitchell Principles, which Sinn Féin had just undertaken to adhere to. 'Sinn Féin is a political party with a very substantial democratic mandate. What they do is a matter for them ... As to the IRA's attitude to the Mitchell Principles per se, well, the IRA would have problems with sections of the Mitchell Principles. But then the IRA is not a participant in these talks' (*AP/RN*, 11 September 1997).

This argument, that Sinn Féin and the IRA were separate entities, was one that the republican movement offered throughout the peace process. It was not, however, one which many accepted and was one which was explicitly rejected on occasions by other parties. In response to the interview, Tony Blair stated that Sinn Féin would be barred from the talks if the IRA broke the Mitchell Principles. According to Blair, 'The two organisations are inextricably linked. One cannot claim to be acting independently of the other' (Bew and Gillespie, 1999: 348). The comments by the IRA spokesperson were the basis of an attempt by the UUP to have Sinn Féin excluded from the talks on 23 September. In the arguments offered by Ken Maginnis, examples were given of statements by the British and Irish politicians, and by SDLP figures, that argued that Sinn Féin were indeed inextricably linked to the IRA. 'Sinn Féin is a monstrous deceit condemned out of the mouths of virtually every other party here; with no commitment to work, as other parties at the table must do, within the accepted constraints which apply to the rest of us; that is . . . strictly committed to the Mitchell Principles' (*Irish Times*, 24 September 1997). Unsurprisingly, given the focus and purpose of the peace process at that stage, the governments rejected the UUP's demands for Sinn Féin's exclusion. However, the attempt was the occasion which allowed the UUP to sit down at the same table with Sinn Féin for the first time at the talks,

Why did the UUP participate in the talks?

By going to demand their exclusion, the UUP tacitly acknowledged their inclusion. This was a notable and important step by the largest unionist party. Ian Paisley's DUP and the smaller UK Unionist Party (UKUP) had walked out of the talks process in July once the governments had published their plans for decommissioning and to move to the inclusive stage of the talks. There was some speculation that Trimble would also withdraw from the process, a stance he refused to take. This was a brave decision, for which Trimble deserves great credit. Godson suggests that Trimble was always determined to remain in the talks process as he 'firmly believed that protest politics had run their course. Unionists had entered the process in order to rid themselves of the burden of the AIA of 1985, and nothing would deflect them from that task' (Godson, 2004: 285). This desire to negotiate a new agreement which would supplant the hated Anglo–Irish Agreement was a driving consideration for Trimble, as was the desire to avoid Unionism being marginalised or denied a voice at the table (Millar, 2004). Trimble believed that the tactics adopted by the main unionist parties after the AIA was signed, effectively seeking to withdraw from and disrupt the political process and refusing to meet ministers until the AIA was abandoned, were not only unsuccessful but had served to marginalise Unionism and potentially damage the Union itself. The situation the UUP found itself in now was different from that which had led to the AIA. A key distinction between this peace process and the one that had led to the AIA, was that the former had the aspiration to create all-party talks which would lead to a comprehensive agreement, whereas the AIA was specifically an intergovernmental accord which excluded the local parties from the negotiating process.

Given that the peace process, however, was reliant on local party participation and was designed to agree new institutional structures which would require local party participation to operate, Trimble's position was quite strong. If the UUP had joined the DUP in refusing to participate in a process that included Sinn Féin, the peace process, as designed, could not have continued. It would not be an inclusive process if the elected representatives of the majority (unionist) community, were not at the table. There would have been a logic to such an approach for Trimble. Given the unionist community's concerns over allowing Sinn Féin into talks, there is little to suggest that the party would have suffered electorally. However, although the peace process as conceived would have collapsed without the UUP's continued participation, this would not mean that no initiatives would have been carried out. Whilst in opposition in December 1996, Mo Mowlam had stated that the status quo was not an option in Northern Ireland (*Independent*, 9 February 1997). Trimble seemed to accept this. He later told Frank Millar, 'Look, the status quo is not an option for us either because the status quo post Anglo–Irish Agreement was the status quo where unionism was weak and marginalized, where the system was being run for the benefit of nationalism and the long-term effect of that was going to be disastrous from the point of view of the union with Britain' (Millar, 2004: 66). Given the views, and frustrations, of the British government towards Northern Ireland, the fear was that the trajectory would be for closer cooperation with Dublin, which unionists believed would further undermine the Union. It was also the case that they would be blamed for the collapse of the process, handing the 'high ground' to republicans, who would argue that unionists were incapable of contemplating a fairer and inclusive Northern Ireland. Indeed, these twin fears of closer cooperation with Dublin and blaming the unionists for failure were ones which would periodically be invoked by the British government to pressure unionists over the coming years.

Trimble was aided in his decision to remain engaged in the talks process by the continued involvement of the two parties linked to loyalist paramilitaries, the PUP and UDP. It might have been considered that those groups would have been particularly opposed to negotiating with republicans and might have been likely to follow Paisley in boycotting the talks. However, there were several differences between loyalist groups and paramilitaries and the DUP. First, at that stage, loyalists had also not decommissioned their weapons, so the argument that you could not sit down with those associated with groups that had weapons had less purchase for them. Second, however, loyalists such as David Ervine were sceptical of mainstream unionists and believed that parties such as the DUP had used loyalist paramilitary groups when it suited them and then distanced themselves from loyalists when it did not. Ervine claimed that 'a fairly senior member' of the DUP had given him a lift a couple of weeks after the IRA ceasefire and had urged that the UVF did not call one. This was because Ervine believed the politician saw the threat of loyalist paramilitaries as useful to 'keep the nationalists frightened, now you don't have to do anything, just a bit of sabre-rattling here and a bit of sabre-rattling there'. Ervine said he 'left the car disgusted' (Ervine, LHCMA). George Mitchell recalls that in one exchange before the DUP and UKUP left the process, in July 1997, the UKUP leader, Robert McCartney, had 'said with emotion: "If this is peace, let us have war". Ervine cut in immediately, with equal passion: "That's easy for you to say, safe as you and your family are in the suburbs. But if there's a war it's we and our sons who'll do the fighting and dying. We want this process because it's our only hope for peace"' (Mitchell, 1999: 186).

This decision by the PUP and UDP to remain in the talks process once Sinn Féin joined, effectively gave Trimble 'cover' and reduced the ability of Paisley to 'outflank' the UUP and portray the UUP as 'selling out' the Union (though this would change as the peace process lurched between crises after the GFA was signed). Interestingly, the withdrawal of the DUP and UKUP was advantageous for the overall process. George Mitchell argued that the DUP and UKUP had sought to wreck the talks from the start, but their withdrawal was a tactical mistake on their part. 'Reaching agreement without their presence was extremely difficult; it would have been impossible with them in the room ... No one can ever know for certain what might have been, but I believe that had Paisley and McCartney stayed and fought from within, there would have been no agreement' (Mitchell, 1999: 110).

Negotiating the Good Friday Agreement

In September 1997 things appeared to be in place to progress the peace process. All the main paramilitary groups were on ceasefire and the parties associated with them were at the negotiating table, along with the largest unionist party, the largest nationalist party, the Alliance Party, Women's Coalition and the Labour Coalition. The structure and duration of the talks had been agreed, the Chair was in place and a parallel commission to deal with the contentious issue of decommissioning had been created. All that was lacking was the political trust, if not the will, between the parties to move the process forward. What is clear from the existing accounts of the negotiations (see for example, Mitchell, 1999; Hennessey, 2000; Godson, 2004; Ahern, 2009; Powell, 2009; Blair, 2011; Campbell, 2013) is that the period between September 1997 and January 1998 saw slow progress. The talks had moved onto substantive discussion in October 1997 and followed the previously agreed three-strand approach. Strand One talks, which dealt with what the new internal structures of governance in Northern Ireland would be, was chaired by the British minister Paul Murphy (and did not include the Irish government, as they dealt with matters internal to Northern Ireland). Strand Two was chaired by Mitchell and dealt with what arrangements should be between Northern Ireland and the Republic, and Strand Three, which dealt with East–West relations between the British and Irish governments, were conducted directly between London and Dublin. In addition, there were two subcommittees, one which considered the progress of decommissioning which was being examined by the Commission headed by John de Chastelain, and one which considered confidence-building measures. The strands were separate but there were periodic plenary sessions to consider overall progress. The agreed approach of the process was that nothing would be agreed until everything was agreed. This was to seek to ensure that parties could not make progress on areas they favoured but stall progress on those they did not support.

There was a real division between some of the parties. The unionists wanted strong internal structures for Northern Ireland but were hostile to strong North–South institutions given their long-standing fear that such structures could be an embryonic all-Ireland government or at least might weaken the Union. An example of this concern can be seen in the unionist reaction to comments by the Irish Foreign Minister, David Andrews, when he stated that proposed North–South bodies 'would have strong functions, executive functions and directional functions, and not unlike a government' (*Irish Times*, 1 December 1997). Republicans, on the other hand, favoured strong North–South bodies (given their aspiration for a united Ireland) but had stated that they did not support internal structures for Northern Ireland, which they saw as a recognition of partition. However, whilst the structures and processes were clear, progress was not. In his memoirs, Mitchell summed up his views as the talks prepared to adjourn for the Christmas break in 1997.

> Rarely in my life have I felt as frustrated and angry as I did on that day. We had been meeting for a year and a half. For hundreds and hundreds of hours I had listened to the same arguments, over and over again. Very little had been accomplished. It had taken two months to get to an understanding on the rules to be followed once the negotiations began. Then it took another two months to get agreement on a preliminary agenda. Then we had fourteen more months to get an accord on a final agenda. We couldn't even get that, and we were about to adjourn for a Christmas break. (Mitchell, 1999: 126)

There were several reasons for this lack of progress, some were attitudinal, and some were procedural. Attitudinally, although the process was an inclusive one, this did not lead to engagement across the range of parties. The UUP refused to speak directly to Sinn Féin and mistrust was a marked feature between many of the participants. This undermined the ability to make progress. This lack of trust and engagement was also not helped by some of the logistics of the process. When the talks were in plenary session, these were held in a large room, with all the parties in attendance, and up to sixty people present, plus note-takers. This, as Mitchell noted, 'was not conducive to a candid exchange of views, let alone to hard bargaining' (Mitchell, 1999: 124). It also did not lend itself to being able to draw up a brief document which outlined the issues which might form the basis of a wider settlement, which it had been hoped to secure before the Christmas break. The first of these issues was addressed by an agreement between the parties that a working group would be created to lead discussions which would be limited to two people from each party. However, even in this smaller formation, progress was limited. The situation was aided by an approach that was to become a notable feature of the peace process, the tabling of documents by the governments for the parties to consider. Despite the aspirations of Mitchell and indeed the governments themselves at the time, the political parties were very reluctant, or unable, to take the lead and draw up agreed documents to be debated. So the governments took on this role and tabled the Heads of Agreement (HOA) document in January 1998.

Although talks were making slow progress, they were not taking place in a vacuum, and events outside impinged upon them. On 27 December the leader of the LVF, Billy Wright, was shot dead inside the Maze prison by the republican group the INLA (who were not on ceasefire or party to the talks). This led to a series of killings over the coming weeks. It illustrated that along with the hope that the peace process and paramilitary ceasefires engendered at this time, there was also the backdrop of fear and sectarianism in play. Some of the killings also illustrated other facets of the situation and the conflict in Northern Ireland, such as how random death could be, how interconnected the communities are in Northern Ireland and how, despite the depressingly high number of deaths in Northern Ireland over the years, killings still had the power to shock and destabilise the region. For example, as part of their 'retaliation' attacks, on 11 January 1998 the LVF killed Terry Enright who was working as a doorman in central Belfast. As well as being a widely respected community worker and amateur sportsman, who was not involved with any paramilitary groups, he happened to be married to Gerry Adams's niece but was killed working at a club owned by the sister-in-law of the PUP's David Ervine. His killing appears to have been a random act by the LVF. His funeral was the largest in West Belfast since the hunger strikers of 1981 (McKittrick et al., 1999: 1423–1424). A few weeks later, on 3 March, the LVF killed Philip Allen and Damien Trainor in a pub in Poyntzpass (and injured two others). The killings attracted widespread attention and condemnation as Allen was a Protestant who was about to be married and his friend Trainor was a Catholic who was due to be his best man. Between the killing of Billy Wright and the shootings in Poyntzpass, twelve others were killed in Northern Ireland, the overwhelming majority of whom were simply caught up in what were usually sectarian attacks by the small loyalist and republican groups who were not on ceasefire.

The killing of Wright, however, caused wider problems in the peace process. Although Wright was not a popular figure within loyalist circles beyond the LVF, his killing in prison by the INLA caused anger within loyalist groups, who were growing suspicious of the direction of the peace process. It was reported that a vote by UFF prisoners in the Maze on 4 January 1998 saw 60 per cent of the prisoners in favour of withdrawing their support from the group's ceasefire. This was a potential crisis, not least because, as Mo Mowlam noted in her memoirs, if the loyalist UFF and UVF rejected the process, their affiliated political parties, the UDP and PUP would have to leave the talks. This would leave Trimble unable to claim he still had the support of a majority of unionist voters. Trimble went in to meet the prisoners and, subsequently, and controversially, Mo Mowlam, at the request of the UDP's Gary McMichael, also went into the Maze to talk to the prisoners. Mowlam had not informed Blair she had agreed to do so before McMichael announced it would happen, which left Blair 'genuinely taken aback'. The government announced its support for the move and did not admit it had not been consulted on the plans (Campbell, 2011: 253–254). At the meeting, Mowlam reassured the UFF prisoners that the process was no threat to the Union and that if there was a lasting settlement the release of prisoners would be examined, provided they were affiliated to a group that was not 'actively engaged in terrorist activity' (Mowlam, 2003: 182–186). Mowlam's actions were successful, and the prisoners recommitted their support to the ceasefire. However, both the UDP and Sinn Féin were temporarily suspended in January and February 1998, due to evidence that the IRA and UFF members had been involved in murders in that period.

Despite the violence and distractions outside the talks, the process reconvened in January to discuss the propositions on the Heads of Agreement document that the two governments tabled. The fact that there were no scheduled suspensions between January and the proposed May deadline (which would subsequently be brought forward to April at George Mitchell's suggestion) and that there was a document on the table to discuss, led to a greater sense of urgency and hope for that stage of the process. Frank Millar's story on the resumption of the talks on 13 January was headlined, 'Peace talks finally reach the beginning' (*Irish Times*, 13 January 1998). The HOA was, according to a joint statement issued by the governments, 'our best guess at what could be a generally acceptable outcome'. It was a brief document whose purpose was to try and shift the discussion onto substantive issues, or, as one British official noted, it was 'a bone for the parties to gnaw on, designed to concentrate minds and get negotiations going in earnest' (*Guardian*, 13 January 1998). The document noted that there would be a 'new British–Irish agreement to replace the existing Anglo–Irish Agreement'; a Northern Ireland Assembly; an intergovernmental council that would include representatives from the British and Irish government, as well as representatives from the proposed Northern Ireland Assembly and devolved institutions in Wales and Scotland; a 'North–South ministerial council to bring together those with executive responsibilities in Northern Ireland and the Irish government in particular areas' and 'implementation bodies and mechanisms for policies agreed by the North–South council'. In addition, it indicated there would be measures for 'dealing with issues such as prisoners, security in all its aspects, policing and decommissioning of weapons' and provisions 'to safeguard the rights of both communities in Northern Ireland' (HOA Document, CAIN).

However, it soon became apparent that some parties found the 'bone' more digestible than others. The UUP received the document positively, Sinn Féin far less so. The disagreements over the HOA were indicative of the disputes that would characterise the negotiations over the following three months in the run-up to the GFA. Whilst the eventual GFA can be seen as largely in line with the HOA, in so far as all the bodies suggested in the document were ultimately created, it was the status and powers of those bodies and the relationship between the HOA and the earlier FWD that was disputed. Unionists were encouraged by the fact that the HOA stated there would be a Northern Ireland Assembly. Sinn Féin had argued against the creation of such a 'partitionist structure' and it was reported that to placate Sinn Féin at that stage the wording should be that there 'could' be an Assembly. The other issue that angered nationalists generally was that the proposed North–South bodies were not stated as having 'executive powers' as they had been in the FWD. This was seen as a dilution of their status by nationalists and taken to be a victory for unionists. Sinn Féin called for the document to be renegotiated. Martin McGuinness stated, 'We are opposed to the document, and we are going into the talks to oppose the document, because we are absolutely convinced that there can be no internal settlement in the North' (*Irish Times*, 19 January 1998).

In the immediate aftermath of the HOA's publication, the Irish government sought to assuage Sinn Féin's concerns and stressed that the HOA was in line with the FWD, with both Bertie Ahern and David Andrews stating that the North–South bodies would be free-standing and have executive functions. A more detailed document was tabled for discussion in Strand Two talks on 26 January by the two governments, which was closer to the FWD, apparently making reference to it. Alastair Campbell suggests that Trimble was furious at what he saw as the reintroduction of the hated FWD and at a meeting was 'screaming abuse at John Holmes (Blair's private secretary) as though it was all his handiwork'. It would appear Blair also felt that the new document pitched too far back towards the nationalists' concerns (and seemed to blame Mo Mowlam for this). In a comment that invites consideration of one of the dynamics in the peace process, Campbell records Blair as saying that Mowlam 'had to understand that DT (Trimble) needed the extra support because the SDLP have the Irish batting for them, and they need a sense of us batting for the unionists because they feel isolated and beleaguered' (Campbell, 2011: 276–277). This concern was one that was periodically in play throughout the process. Given that all sides were essential to the negotiations, as an inclusive process required inclusion, the belief by any of the main participants that their position was undermined to the point that it might become untenable had severe implications for the wider talks and possible agreement. Whilst both governments realised this, the relations between the governments and the Northern Irish parties were different. Dublin frequently took on the role as the defenders of nationalism which, on occasion, forced the British to seek to act in ways that would reassure unionists. The British were not, however, as comfortable in playing this role towards unionists as the Irish were for nationalists. The British consistently sought to portray themselves as neutral in their handling of Northern Ireland (a stance which at times infuriated unionists) but they were conscious of this need for 'balance', although unionists often questioned whether this was achieved.

The disagreements over what form the North–South structures should take was not resolved in the Strand Two talks at that stage and became the issue which nearly scuppered the process in the final week of the negotiations in April. The final few days of the talks were frenetic. All accounts of the talks record the importance of the engagement by the two Prime Ministers, who decided to travel to Stormont Buildings on the Tuesday of the final week and become directly involved in the negotiations. It was far from clear at that stage that there would be a successful conclusion to the talks, indeed it was a crisis in the process which led to their decision to travel to Belfast. On Monday 6 April, three days before the proposed Thursday deadline, George Mitchell tabled a draft of a possible agreement. Originally, he had hoped to get the draft to the parties on the previous Friday, but the text of Strand Two on North–South relations had not been agreed by the governments. On Sunday evening Mitchell was given the Strand Two section by the British and Irish officials but told 'to put this into the agreement without changing anything – not a single comma, but we want you to identify it as your draft, not ours'. Mitchell records that this was the first time that he had been given such an instruction. Mitchell and his co-chairs, de Chastelain and Holkeri were 'upset and concerned' by the instructions. However, despite their concerns, they decided to do as the governments requested, which they suspected was for the governments to have a 'buffer between them and the document they had just negotiated' (Mitchell, LHCMA). The document did not include the annexes, which were a list of areas that it was proposed would be dealt with by the North–South bodies. These were only provided to Mitchell late on the Monday and then the entire draft agreement was distributed to the parties. It was at that stage that it became apparent there was a serious problem, with the unionists distinctly unhappy with the Strand Two proposals. The problem, for the unionists, was the extent of the proposed Strand Two bodies, which ran to over fifty areas. (For a full outline of the proposals, see Hennessey (2000: 161–165).) There was a difference in aspiration between nationalists' and unionists' positions over the North–South bodies. Nationalists, championed by the Irish government, believed that the structures should be in line with the proposals in the FWD – a free-standing North–South Ministerial Council, created by legislation in Westminster and Dublin, with executive powers in a wide range of stated areas. As a result, the body would have meaningful powers and could not be collapsed or controlled by the proposed Northern Ireland Assembly (where unionists would have the majority of seats). On his way to London to negotiate the North–South bodies, Ahern had made his commitment to a strong North–South dimension clear. 'My compromises are over ... As far as I am concerned, the framework document is what has to stand. That is why we are still negotiating and working on it. I would like to be able to tell you that we will be able to surmount this. I don't know if we can' (*Observer*, 5 April 1998). For unionists, however, the structures envisaged by nationalists were seen as an embryonic united Ireland. They wanted a North–South council of a more advisory nature, which was created by, and answerable to, the Northern Ireland Assembly.

The proposals which appeared in Mitchell's draft late on Monday 6 April were far too close to the FWD model for unionists, with the UUP's John Taylor stating he would 'not touch it with a 40ft pole'. It was not, however, just the UUP who had problems with the document, the APNI's leader John Alderdice's rejection, though less colourful than Taylor's, was clear. He argued the 'paper takes us backwards rather than forwards in our search for agreement' (*Guardian*, 8 April 1998). It was this crisis that led Blair and Ahern to travel to Belfast and directly involve themselves in the talks. Blair records that when he met Mitchell in Belfast and was told 'that he thought the deal was undoable' he 'then and there took the decision to take complete charge of the negotiation' (Blair, 2011: 167). Mitchell himself has recorded the importance of the two Prime Ministers leading the talks, as it 'had a profound effect on the participants, the knowledge that the Prime Ministers would come, get involved in every detail with them, place themselves in great political risk'. Not least, as Mitchell notes, because at that stage the signs were not good that a deal was possible (Mitchell, LHCMA).

This begs the question, why did Mitchell table such a problematic Strand Two draft in the first place? The account in Alastair Campbell's diary lays the blame at the senator's feet. He records that Blair 'was furious' when the row broke on the Tuesday as he believed that 'both Mitchell and the NIO had not handled the Ulster Unionists properly'. Blair's frustration rose when he read the draft on the plane to Belfast as it was clear 'the areas for coop-eration were too numerous and too all-encompassing'. According to Campbell, Blair and Ahern 'had not actually negotiated all this, but Mitchell insisted it was all in there' (Campbell, 2011: 262–263). What Campbell's account does not cover, however, is the intense negotiations that had been occurring throughout the weekend, negotiations in which Blair was heavily involved. Blair's own account also fails to note the talks that he had had with Ahern over the weekend. However, Mitchell's account notes that it was the British and Irish governments who stated that the draft of Strand Two and the subsequent annexes needed to be included as presented to him. Jonathan Powell's account does offer something of a corrective to Campbell's suggestion that it was Mitchell that had 'insisted' the draft and annexes were included, and that the NIO had erred in handling the issue. Powell notes, on the helicopter to the talks, 'Tony was looking for someone to blame and he said that John Holmes had let him down. I gave him quite a sharp lecture. The week before he had been singing John's praises and now he said he had lost all faith in him. He had in any case agreed the text of the draft himself.' Powell does, however, claim that the annexes had not been negotiated by the two governments, but by British and Irish officials, and had been included in the draft document at the insistence of the Irish government (Powell, 2009: 91). The question can still be asked, however, why include such a problem-atic document in the draft? John de Chastelain, like Mitchell, noted that they realised it was an unacceptable document as soon as they received it, but like Powell, nods towards Blair's involvement in its drafting. 'We felt the paper was far too "green". Tony Blair was reported to do so as well. Well, it was his paper!' (Godson, 2004: 327). Some of the local politicians involved in the talks believed that it had been deliberately used as a negotiating tactic. David Ervine saw the draft in a similar vein. He later argued it was a 'brilliant tactic' by the governments. 'By the creation of what was a very "green" tinted, in other words, pro-republican document, what they did was get us to negotiate away from something' (Ervine, LHCMA). The UUP MP and negotiator, Jeffrey Donaldson, was of this view (Godson, 2004: 334) as was the SDLP's Seamus Mallon (Mallon, LHMCA). Whether the draft was designed to concentrate minds and insert something that the unionists could negotiate out, to give them a sense of 'victory' or was a serious (but poorly thought through) offering by the two governments, can be debated. What is clear, however, is that the British government, and Tony Blair, had been instrumental in its development, and claims that it was simply an error on Mitchell's part to table it are not convincing. It led to a crisis in the process, which necessitated the direct involvement of the two leaders. Blair has noted that it was not originally envisaged that they would get involved in the talks. 'I was due to stay a day to give an agreed deal my endorsement, the detailed work having been done by officials' (Blair, 2011: 166). However, given that the draft had the fingerprints of the two leaders on it, it would require their participation to alter the documents, hence their decision to travel to Belfast.

The final four days of the talks were somewhat chaotic and unpredictable, with Adams suggesting it was not clear that a deal would be done until fifteen minutes before the televised plenary at 5 p.m. on Friday 10 April, when Trimble finally confirmed to Mitchell that the party would support the proposed agreement (Adams, 2004: 366). Given the intensity of those days, the competing objectives of the participants and of the accounts that exist of the talks, it is impossible to fully outline what took place and exactly why the parties eventually decided to go with the agreement. As Alastair Campbell, who was with Blair throughout those days in Belfast, observed in the 2013 edition of his diaries, 'There have been plenty of accounts of these crucial days written, but just as at the time I could not really work out how it all came together, so I can't now' (Campbell, 2013: 117). It is, however, possible to chart the issues which divided the parties during the talks, identify how they were resolved (or at least what the GFA said about them, which is not always the same thing) and offer some thoughts on the resulting agreement.

North–South bodies

As noted, this was the issue which precipitated the crisis in the days running up to the deadline. This became the key logjam which had to be removed if there was to be an agreement. Mitchell is clear on its importance in his memoir, noting if, 'Ahern insisted on the Strand Two provisions he had worked out with Blair, there would not have been a Good Friday Agreement' (Mitchell, 1999: 171). It was far from inevitable that Ahern would agree to do so. Adams claimed that when he spoke to Ahern after the draft had been published, the Taoiseach 'assured me that the Irish government had agreed positions with the British government and intended sticking to them'. For their part, Sinn Féin made it clear to the Irish government 'that any dilution in Strand Two would be disastrous' (Adams, 2004: 355–356). Ahern was in a difficult position. He had publicly stated that his concessions were over, had agreed directly with the British a draft of Strand Two, had assured Sinn Féin that he would protect it and was under pressure from some of his own officials to stand firm on the draft. To add to the Taoiseach's difficulties, his mother had died suddenly of a heart attack early in the morning of Monday 6 April. He spent the next few days shuttling between Dublin and Belfast whilst his mother was buried, and he led the Irish government's negotiations. Yet Ahern did agree to the reopening of talks on the Strand Two draft. This was presented by some commentators as a major victory for British pressure and unionist demands. Godson records that after Ahern agreed to reopen negotiations on the draft, Trimble stated, 'I have just witnessed the ritual humiliation of the Irish Prime Minister' (Godson, 2004: 333). Thomas Hennessey claimed Trimble stated that Blair attributed the change in tack from the Irish to the fact that 'he had informed Ahern that unless the Irish agreed to the unionist model of Strand Two, he would declare the talks finished and blame the Irish government' (Hennessey, 2000: 167). There are problems with such analyses. The British government may have found it difficult to conclusively pin the blame on the Irish if talks had broken down over the Mitchell draft, given that they had effectively been its co-authors. Similarly, Godson's claim that the agreement to renegotiate Strand Two by the Irish was 'possibly a clear demonstration of the muscle of the British state in a negotiation with its Irish counterpart' is questionable (Godson, 2004: 333). Although the Irish did agree to reopen the talks, this did not necessarily mark a capitulation by them, more perhaps an acknowledgement of the wider reality they faced. As Hennessey suggested, it 'went to the heart of the peace process. Was this to be an intra-nationalist agreement which kept Sinn Féin happy or the chance for an historic nationalist–unionist settlement which might not occur again? Ahern ignored his aides and chose the latter' (Hennessey, 2000: 167). If the impact of Ahern refusing to renegotiate Strand Two with the unionists had been the end of the process, it might have burnished his credentials amongst elements of nationalism, but to what wider end? Given there is nothing to suggest that Unionism's rejection of the proposals was a negotiating ploy, such a stance would have broken the talks, something which was not in the interests, by that stage, of anyone but hard-line unionists and republicans that were not party to the talks. Ahern's own account of the decision suggested that whilst he was willing to reopen the talks, he was not willing to move entirely to the unionist position. He stressed to Blair that the proposal to change Articles 2 and 3 of the Irish constitution, which claimed Northern Ireland as part of the Republic's state, was historic and he was not willing to have 'North–South institutions turning into chat shows'. Ahern claimed that his position was that 'the text could be revisited but the substance had to be maintained' (Ahern, 2009: 221). Ahern stressed that he would be unable to get agreement in the Republic, and indeed within his own party, to change the constitution, without substantial North–South institutions being created. However, he also saw himself as being in a relatively strong bargaining position, given the desire for unionists that Articles 2 and 3 be removed from the constitution. His view was that 'in lots of ways I held the biggest card. I held the card that was whether we were going to recognise Northern Ireland as an entity and were going to make the constitutional change or were not. So, I was quite happy with the card that I had to play' (Ahern, LHCMA). In a comment which portrayed Ahern's noted pragmatism, he also suggested that the argument about the powers of North–South bodies was perhaps not as important as was being suggested at that time. He claims he suggested to Blair, 'To be honest Tony ... if we get an agreement people are going to wonder what all the fuss was about North/South stuff. It's not like we are not already doing it in the EU' (Ahern, 2009: 221–222). It is worth noting, however, that he did not see them as so unworthy of fuss that he would meet unionists' demands that they be simply advisory structures created by the Northern Ireland Assembly (NIA) post-Agreement.

The eventual shape of North–South structures in the GFA represented a compromise between the original proposals in the Mitchell draft and what unionists had indicated they favoured. The new North–South Ministerial Council (NSMC) was to be created by legislation at Westminster and Dublin, rather than by the NIA, and 'Participation in the Council to be one of the essential responsibilities attaching to relevant posts in the two Administrations' (Belfast Agreement, 1998: 14). This addressed nationalist fears that the NIA may refuse to subsequently create the NSMC, or unionist ministers would simply refuse to engage with it. However, the body was not as independent from the new NIA as the original draft had suggested. Although decisions would be taken in the Council, the ministers were 'to remain accountable to the Assembly and Oireachtas respectively, whose approval, through the arrangements in place on either side, would be required for decisions beyond the defined authority of those attending' (Belfast Agreement, 1998: 15). As a result, the NSMC was effectively answerable to the NIA and the Dáil, addressing one of Unionism's key demands. The list of possible areas for cooperation had also been notably slimmed down from the fifty originally proposed to twelve (Agriculture; Education; Transport; Environment; Waterways; Social Security/Social Welfare; Tourism; Relevant EU programmes; Inland Fisheries; Aquaculture and Marine Matters; Health and Urban and Rural development). The existence of the NSMC was dependent upon the functioning of the NIA (and vice versa). The agreement stipulated, 'It is understood that the North/South Ministerial Council and the Northern Ireland Assembly are mutually interdependent, and that one cannot successfully function without the other' (Belfast Agreement, 1998: 16). This addressed concerns from both nationalists and unionists that the 'other' may collapse the institution they did not support but continue to work the one they did. Although the differences over the Strand Two arrangements had been fierce, ultimately they were largely thrashed out by talks between the UUP and Dublin.

Strand One

The progress over Strand Two allowed progress to also be made over what the internal governance of Northern Ireland would look like. There had been a notable difference between the proposals of the unionists and SDLP for the devolved structure to be created at Stormont. Unionists favoured a committee-based system, where membership and allocation of Chairs were proportionate to party strength in the Assembly. This, from a unionist perspective, would have had the advantage that they would not be sharing power with Sinn Féin in a cabinet. The SDLP, however, pushed for a more formal power-sharing structure with departments, headed by ministers and with a cabinet structure. It was this model that finally won out. The unionists became persuaded that, internationally, it might make sense to have ministers representing Northern Ireland rather than Committee Chairs. However, perhaps more importantly, the issue also illustrates the interrelated nature of the talks process. The unionists were aware that they had made notable gains from nationalism in Strand Two, so they appreciated that there was a need to make concessions in Strand One. Reg Empey, who led the UUP in the Strand One talks, acknowledged this when he argued to his colleagues, 'We can't push the SDLP to the limit. We'd then be doing to them what the SDLP and the Irish and Whitelaw did to Faulkner [in 1973]' (Godson, 2004: 338–339). This was a reference to the belief that the then leader of the UUP, Brian Faulkner, was pressurised into accepting a deal at Sunningdale which he could not persuade Unionism to accept, leading to the collapse of the future power-sharing Executive in 1974. This is an interesting illustration of the fact that the parties themselves were aware that they needed to negotiate a balanced package, and compromises were necessary. It also appears that Trimble was not convinced that he was effectively signing up to structures under the Agreement that would necessitate having to share power with Sinn Féin. He subsequently told Frank Millar, 'on that Friday afternoon there was a fair probability that Sinn Féin would reject the Agreement and Sinn Féin did not actually accept the Agreement on 10 April 1998 (Millar, 2009: 154).

As a result of this concession by the UUP the structures of the new devolved government were agreed. There was to be a 108-member Assembly and votes on 'key decisions' would be structured to ensure that decisions had cross-community support – either parallel consent where a majority of those who voted and a majority of those unionists and nationalists who voted had to support a measure, or a weighted majority where 60 per cent of members who voted had to support a proposal to include 40 per cent of the nationalists and unionists who had voted. Upon taking their seats all Members of the Legislative Assembly (MLAs) had to designate as unionist, nationalist or other, for the purpose of cross-community voting. Those issues which required cross-community support included votes for who would chair the NIA, who would become First Minister (FM) and Deputy First Minister (DFM) and budget issues. In addition, a decision would be one that required cross-community support if thirty or more MLAs signed a 'petition of concern'. These measures were designed to make sure that no one party or tradition could dominate the decision-making or legislative process in the NIA and was largely perceived as a safeguard for nationalists. The Agreement also stipulated that there would be an Equality Commission 'to monitor a statutory obligation to promote equality of opportunity in specified areas and parity of esteem between the two main communities, and to investigate individual complaints against public bodies' (Belfast Agreement, 1998: 12).

Despite the terminology, the roles of First and Deputy First Ministers were equal and the two had to be jointly elected. In addition to the FM and DFM there would be ten ministers with departmental responsibilities; together these twelve ministers would make up the Executive Committee (subsequently this was commonly known as the Executive). All ministers had to take a pledge of office, which included the commitments to 'non-violence and exclusively peaceful and democratic means' and 'to serve all the people of Northern Ireland equally, and to act in accordance with the general obligations on government to promote equality and prevent discrimination' (Belfast Agreement, 1998: 12) and were bound by a code of conduct.

Strand Three, East–West relations

The negotiation of Strand Three was the least problematic of the talks process and was largely agreed directly between the two governments. There were two new proposed structures. A British–Irish Council (BIC), which was a consultative body that would bring together representatives from the British and Irish governments along with those from the devolved institutions of Northern Ireland, Scotland and Wales, the Isle of Man and the Channel Islands, 'if appropriate'. This was a body which was favoured by unionists as it enabled them to argue that Northern Ireland was not being treated differently from the other constituent parts of the UK. The other institution was the British–Irish Intergovernmental Council (BIIGC). This body was to 'subsume both the Anglo–Irish Intergovernmental Council and the Intergovernmental Conference established under the 1985 Agreement'

(Belfast Agreement, 1998: 18). This was seen as an important development for unionists as it enabled them to argue that they had negotiated the replacement of the hated AIA. They also insisted that the previous base of the IGC secretariat, Maryfield, be closed. Blair claimed that this demand originally caused confusion in the negotiations as 'we thought they were saying "Murrayfield" had to close, and even I winced at the prospect of demolishing the Edinburgh home of Scottish rugby ... ' He noted, however, it 'was a measure of our now complete isolation in the negotiating cell that I neither asked why Unionism might want to erase a rugby pitch, nor was unprepared to do it' (Blair, 2011: 174). The BIIGC would continue to consider issues related to Northern Ireland that had not been devolved to the NIA. In many respects the new Strand Three arrangements were a reworking of existing structures. Given that both governments had been committed to close intergovernmental cooperation on Northern Ireland since at least the AIA of 1985, it was comparatively straightforward to negotiate.

Prisoners, decommissioning and policing

The negotiations over the three main strands did not see an intensive input from Sinn Féin. Whilst the Irish government had consulted Sinn Féin (and the SDLP) over the proposed Strand Two arrangements, the main negotiation had been conducted originally between the British and Irish government and then, post the problems over the Mitchell draft, between Irish officials and the UUP leadership. The Strand One negotiations over the proposed devolved arrangements for Northern Ireland were largely conducted between the UUP and the SDLP, and overseen by the British NIO minister, Paul Murphy. Sinn Féin had largely absented themselves from that process on the grounds that they did not support the creation of 'partitionist' structures for Northern Ireland. This was clearly an untenable position, and it appears to be one that they themselves realised was not deliverable; there clearly was going to be a devolved government in Northern Ireland if there was an agreement. Indeed, Mallie and McKittrick note that Adams had discussed with McGuinness the fact that they were likely to be serving in a Stormont-based Assembly if there were an agreement, during a walk in the grounds that week. The authors noted that the stance that they 'wanted nothing to do with an essentially partitionist body ... turned out to be a tactical position which they later simply dropped' (Mallie and McKittrick, 2002: 266). The reason that they felt the need to take a clearly untenable position was that, as Adams recalled, 'the broad slogan for a long time had been no return to Stormont' (Adams, LHCMA). To be seen to be negotiating a 'partitionist structure' would have been problematic for the rank and file of the republican movement, but subsequently, engaging with one that was part of a wider package which contained identifiable gains for republicans was less problematic.

Prisoners

The issue that became one of the main areas where republicans sought to secure an identifiable gain was in the early release of prisoners. Whilst the British had accepted that early release needed to be part of the deal, the question was how 'early' would the releases be? Republicans were pushing for a year, and the British were offering three years. In the final run-up to the agreement, the British were prepared to agree to two years, but republicans were still pressing for a year. To try and increase pressure on the British, Sinn Féin sought to persuade the PUP and UDP to 'come onboard in a joint effort to get the prisoners out earlier' (Adams, 2003: 360). The loyalists considered this, and David Ervine notes that it was discussed in their room between the forty people there, some of whom were keen to try and get their colleagues out as soon as possible. However, the decision was taken not to support a demand for release in a year. The reason for this illustrates an awareness of the wider political and social context the talks were operating in. It was not only that such a move would have led to IRA prisoners, many of whom had been sentenced for murder, being let out in a short period of time. This would have inevitably been problematic for many within the unionist community. Ervine also notes that the release of loyalists would have been contentious for many. He argued, 'we would all love to fool ourselves that the prisoners are wonderful and that our community loves us, and I am not so sure that that is quite the case and we knew that. Those of us who had political sense knew that' (Ervine, LHCMA). The British were sensitive to the issue of prisoners. Jonathan Powell noted that himself and Alastair Campbell did not support the argument that they should be released within a year as they were worried about the response of the British public, who were 'not at all prepared for the extraordinary act of releasing murderers'. This was a concern shared by the NIO official John Steele, who Blair records as stating 'in civil servant language' that 'it wouldn't be "frightfully helpful"', which Blair translated as 'the whole business was barking' (Powell, 2009: 100–101; Blair, 2011: 172). However, at that stage, the British were concerned that Sinn Féin may refuse to sign up to the deal. Mowlam argued for a year, on the basis that the 'flak' over the issue would be the same whether the decision was for twelve or twenty-four months, and so it made sense to go for the shorter period in order to 'make some progress on other issues with Sinn Féin' (Mowlam, 2003: 222). Blair and Powell both suggest that Mowlam told Sinn Féin that the government agreed to the one-year timescale. Blair subsequently believed that this would not be possible and decided to 'renegotiate' with Adams. The compromise they reached was that Blair 'privately assured him we would do it within one year if conditions permitted but publicly and officially it would be two years' (Adams, 2003: 361; Blair, 2011: 171). This effectively resolved the issue and gave Sinn Féin (and the loyalists) a notable benefit that they could use to persuade their supporters to accept the deal; if they signed up to the Agreement, all prisoners would be out within two years.

Decommissioning

The Mitchell Report had succeeded in shelving the issue of decommissioning and the parallel process that had been designed to separate the issue from the wider talks enabled progress to be made during the negotiations. However, it was inevitable that the Agreement would have to deal with the issue. As was to become clear over the next few years, the GFA addressed but did not resolve the problem. There was widespread agreement that the issue needed to be part of an overall settlement of the conflict, so the proposed Agreement contained a section on decommissioning. The key clause affirmed that:

> All participants accordingly reaffirm their commitment to the total disarmament of all paramilitary organisations. They also confirm their intention to continue to work constructively and in good faith with the Independent Commission, and to use any influence they may have, to achieve the decommissioning of all paramilitary arms within two years following endorsement in referendums North and South of the agreement and in the context of the implementation of the overall settlement. (Belfast Agreement, 1998: 25)

At one reading this could have been taken to suggest that all parties had accepted the need for decommissioning and agreed that it would occur within two years of the Agreement, under the supervision of the Commission. However, this was not how the wording was seen by all those who negotiated it, given, as Hennessey noted, this section was 'the most ambiguous area of the Belfast Agreement' (Hennessey, 2000: 185). The problem lay in the relationship between Sinn Féin and the IRA. Sinn Féin's position was that they were a separate entity; a political party that had an electoral mandate and held no weapons. Whilst they might 'work constructively and in good faith' to use 'influence' with the IRA to achieve decommissioning, they could not compel them to disarm. If the IRA did not choose to do so, then this was not the fault of Sinn Féin. Sinn Féin saw its participation in the structures proposed under the Agreement as due to their electoral mandate, and not connected to whether the IRA decommissioned. By their reading of the Agreement, decommissioning was not linked to the question of who should be in government.

This was not a view of the relationship between decommissioning and office-holding that unionists had. In the UUP's view, Sinn Féin was intrinsically linked to the IRA and, as a result, the issue of decommissioning was directly related to that of office-holding. Indeed, David Trimble believed that he had received such a commitment from Tony Blair when he and his colleague, Jeffrey Donaldson, had met the Prime Minister and John Holmes at Chequers two weeks before the GFA was concluded. Trimble was adamant that the government's position was that Sinn Féin could not serve in government before the IRA decommissioned. However, when Trimble saw the final draft of the Agreement the section on decommissioning did not specifically link the two issues. Trimble claims he then challenged Blair on the lack of specificity on this and was told that it was too late to unpick the text of the Agreement. Frank Millar asked whether Blair had 'suckered' him over decommissioning. 'Did Blair sucker us? I don't know, he may very well have been genuine both at Chequers and in the last week' (Millar, 2004: 69–70). This ability to have been 'genuine' whilst apparently advocating two diametrically opposed positions was not as irreconcilable as it may sound when looked at in the context of the final, frantic hours of the GFA negotiations. Blair himself recorded that he was 'sprinkling concessions around like confetti' during the talks. The quest was for an agreement that all would endorse (or at least not overtly reject) rather than intellectual and moral clarity. As it was apparent during the talks that Sinn Féin would not sign up to a deal that explicitly linked decommissioning and office-holding, the governments constructed a form of words which suggested a necessity for decommissioning but did not state it categorically. However, when it then subsequently appeared that the UUP would not sign up to an agreement on that basis, there became a necessity to find a way to get them back onboard, without losing Sinn Féin. This was achieved by Tony Blair offering a side letter to Trimble which suggested a closer linkage between the two issues than that in the GFA. The letter stated, 'I confirm that in our view the effect of the decommissioning section of the agreement, with decommissioning schemes coming into effect in June, is that the process of decommissioning should begin straight away' (letter from Blair to Trimble, CAIN). This was enough to persuade Trimble to agree to endorse the Agreement. He was aided in taking this stance when another senior figure, John Taylor, indicated it was sufficient to secure his support. It was not, however, universally accepted within the UUP. Jeffrey Donaldson did not accept the position and left the talks before the final plenary. For the UUP, the letter indicated that Blair would ensure that Sinn Féin would not be allowed into government if the IRA did not decommission; for Sinn Féin, the letter had no status as it was not part of the Agreement. The letter was instrumental in saving the Agreement but was also a hostage to fortune when decommissioning did not occur within the two-year time period. Powell notes that such was the haste to get the letter to the UUP, due to the fear that they might withdraw from the process, that he forgot to save it and they had to ask the UUP for it back subsequently, so they could make a copy for the files (Powell, 2009: 106).

Policing and justice

The other area that nationalists argued needed to be addressed to create a more equitable and inclusive Northern Ireland was related to the justice system. Many saw the issue of policing as being closely related to the wider problems in the political structures and attitudes in Northern Ireland. Seamus Mallon, who was deputy leader of the SDLP and a key participant in the talks progress, had served for a long time as the party's spokesperson on justice and held this view. His memoir contains an interesting examination of the nationalist community's view of the RUC as 'the Other' and noted that he had always resisted calls that the party urge Catholics to join the RUC (the force was by the 1990s over 90 per cent Protestant). Mallon's argument was that 'the policing problem could not be solved in isolation from the political process, bad politics and bad policing were interlocked in the old Northern Ireland' (Mallon, 2019: 3012). As a result of such attitudes, reform of the policing and justice systems was an important objective for nationalists in the negotiations. Reflecting these aspirations, the Agreement stated there was, 'the opportunity for a new beginning to policing in Northern Ireland with a police service capable of attracting and sustaining support from the community as a whole'. It stated there would be an independent commission to make 'recommendations for future policing arrangements in Northern Ireland including means of encouraging widespread community support for these arrangements'. There would also be a 'parallel wide-ranging review of criminal justice' (Belfast Agreement, 1998: 26). These undertakings in the text were designed to address areas which were primarily of concern to nationalists. Like many aspects of the text, they did not settle issues to the satisfaction of the parties but offered a prescription as to how contentious issues would be addressed in the post-Agreement Northern Ireland.

The Agreement also committed the British government to return Northern Ireland to 'normal security' arrangements as soon as possible. This would include 'the reduction of the numbers and role of the armed forces deployed in Northern Ireland to levels compatible with a normal peaceful society; the removal of security installations; the removal of emergency powers in Northern Ireland; and other measures appropriate to and compatible with a normal peaceful society.' Similarly, the Republic would consider its own Offences Against the State Acts and reform and remove 'those elements no longer required as circumstances permit' (Belfast Agreement, 1998: 25–26). The rationale behind these proposals was that if Northern Ireland was transitioning to a post-conflict society, the previous security measures introduced to deal with the violence would no longer be required, so could be removed. There was, again, a difference in outlook between the parties over to what extent some of the measures had been required. The British state and unionists argued, for example, that security installations and watchtowers were a response to the security situation, while republicans saw them as oppressive structures seeking to intimidate nationalist areas. Their removal would, however, eradicate some of the most obvious physical manifestations of the conflict. There were also proposals related to the equality agenda in the Agreement. These included a pledge to support and promote the Irish language (and Ulster-Scots), create a new Equalities Commission, a Northern Ireland Human Rights Commission and an undertaking by the British government to incorporate the European Convention on Human Rights (ECHR) into Northern Ireland law.

Evaluating the GFA

The undertaking by the parties to pledge to support the Agreement at the final plenary on Friday 10 April was something that had seemed uncertain even an hour before the session. The only exception was Sinn Féin. Adams told the plenary,

> I have always made it clear that our negotiating team will go back to the ard comhairle (national executive) of Sinn Féin. We will assess the document in the context of our peace strategy; does it remove the causes of conflict? Can it be developed and is it transitional? As in the past, we will approach this development in a positive manner. But for now, it is time to draw a breath. It is time to reflect. Republicans and nationalists will come to this document with scepticism but also with hope. They will ask does it offer a chance of a way forward. Is it a new beginning? Sinn Féin will ask all those questions also. When we have democratically come to a conclusion, we will let you know. (*Irish Times*, 11 April 1998)

He did not, as he suggested in his memoir, tell the plenary, 'our delegation would be urging support' (Adams, 2003: 366). However, Adams's comments were taken as a positive outcome by the governments who were aware that Sinn Féin would not endorse the document on the day. The party's special conference in Dublin did vote to support the deal on 10 May.

In line with many other aspects of the peace process the motivations of each party were, in many ways, contradictory, what had been agreed was contested, and who had won and lost disputed. David Trimble could assert that, 'We rise from this table knowing that the Union is stronger than it was when we first sat down. We know that the fundamental act of union is there intact' (*Irish Times*, 11 April 1998). Republicans, however, could portray the GFA not as a 'settlement' but as a step on the road towards a united Ireland, a point Danny Morrison, former Sinn Féin director of publicity, made after the decision to endorse the deal. According to Morrison, Sinn Féin was a 'party with a large mandate in the North and which is going to enter Stormont and be eligible for high office – but which rejects the union-ist veto, refuses to recognise the six-county state, demands an end to British rule, and whose key national objective remains Irish reunification' (*Guardian*, 11 May 1998). The successful conclusion of the negotiation of the GFA was, in many ways, a surprising achievement. Paul Dixon has rightly noted that the remarkable thing about the Agreement 'was that it fell so far short of the polarised, publicly stated positions of both Sinn Féin and the Ulster Unionist Party' (Dixon, 2019: 155). Both sides could point to 'gains'. For unionists, the commitment by the Irish Republic to remove its constitutional claim over Northern Ireland; the replacement of the AIA; the enshrinement of consent and its linkage to Northern Ireland as a political unit; and the neces-sity that any additional expansion of North–South bodies required the approval of the NIA were all notable 'wins'. For nationalists, in general, the commitment to a devolved power-sharing government in Northern Ireland, North–South structures created by Westminster and Dublin, the equality agenda, the acknowledgement of Ireland's 'right to self-determination' (albeit with the necessity for concurrent agreement in Northern Ireland and the Republic) and the proposed changes to policing and the justice system, were seen as positive outcomes. For republicans (and loyalists), the decisions on prisoner releases were notable concessions. But all sides had made signif-icant compromises. Unionists had to agree to: power-sharing which would, in all likelihood, see them in government with Sinn Féin; the creation of North–South structures which they could not collapse without bringing down the other devolved structures; a Commission which would lead to major changes to the Royal Ulster Constabulary (RUC); an equality agenda that could include the promotion of the Irish language and steps that would be seen as undermining elements of their culture; the release of IRA prison-ers and remaining ambiguity over decommissioning. Nationalists had had to accept the removal of the constitutional claim from the Republic and North–South structures which did not have the executive powers that they had hoped for. Republicans also had to accept some unpalatable compro-mises. Despite the claims of Morrison, they effectively did sign up to a 'partitionist' structure with the proposals to create a devolved government at Stormont; the wording on consent went against their long-held claim that the island of Ireland had to be treated as a single unit in terms of self-determination; and decommissioning was included as an issue that had to be addressed. Indeed, Paul Bew later posed the question, 'how could a revolutionary movement settle for such a prosaic, even dull outcome, which fell so drastically short of its stated objectives?' (Bew, 2007: 551). It is of course impossible to categorically answer this question, which relates back to issues as to the reasons why the IRA ended their armed campaign and the stalemate/defeat issues raised in Chapter 1. Arguably, once that decision had been taken, the republican movement was on a course that would inevitably lead to compromises and an outcome notably short of their long-stated objectives of achieving a 32-county socialist Republic. Few could have believed that ending the armed conflict was going to lead to an inclusive talks process that would secure that objective. However, given the lack of progress towards that outcome using violence, it was not persuasive to argue, as some dissident republicans tried, that ending the armed campaign had delayed a united Ireland.

Bew's question does raise the possibility that another option for Sinn Féin would have been to simply refuse to endorse an outcome that fell so far short of their stated objectives. However, what would be the likely outcome of such a stance? As argued previously, the peace process was, to a large extent, based on the objective of securing the end of violence by the IRA in order to create a talks process which would include them and reach a negotiated settlement. However, this was not to be achieved at any cost. The DSD, FWD, HOA and Mitchell drafts had all been largely in line with what eventually was in the GFA. It was clear there was going to be devolved government in Northern Ireland, that consent would have a Northern Ireland focus, that there would be North–South bodies, albeit of varying proposed powers, and that Articles 2 and 3 of the Irish constitution would have to be altered. So it is not the case that Sinn Féin could have believed when the IRA ceasefire was called that the talks process would achieve anything markedly different to what was on the table on 10 April 1998. To reject the deal would have only left them isolated. Their rejection may well have led to a collapse of the peace process and an inability to create the structures proposed in the GFA, but it is unlikely that the result would have been a new process which led to an outcome closer to their stated objectives. The gains in the areas of prisoners and the equality agenda were eventually deemed sufficient by Sinn Féin to endorse the Agreement. These, along with the claims that the struggle would go on to secure a united Ireland, was Sinn Féin's new approach. It was to become, as will be discussed, a highly effective one, in terms of the party's electoral support, north and south of the border. Sinn Féin, like the other parties, decided to endorse an agreement about which they had notable reservations.

There were several other factors which also helped the talks process to come to a successful conclusion. The fact that there was what appeared to be a hard deadline, albeit one that slipped by a day, meant that the talks could not go on indefinitely. George Mitchell had made it clear that he was leaving for the Easter weekend and that was to be the end of the process. This did not mean, of course, that the parties had to reach an agreement by then, but it did mean that the process had to end by then. It was clear that no party wanted to shoulder the blame as the one that had collapsed the talks, a threat which the governments used against parties during the final days. There was also the helpful support of President Bill Clinton. Clinton phoned both David Trimble and Gerry Adams in the final hours to seek to persuade them to do the deal and was in close contact with the two governments throughout the negotiations. The intensity of the talks, the deadline and the international attention they were attracting built a momentum that helped them reach an agreement.

The talks were really a series of mini negotiations between a changing cast of parties and individuals throughout that final week, with some unlikely people negotiating with each other. For example, Bertie Ahern claims that at one stage he was talking with loyalists and some republicans were also present, when one of the participants observed that 'We've worked out you're the only person in the room who hasn't killed anyone' (Ahern, 2009: 224). The only groups who did not negotiate directly were the UUP and Sinn Féin as Trimble's party refused to talk to Adams's. The negotiations were increasingly led by the two Prime Ministers and the party leaders with others, such as the NISS, Mo Mowlam, playing a less direct role. Though Blair did note that Mowlam made a major contribution in the final hours when Sinn Féin suddenly produced forty pages of proposed amendments, much to Blair's annoyance. 'It was here that Mo played an important part in the negotiations. Mo's idea of negotiating with Sinn Féin was rather smart. She heard them out, took receipt of the document, as it were, then ignored the overwhelming majority of the points, focusing on one or two things that might matter. The rest sort of fell by the wayside' (Blair, 2011: 172). However, Ahern's account of the same instance paints a rather different picture. 'Mo Mowlam went absolutely crazy. I've never seen anything quite like it. She was shouting and swearing at Adams' (Ahern, 2009: 225).

How far the talks and subsequent agreement were perceived as changing the political landscape in Northern Ireland was illustrated by the apparent marginalisation of Ian Paisley and the DUP. The night before the talks concluded, Ian Paisley led a delegation into the grounds of Stormont to denounce the process and what he argued was the betrayal of the Union. However, at that stage, his appeared to be a voice in the wilderness. George Mitchell records a British official saying to him, 'Once he would have brought thousands, tens of thousands with him. Now he has a few hundred. And look at those loyalists. Many of them thought him a god. They went out and killed, thinking they were saving the Union. Now they've turned on him. It's the end of an era' (Mitchell, 1999: 177). In a piece in the run-up to the subsequent referendum of the GFA, Ronan Fanning noted, 'poor Dr Paisley, he resembles nothing so much as a beached whale, a once fearsome Moby Dick who now excites only pity as he thrashes about in the shallows' (*Sunday Independent*, 24 May 1998). Yet within five years, the DUP would displace the UUP as the largest unionist party, within ten years they would have twice as many seats in the NIA as the UUP and within twelve years the UUP would have no MPs in Westminster and the DUP's representation there would have quadrupled to eight.

The peace process, which had begun as a quest to entice the IRA from violence and build an inclusive process that would allow Sinn Féin a seat at the table, took on a different complexion once the GFA was agreed. The process was still designed to keep the IRA from violence and to be an inclusive process, but other issues became more apparent and more problematic. As already noted, Unionism, and particularly the UUP, had made many concessions during the talks. What happened over the coming months and years, was that the wider unionist community found it increasingly less persuasive that the gains had justified the concessions. The 'constructive ambiguity' that was such a feature of the GFA, and one of the reasons it was possible to get the parties to sign up to the deal, would inevitably not be allowed to stand. Once the Agreement was unpacked and moves made to create the proposed structures, and parties looked to hold other parties to the obligations they felt were given during the talks, incompatible positions would be more difficult to maintain and clarity would be necessary. This was to begin almost immediately.

4

Implementing the Agreement, from exaltation to exasperation, 1998–2003

The euphoria that greeted the negotiation of the GFA was marked and widespread. Almost overnight Northern Ireland became the poster child of conflict resolution, a case to be invoked and emulated across the world, though often presented in a rather muddled and unconvincing way (O'Kane, 2010). A conflict long viewed as having no solution was suddenly an apparent exemplar of best practice and an international beacon of hope. The national and international press, which had been camped outside Castle Buildings, reported the historic achievement. Writing in the *Irish Times,* Frank Millar summed up the view of many when he noted, 'Think of all the bad days we've known here. Bloody Sunday, Bloody Friday, Bloody Monday. This really will be Good Friday' (*Irish Times*, 11 April 1998). The euphoria and praise were justified; the conclusion of the deal was a stunning achievement and those that negotiated it deserved the plaudits they received. The two local leaders who arguably did the most during the negotiations to secure the deal, David Trimble and John Hume, were the joint recipients of that year's Nobel Peace Prize. Yet once the initial relief and jubilation passed, the practicalities of getting the deal endorsed and, more problematically, creating the proposed structures, proved to be far more difficult than had been expected on 11 April. This chapter will examine why in the five years following the drafting of the GFA, the parties that were the main architects of the Agreement became marginalised, and those that were most sceptical of it, and least committed to implementing all elements of it, became the largest parties in Northern Ireland. It will demonstrate how the very ambiguity that had enabled the Agreement to be passed became the barrier to allowing it to be implemented. The issues that had been sidelined during the talks, notably decommissioning and police reform, became the ones which dominated the political landscape. The differences over these issues led to increasing mistrust between the political parties and their electorate.

The necessity of the parties to be able to 'sell' the Agreement to their electorate and to portray it as in line with their prescriptions for Northern Ireland placed a strain on the politics of the region. There was a necessity for the Agreement to be passed in concurrent referenda in the north and south of Ireland. These referenda were scheduled for 22 May 1998. It might have been expected that such an endorsement would have been a foregone conclusion. An Agreement, negotiated and endorsed by the main parties in Northern Ireland and the British and Irish governments, which was designed to bring about an end of a thirty-year conflict that had killed thousands of people, and injured tens of thousands, would surely be a popular outcome.

However, given the mistrust that still existed between the parties and traditions, it soon became apparent that the vote could be closer than expected. Although the talks had led to all parties having gains they could sell, it had also led to all parties having 'losses' that they had to be able to justify. As discussed in the previous chapter, Sinn Féin had settled for an outcome well short of its original position. Their position was well summarised by the former British diplomat, Sir David Goodall, who had long been involved in shaping British policy towards Northern Ireland and had been a key player in the negotiations which led to the 1985 AIA. Writing before the referenda, Goodall noted the issue for Sinn Féin was whether the freeing of prisoners, the equality agenda, 'hypothetical restructuring' of the RUC and the chance to become the dominant nationalist party in Northern Ireland, 'are gains sufficient to justify relegating the historic objective of a united Ireland to a more distant future and to provide a satisfactory answer to the agonising question, "What did Johnnie die for?"' (*The Tablet*, 25 April 1998). This was the crux of the problem for Sinn Féin.

The unwillingness of the republican leadership to openly endorse the Agreement ahead of Sinn Féin's special conference, and the portrayal of the Agreement and the end of violence as just new tactics in the ongoing struggle to achieve a united Ireland, were indicative of the predicament the leadership faced. The GFA was not universally welcomed by republicans, some of whom saw the gains as insufficient to justify the end of the IRA's campaign and claims that it was a staging post on the way to a united Ireland as unpersuasive. The fear that the answer offered by Sinn Féin to Goodall's question would not be satisfactory led to the party line being that whilst they supported a Yes vote in the referenda, it was not a decision taken lightly and their endorsement of the deal was far from effusive. An editorial in *An Phoblacht* a day before the referendum in Northern Ireland argued that 'republicans have severe reservations and concerns about several aspects of the Good Friday document. While the party is supporting a Yes vote North and South it recognises the individual right of any republican to vote No if that is their wish.' It also stressed the line that this was not a settlement. 'The Good Friday document and the referenda are only the beginning of a political process. It is the intention of republicans to turn that process into a transitional phase towards Irish unity.' The paper argued, 'Real democracy and a lasting peace will be achieved when the British government has removed itself from our shores and when the Irish people – Catholic, Protestant and Dissenter take charge of our own destiny and map out a future as equals on this island' (*AP/RN*, 21 May 1998).

There was a concern in London and Dublin that republicans might not be able to persuade their constituency to support the deal or prevent a notable split within the IRA. The nationalist SDLP were more fulsome in their support for the Agreement, but their course and demands had been different to those of Sinn Féin. Whilst both parties favoured a united Ireland, the SDLP had always rejected the use of violence, whereas republicans had argued that not only was it necessary, but that it was the only way to achieve unity. So the GFA was a harder sell for Sinn Féin. As a result, there was a belief that republicans needed some clear evidence of the benefits that they had secured. It was this rationale that explained the decision by the Irish government to release the Balcombe Street gang to attend the Sinn Féin conference considering whether to back the Agreement.

The reaction to the attendance of the Balcombe Street gang at the conference highlighted the problems with trying to maintain support for the Agreement between parties and traditions in Northern Ireland whose aspirations and interpretation of the past were so different. The four members of the Balcombe Street gang had been responsible for a bombing and shooting campaign in London in 1974–1975. They had been involved in a six-day siege in Balcombe Street where they held a married couple hostage in their flat after staging a gun attack on a Mayfair restaurant. They eventually surrendered to the police and in 1977 were convicted of seven murders and sentenced to over 600 years' imprisonment for their campaign. They had been transferred by the British government to a prison in the Irish Republic the week before the conference (which Blair claims was 'unwisely' decided by Mowlam) and were released by the Irish on a 24-hour pass to attend the event (again, according to Blair, without telling the British) (Blair, 2011: 179). In addition, the British had released several IRA members from the Maze, including Padraig Wilson, the IRA's leader in the prison, to attend the event to encourage the party to support a Yes vote in the forthcoming referendum in Northern Ireland. Powell claims that decision was also Mowlam's, along with the release of loyalist Michael Stone to attend a UDA/UDP rally in Belfast (Powell, 2009: 116). The presence of the men had a notable impact on the mood in the hall; they were embraced warmly on the stage by the Sinn Féin leadership of Adams and McGuinness and their hands held aloft. They were given a ten-minute standing ovation by the delegates and described by the Sinn Féin president as 'our Nelson Mandelas' (Bew and Gillespie, 1999: 363). The conference vote in support of the deal was subsequently passed with 96 per cent approval.

Whilst for Sinn Féin delegates the men may well have been heroes and political prisoners who had been caught up in a noble struggle against the oppressive British state, the unionist community watching the footage back in Northern Ireland viewed the spectacle very differently. For them, these were murderers and terrorists who had used unjustified violence to kill and maim innocent civilians and had been released a long time before their sentences had been served. The event was seen at the time as undermining support for the GFA amongst unionist voters, who were, of course, critical in securing the passing of the referendum scheduled for less than two weeks later. Blair claimed the incident 'very nearly wrecked the train as it was leaving the station' (Blair, 2011: 179). Powell noted that moderate unionists 'thought that if this is what the agreement meant, they were not for it' (Powell, 2009: 116). The criticism that incident garnered did lead to some reflection. Adams noted a few days later that he had 'misjudged the raw emotion of delight which gripped the Sinn Féin Ard Fheis when those four men came in', though he added that he didn't regret inviting them (*BBC News*, 20 May 1998) and Bertie Ahern noted that the appearance of the gang could have been handled 'in a calmer way' (*Irish Times*, 13 May 1998).

The incident highlighted that the concessions that all sides had made were not abstract, and although in the intense negotiations at Castle Buildings the leaders may have been persuaded that they were necessary and justified, the wider electorate had not been party to those talks. They did not know what was in the Agreement until it was published (a copy was delivered to every address in Northern Ireland) and they needed reassurance as to what it meant in practical terms. Fortunately, Trimble had sought and received the endorsement of his party's ruling Ulster Unionist Council for the deal the week after the GFA was concluded by 540 votes to 210 (*Independent on Sunday*, 19 April 1998), which was before the Sinn Féin conference. The increasing perception that the referendum vote in Northern Ireland might be tight led to a concerted effort by not only the parties, but also the two governments, to persuade voters to support it. Tony Blair was personally heavily involved in this. He visited Northern Ireland with his predecessor, John Major, and Major's successor as Conservative leader, William Hague, to urge support for the deal. Blair's role in the referendum campaign and the promises he appeared to make during it has received detailed consideration by Paul Dixon. Dixon argues that Blair undertook an 'honourable deception' during that campaign by suggesting outcomes that were not actually mandated by the GFA. He points out that the former Prime Minister notes in his memoirs that he 'took horrendous chances in what I was telling each the other had agreed to – stretching the truth, I fear, on occasions past breaking point' (Dixon, 2013: 109). This was perhaps most clearly demonstrated in Blair's actions in the final twenty-four hours before the referendum vote in Ireland. The Prime Minister appeared with Trimble and Hume and unveiled five pledges in his own handwriting. These were: 'no change to the status of Northern Ireland without the express consent of the people; the power to take decisions to be returned from London to Northern Ireland, with accountable North–South cooperation; fairness and equality for all; those who use or threaten violence to be excluded from the government of Northern Ireland; and prisoners to be kept in prison unless violence is given up for good' (*BBC News*, 21 May 1998). It was the final two pledges which were potentially problematic. The fourth one appeared to link serving in government with the end of violence, and for many would be taken to mean that Sinn Féin could not enter government until the IRA had decommissioned. The last pledge, which linked prisoners to giving up violence 'for good' also suggested a link to the decommissioning of weapons. In an interview that day, Blair appeared to go even further in linking the issues. When asked if he meant Adams would be unable to take a seat in government if the IRA had not 'renounced violence' he replied 'absolutely'. On decommissioning he stated that it was 'merely one test amongst many others, all these bombings, killings, beatings, targetings have got to stop. There is no question of people being allowed to employ some dual strategy of the ballot box on one hand and the gun on the other' (Dixon, 2013: 123). This interpretation was difficult to square with the text of the GFA. As previously discussed, the Agreement simply stated that parties would 'use any influence they may have, to achieve the decommissioning of all paramilitary arms within two years'; it did not state that there had to be decommissioning before a government was created. Yet Blair's 'pledges' and comments to the people of Northern Ireland seemed to suggest that Sinn Féin's participation in government, and the release of prisoners, were conditional on actions by the IRA.

Those around Blair (and, as his memoirs suggest, the Prime Minister himself) knew that his suggestions were based on a highly questionable interpretation of the Agreement they were asking the electorate to endorse. Alastair Campbell records in his diary that in an interview with the journalist Eamonn Mallie that day, Blair, 'went further than ever' in linking decommissioning 'with prisoner releases. Both John H[olmes] and I winced a little, worrying that he was making too many promises' (Campbell, 2013: 140). However, by that stage, the concern in British circles that the Agreement might be rejected in the referendum in Northern Ireland meant they were willing to risk making 'too many promises' to try and get unionist voters to back the deal. The Orange Order, DUP and UKUP were opposing the agreement and Blair was concerned that they might be successful in persuading a majority of unionists to vote 'No'.

Once the results of the referenda were in, it appeared that the campaign had been a success. The vote in the Irish Republic for the Agreement, and to change Articles 2 and 3, was overwhelming, with over 94 per cent of those who voted endorsing the deal and less than 6 per cent rejecting it, on a 55.59 per cent turnout. Perhaps predictably, the vote in NI was closer but there was still an overwhelming majority in favour of the deal, with over 71 per cent endorsing it and under 29 per cent voting to reject it. Turnout was an impressive 80.98 per cent (the highest ever turnout since 1921) (Bew and Gillespie, 1999: 365). There appeared, however, to be a notable difference in terms of support from Catholics and Protestants in NI. The DUP's Peter Robinson claimed that 56 per cent of Protestants had rejected it, whilst Trimble asserted that 'a majority' of unionists had backed the deal (though he did note 'not as big a majority' as he would have liked) (*Observer*, 24 May 1998). Given the voting system employed, it was impossible to state categorically the proportions of each community that backed the vote, but exit polling suggested that a slim majority of Protestants (and up to 95 per cent of Catholics) had backed the deal (*Observer*, 24 May 1998; Bew and Gillespie, 1999: 365). The divisions within Unionism in Northern Ireland over the GFA were highlighted by the election results for the newly devolved Assembly, which were held on 25 June. The avowedly anti-Agreement DUP polled 18.14 per cent of the vote and the other smaller anti-Agreement unionist party, the UKUP, got 4.51 per cent. The UUP's share was its lowest ever at 21.25 per cent. The SDLP polled 21.97 per cent (the first time a nationalist party had topped the poll in a Northern Ireland-wide election). Sinn Féin's strong growth continued, with the party receiving 17.63 per cent of the first preference votes. The APNI received 6.5 per cent, the UVF-linked PUP achieved 2.55 per cent and the UDA-linked UDP only secured 1.07 per cent. The Women's Coalition polled 1.61 per cent. Once the count was complete, the result was an Assembly in which the UUP was the largest party with twenty-eight seats, the SDLP had twenty-four; DUP, twenty; Sinn Féin, eighteen, APNI, six; UKUP, five; the Women's Coalition and PUP had two seats each and three independent (anti-Agreement) unionists were elected. This meant that pro-Agreement parties had secured 80 of the 108 seats in the new Assembly. This appeared on paper to be a strong endorsement of the Agreement. However, the numbers were somewhat deceptive. First, there was distinct, and growing, unease within the UUP over the Agreement. Second, although the majority of parties elected did indeed back the Agreement, what was missing was a shared perception of what the Agreement committed them to. The ambiguity in the GFA, which was such a vital part in getting the parties to sign up to it, was starting to become a barrier to its implementation.

The fault lines

Several fault lines soon began to emerge which were to undermine the support for the Agreement and the ability to create and sustain the proposed devolved structures in Northern Ireland. These were the challenges of continuing violence, parades, the relationship between sitting in government and decommissioning, and reform of the RUC. At one level these were separate issues. However, the fact that they were happening around the same time and that many of them were issues that the GFA had sought to deal with meant that they had a detrimental impact on the peace process and further undermined the chances of fully implementing the deal.

Continuing violence

Although the peace process had managed to entice the main armed groups away from violence, there remained a core of individuals and groups who continued to use violence for political ends. This was particularly an issue within militant republicanism. There had been a leakage of some notable figures from the IRA over the direction of the peace process from the early 1990s. Whilst many of these simply left active engagement, others looked to create or join alternative variants of the IRA, which would keep the 'armed struggle' alive. This idea of the 'split' had been a background consideration for the governments during the talks and had been a factor that was regularly raised by Sinn Féin's delegation during the process as a reason why there were limits to how many concessions the party could make. There had been a significant split in 1997 when Sinn Féin had endorsed the Mitchell Principles, leading to several prominent figures leaving the Provisional movement. Some of these formed another political organisation, the 32-county Sovereignty Movement, which, according to Marisa McGlinchey, 'shared an ideology' with the newly formed armed group the Real IRA (McGlinchey, 2019: 71). McGlinchey, who interviewed many of the key individuals associated with the groups which emerged from the Provisionals in this period, has stressed the importance of the issue of consent in the split. For many who were critical of the path that Adams and McGuinness had set the Provisionals on, 'the acceptance of consent' was the key decision in what they saw as the betrayal of republicanism, even 'more fundamental than final IRA decommissioning in 2005' (McGlinchey, 2019: 95). Bertie Ahern claims that throughout the negotiations leading to the GFA and in its immediate aftermath he was getting security reports of the activities of people who were previously senior members of the IRA. He was receiving reports that Kevin McKevitt (former quartermaster general of the Provisional IRA) 'was in Clare, and the next night he was in Kerry, and the next night he was in Cork, so he spent all that winter of 1997 to 1998 going around the country talking to groups and PIRA activists. McKevitt knew them and was asking eight or ten key guys to pull away from the leadership, and that was a very worrying time' (Spencer, 2020: 249). Quite how worrying the activity of disgruntled former IRA members who rejected the idea of abandoning the armed struggle (or dissidents as they became commonly known) could be was catastrophically illustrated in Omagh on 15 August 1998, when the Real IRA (RIRA) detonated a bomb in the centre of the town. The explosion led to the largest single loss of life in Northern Ireland during the conflict, with twenty-nine people killed and over two hundred injured. This was not an isolated act, there had been at least a dozen acts of violence by republicans in the period between the signing of the GFA and the Omagh bomb. These included two previous large town-centre bombings, one in Armagh (by the INLA) in June and one by the RIRA in Banbridge two weeks before the Omagh bombing. Smaller loyalist groups also carried out actions in this period too. The impact of the Omagh bomb, however, was more pronounced, due to the high death toll. In the immediate aftermath, the attack was widely condemned, including by Martin McGuinness and Gerry Adams. The RUC chief constable told Tony Blair that 'it was McKevitt and the Real IRA' who carried out the attack (Campbell, 2013: 156). The bomb actually had the opposite impact to that which the RIRA would have intended; it united people in condemnation and made it harder to justify continuing an armed campaign. The RIRA called a ceasefire in the days following the attack, as did the INLA a week after the bomb. Dissident republican violence was, however, to remain a real problem throughout the coming years in Northern Ireland, but the immediate aftermath of Omagh did see a reduction in their activity for a period. In response to the attack, both the Irish and British parliaments were recalled and new terrorist legislation was introduced, designed to make it easier to convict those believed to be involved in proscribed organisations. Despite the new legislation, those responsible for the Omagh bomb were never convicted for the deaths it caused. One man, Colm Murphy, was convicted in Dublin in 2002 of conspiracy to cause the bombing and sentenced to fourteen years, but no one was ever successfully prosecuted for the murders committed that day. The families of some of those who died, successfully brought a civil case against four men, Michael McKevitt, Liam Campbell, Colm Murphy and Seamus Daly, who were found liable for the bomb in 2009 and ordered to pay compensation totalling £1.6m, which was never paid (*Irish Times*, 12 August 2018). McKevitt was convicted in 2003 of 'directing terrorism' and membership of a proscribed organisation (the RIRA) in the Republic and served sixteen years, but these charges were not specifically related to the Omagh bomb. Campbell and Murphy also served prison sentences in the Irish Republic for IRA membership, not specifically related to the Omagh bomb.

Parades/Drumcree

It was not, however, just the organised actions of republican and loyalist armed groups in this period that was having a destabilising impact. The marching season in Northern Ireland had caused disturbances and tensions over the previous few years, notably at Drumcree. In July 1995 the proposed traditional Orange Order march along the Garvaghy Road after a service at Drumcree church in the town of Portadown was met with protests from local residents. After a stand-off, a compromise was reached, and the local Orange Lodge was allowed to march but without bands. The sight of David Trimble and Ian Paisley hand in hand after the local Orange Order had been allowed to walk the road was criticised as triumphalist by many. Trimble's explanation was that he, as the local MP, could not allow Paisley to upstage him and it was not meant as a triumphalist gesture. (See Godson (2004: 131–145) for an account of the episode and Trimble's role in it.) Although Trimble denied that his profile-raising activities at Drumcree had any connection with his successful UUP leadership bid two months later (Godson, 2004: 145) others believe it 'catapulted him into the leadership' (Patterson and Kaufmann, 2007: 222). The following year the situation deteriorated further. There was a difference between the Orange Order and the residents' organisation over what had been agreed the previous year. The residents believed that an agreement had been reached in 1995 that they would acquiesce to the march that year on the understanding that it would not be allowed to happen the following year. The marchers claimed that there was no such agreement, and tensions soon increased. The RUC originally banned the Orange Order from marching along the Garvaghy Road but reversed the decision in the face of growing numbers of protestors who were pouring into the area and the spreading unrest that was happening in other areas of Northern Ireland. The main unionist parties withdrew from all-party talks during the period. The decision to reverse the ban and allow the march-through led to anger and several days of rioting in nationalist areas. It also drew widespread criticism and put a strain on British–Irish relations. The Irish Taoiseach, John Bruton, told the Dáil, 'The authorities of a democratic state – any state – cannot afford to yield, or to be perceived to yield, to force or to the threat of force, cannot afford to be inconsistent and cannot afford to be partial in the way in which they apply the law. These basic tenets of democratic statecraft were, I have argued, breached in the case of the Portadown parade' (Dáil Éireann, *Debates*, 25 July 1996, vol. 468, col. 1123). The following year, 1997, was the first march under New Labour, but was again problematic. Mo Mowlam recalls in her memoir that although she had the power to overrule the decision taken by the RUC, she felt that it had to be their call. The decision was simply based upon which side posed the biggest threat and the decision was that banning the march rather than clearing the road of protesting residents and letting it through, would cause the most disturbance, so it was allowed (Mowlam, 2002: 94–95). Mowlam had promised the Garvaghy residents that she would personally visit to tell them what the decision was but as it was taken so late the night before the proposed march, the security situation would not allow her to keep her pledge; for which she was highly criticised by the residents subsequently. Again, in 1997, like previous years, the outcome of the march was widespread rioting throughout nationalist areas in Northern Ireland.

Given that the marches of 1995–1997 had taken place at times of heightened tension due to problems in the peace process (and in 1996 and 1997 during a period when the IRA was not on ceasefire) it might have been hoped that by 1998, with the backdrop of the GFA, things would be calmer. However, the problems that had plagued the efforts to resolve the dispute continued. There was still a strong strand of Unionism that saw the GFA as a sell-out and concessions to terrorism. The sense that their identity and traditions were under attack meant, for many loyalists, that Drumcree became, if anything, more important as a statement of values and resistance. The decision by the newly created Parades Commission to reroute the march, which was announced at the end of June, led to increased tension and a stand-off between the Orange Order and RUC. Over the coming weeks, tensions mounted and violence increased, much of it directed by loyalists against members of the RUC. By 8 July the RUC reported there had been more than four hundred attacks on the security services, including twelve shooting incidents and over twenty-five bombings (Bew and Gillespie, 1999: 371). The spiralling violence attracted international attention on 12 July when a Catholic family's house in Ballymoney was the target of a sectarian arson attack (one of 137 arson attacks on Catholic homes by loyalists that took place that week (*Belfast Telegraph*, 4 November 2019). Three brothers, Richard, Mark and Jason Quinn, aged between 8 and 11 were killed. The Orange Order denied that the murders had any link to Drumcree. However, the stand-off had increased tensions in Northern Ireland. In the days before the attack, five other Catholic homes in Ballymoney had received envelopes containing bullets from the UVF ordering them to leave. The deaths of the Quinn brothers saw widespread calls for the protest at Drumcree to be abandoned, including from David Trimble and the Archbishop of Armagh, Robin Eames (McKittrick et al., 1999: 1434–1435). Many loyalists took this step, though some remained to protest at the failure to allow the march. In 1999, 23-year-old Garfield Gilmour was sentenced to three life sentences for the attack, which the judge blamed on the UVF (*Irish Times*, 30 October 1999).

The events at Drumcree in the run-up to, and immediate aftermath of the GFA illustrate the divisions and mistrust which existed within Northern Ireland at that time. Parades had long been, and would continue to be, contentious in some areas and the summer marching season was a time when tensions between the two traditions in Northern Ireland increased and sectarianism became more pronounced. It can, of course, be debated whether they were the causes of such tensions or an opportunity for them to be vented. However, the changing demographic character of some areas in Northern Ireland and the tendency of communities to live in segregation, often in very close proximity to each other, produced conditions that facilitated sectarian conflict. By 1998 there were two parallel emotions in play in Northern Ireland. Celebration and hope for those who saw the new Agreement as an indicator of the end of the Troubles, and a harbinger of peaceful coexistence and parity of esteem between the two traditions in Northern Ireland; and mistrust and fear for those who saw the GFA as marking either a victory for one tradition over the other or as a part of a continuing struggle for the advancement of their tradition. The Orange Order had rejected the GFA, seeing it as both detrimental to the Union and an attack on the traditions and institutions that they believed were instrumental to their Britishness and their community. For them, the right to march down their traditional route was essential. As a result, they were not willing to compromise and see the march rerouted, nor engage with the residents' association, which they saw simply as a Sinn Féin/IRA front. For the nationalists who lived on the Garvaghy Road, the Orange Order march was a triumphalist incursion into their area that should no longer be tolerated when there was meant to be parity of esteem. However, opposition to it was also increasingly viewed as part of the republican struggle. The residents' association was led by Breandan MacCionnaith, who had served a prison sentence in the 1980s for involvement in an IRA bombing of Portadown (one of the main reasons that the Orange Order refused to engage with the group). He was seen as an especially awkward and intransigent individual, particularly by those on the British side. In his memoirs, Tony Blair notes that the 'Drumcree people were the unreasonable of the unreasonable of the unreasonable. In the premiere league of unreasonableness they left every other faction, in every other dispute, gasping in their wake.' On MacCionnaith, Blair argued, 'He was so unreasonable that in the end I became rather intrigued by him … He took unreasonableness to an art form' (Blair, 2011: 160–161). Blair's comments encapsulate the exasperation and frustration that British politicians have often felt when dealing with Northern Ireland.

But, like so many other issues related to the conflict and the peace process, Drumcree was about far more than what it appeared to be focused upon, the right to march along a short length of contested road. It became one of several battlegrounds on which the wider mistrust and inter- and intra-community battles were fought. The role of Sinn Féin in the dispute was widely suspected and criticised by those in the Orange Order and the DUP who opposed the GFA. Gerry Adams was quoted in a Raidió Teilifís Éireann (RTE) documentary of having told a Sinn Féin conference in November 1996,

> Ask any activist in the north, "did Drumcree happen by accident?", and they will tell you, "no". Three years of work on the Lower Ormeau Road, Portadown, and parts of Fermanagh and Newry, Armagh and in Bellaghy and up in Derry. Three years of work went into creating that situation and fair play to those people who put the work in. They are the type of scene changes that we have to focus on and develop and exploit. (*Irish Times*, 6 March 1997, and comments of Peter Robinson in the House of Commons, 27 October 2009, col. 216)

Similarly, the DUP and the Orange Order used the dispute to highlight what they felt were the inequities of the GFA, the dangers of seeking to make concessions to republicans (who had not even decommissioned their weapons or stated their war was over) and to put pressure on the UUP for having done so. The GFA may have been agreed, but the peace had not been secured.

Guns and government

The issue of what had been agreed on decommissioning on Good Friday and what the relationship was between decommissioning and sitting in the Executive had to be clarified. The position of the parties on the link between decommissioning and seats in government hardened in the immediate aftermath of the GFA. Republicans stressed that the IRA would not decommission, and that Sinn Féin were not the IRA and therefore had no arms to dispose of. Adams told the Sinn Féin ard fheis in May 1998,

> The IRA has made it clear that it will not surrender its weapons. So, have all the other armed groups including the British forces. Sinn Féin is not an armed group. We are not the IRA. We want to see all the guns taken out of Irish politics and we will continue to work for that. We go into this next phase of struggle armed only with whatever mandate we receive, armed only with our political ideas and our vision of the future. (*AP/RN*, 14 May 1998)

Yet the UUP insisted that they would not sit in government with Sinn Féin until there was decommissioning.

Although the Executive was created in 'shadow' form in July 1998, and Trimble nominated as First Minister with the SDLP's Seamus Mallon as Deputy, a way to break the impasse over decommissioning needed to be found before power could be devolved. Various proposals were suggested to try and resolve the crisis. Theoretically there were various possible ways that the issue could be overcome. Most obviously, it would have no longer been an issue if the IRA had decommissioned. However, they were unwilling to do this. Second, it would have ceased to be a major factor if the UUP had announced that they were no longer concerned with decommissioning and were happy to enter into government with Sinn Féin regardless of whether the IRA decommissioned their weapons; a stance they were unwilling to take. Another possibility was for the SDLP to side with the UUP and announce that they would support the exclusion of Sinn Féin from government and continue to sit in the Executive themselves if the IRA did not decommission its weapons. Seamus Mallon, in his memoirs, suggested that he appreciated the UUP leader's difficulties over decommissioning and 'genuinely wanted to help Trimble with the problems decommissioning were causing him'. As a result, in November 1998 he told his party's conference 'that the SDLP would support the exclusion of Sinn Féin ministers from government in the North if republicans failed to meet their decommissioning obligations' (Mallon, 2019: 2642). Mallon's speech actually noted concerns that Sinn Féin would 'fail to honour their decommissioning obligations under the agreement within the specified two-year period'. In the speech, Mallon noted that he did not believe that Sinn Féin would fail to meet their obligations but stated, 'no one should have any doubt that if it did happen the SDLP would rigorously enforce the terms of the agreement and remove from office those who had so blatantly dishonoured their obligations' (Mallon, CAIN). However, from the UUP's perspective this was not overly reassuring. Mallon's position was that Sinn Féin had up until the end of the two-year period mentioned in the GFA before the SDLP would support their exclusion. In November 1998, the UUP's position was that the IRA must decommission before they would share power with Sinn Féin. Mallon's commitment in the speech was, by his own account, also somewhat out of line with the view of other key nationalist figures. 'I knew quite quickly after the speech that it was approved neither by John Hume nor the Irish government. Both of them thought that as long as the IRA's guns were silent, there was no major issue' (Mallon, 2019: 2624). The problem was that, although this may have been their view, if the UUP could not be convinced of this, then it would be impossible to create the devolved power-sharing institutions that had been agreed on Good Friday 1998.

The position of Sinn Féin was not only that the issue of decommissioning was not linked to their right to sit in the Executive, but that it would be counterproductive for them to state that the IRA should decommission. Republican 'insiders' argued that the lives of Adams and McGuinness would be in danger if they called for IRA decommissioning (*Guardian*, 5 February 1999). The line that Sinn Féin's leadership took was that the issue could split the movement. Alastair Campbell's diary records a fraught meeting between Blair, Adams and McGuinness in July 1999. The IRA had issued a statement on 21 July claiming unionists were obstructing the creation of the institutions and were 'opposed to a democratic peace settlement'. In what the British took as a 'veiled threat to return to violence' (Campbell, 2013: 235) the IRA noted that the first ceasefire had 'floundered on the demand by the Conservative government for an IRA surrender. Those who demand the decommissioning of IRA weapons lend themselves, in the current political context, inadvertently or otherwise, to the failed agenda which seeks the defeat of the IRA' (IRA, CAIN). At the meeting with Blair the next day, Adams had indicated to the PM that 'as an organization they were not as disciplined as we sometimes thought'. McGuinness also suggested that Blair and Trimble 'have to come to terms with the fact that they have more influence on the IRA than him or Gerry' (Campbell, 2013: 230–231). As a result of these differing positions over the issue of decommissioning, the peace process became logjammed in 1999.

The attitude of the two governments to decommissioning in this period illustrated the pragmatism that underpinned their approach to the peace process. They were driven by what they thought would move the process forward rather than what they thought was 'right'. The policy of both governments in the months following the signing of the GFA was to try and increase pressure on the IRA to begin decommissioning. In February 1999 Ahern had stated that it was not possible for Sinn Féin to be part of the Executive 'without at least a commencement of decommissioning'. He also explicitly rejected the argument that there was no start date for decommissioning only an end date of May 2000 as 'illogical, unfair and unreasonable' (*Sunday Times*, 14 February 1999). This was very much the stance taken by the UUP at that stage. John Taylor asserted the following month that 'There is no question of the Ulster Unionist Party agreeing to an executive involving Sinn Féin until there is some prior decommissioning. That has been our position. That remains our position and those who are saying otherwise are misrepresenting the Ulster Unionist Party' (*Guardian*, 31 March 1999). In April 1999 the two governments drew up the 'Hillsborough Declaration' after three days of intensive talks with the parties at Hillsborough in Northern Ireland. The proposal was for a choreographed sequence which would see the mechanism triggered to allow ministers to be nominated but they would not take office until power was devolved. Within a month of these nominations, there would be a 'collective act of reconciliation' which would 'see some arms put beyond use on a voluntary basis, in a manner which will be verified by the Independent International Commission on Decommissioning' and also 'acts of remembrance of all victims of violence'. Around the same time, powers would be devolved, and the institutions proposed in the GFA would be created (CAIN). Despite the intense focus on the negotiations by the two governments and the pressure applied to all sides to accept the deal, the initiative failed, primarily because Sinn Féin were believed not to be able to sell the proposals to the grass roots of the republican movement. Sinn Féin subsequently claimed that, as Gerry Kelly told an Easter commemoration in Sligo a few days later, 'Sinn Féin was not involved in negotiating it nor in agreeing to it' (*The Irish Times*, 5 April 1999). It is true that Sinn Féin had not agreed to the draft proposals, but they had been involved in the negotiations which led to it (though it was ultimately an intergovernmental document). The two governments suspected that many of the members of the IRA's Army Council were in Hillsborough Castle during those talks and, at one stage, Ahern believed that Adams and McGuinness were trying to persuade them to agree to the proposed steps (Campbell, 2013: 203). Despite the hope that the two governments had for movement by the IRA at Hillsborough it became increasingly apparent that the IRA were not willing to decommission in advance of entry into government.

Due to the refusal of the IRA to decommission, the approach of the governments altered. Given that they had proved unsuccessful in persuading the IRA to decommission any weapons before Sinn Féin could enter government, the focus now became on getting unionists to agree to enter government before weapons were decommissioned, if there appeared to be an undertaking that decommissioning would then occur. Despite his previous assertions that it was not possible for Sinn Féin to be in government before decommissioning commenced, by June, Ahern was stating that decommissioning was only possible 'in the context of a confidence in functioning democratic institutions' (*Irish Times*, 23 June 1999). This brought Ahern more into line with Sinn Féin's analysis. McGuinness claimed after Hillsborough that if the government did not move away from the attempts to make decommissioning a condition of government, 'and back to the letter and the spirit of the agreement, then the Good Friday Agreement is dead' (*Irish News*, 19 March 1999). Indeed, McGuinness subsequently argued that it was not the lack of decommissioning which was hindering the creation of devolved government, but the lack of the devolved government that was a barrier to possible decommissioning. He claimed that the failure to set up the institutions meant that he could not seek to use his influence with the IRA 'because we are working in the context of the non-implementation of the Good Friday Agreement and that it is absolutely essential that David Trimble be told that that is an impossibility' (*Irish Times*, 24 June 1999).

In July 1999, the governments published *The Way Forward*, which was the result of another intense round of negotiations with claims that Blair had held 120 meetings related to Northern Ireland over the previous five days (*The Sunday Times*, 4 July 1999). The plan by then was to truncate the process suggested in April but, crucially, create the devolved government before decommissioning commenced. The proposal was for the d'Hondt process to nominate ministers to be run on 15 July, powers devolved three days later and the Chastelain Commission to then have urgent talks with the IRA contact, confirm the start of decommissioning and report on progress in September and December, to make sure that the process was completed by May 2000. In an attempt to reassure the UUP, the governments introduced a 'failsafe clause' which asserted that the institutions would be suspended if progress was not made. Speaking in support of the proposals, Blair sought to stress that, by accepting the proposals, decommissioning would begin almost immediately. Speaking in the House of Commons he quoted de Chastelain's observation that he expected an 'unambiguous statement' that decommissioning would be completed by May 2000 within days of the institutions being created, and that there would be an act of decommissioning within weeks. The Prime Minister asked the Commons, 'After 30 years of bloodshed, grief-stricken families and terror-torn communities, is it not worth waiting 30 days to see whether the undertakings are fulfilled?' He also repeated his commitment to the suspension option. 'Should default occur, the institutions are suspended automatically while we find a way forward. We are then, in effect, back to where we are now, but with these two vital differences: the blame for default is clear, and the parties are then free to move on in an Executive without the defaulting party' (*Hansard*, 5 July 1999, vol. 334, cols 640–641).

There were problems, however, with Blair's reassurances. Sinn Féin rejected the government's position. Adams stated that the suggestion that the government would exclude Sinn Féin from the Executive if the IRA did not decommission was 'not possible'. 'There is no question of the British government introducing legislation to expel Sinn Féin, Mr Blair knows this would be a breach of the Good Friday Agreement' (*The Herald*, 6 July 1999). In reality, what Blair seemed to be suggesting was that the other parties could agree to continue in an Executive without Sinn Féin if the IRA did not decommission. However, given that the SDLP's position appeared to be that the IRA must decommission by May 2000, logically they would not support the exclusion of Sinn Féin before that date. This meant that a failure by the IRA to decommission would lead to the collapse of devolution. As a result, unionists were not reassured by the government's 'failsafe clause'. Unionists had long objected to the proposal of suspending the institutions on the grounds that it punished others for a failure of the IRA to decommission. The UUP's ruling Executive subsequently voted to reject the proposals and David Trimble announced on 14 July that his party would not participate in the d'Hondt process the following day. The decision of the UUP to block the nomination of ministers exposed the deepening crisis in the peace process, and Seamus Mallon resigned as Deputy First Minister. In his resignation statement, Mallon was highly critical of the UUP.

> They use this crisis to bleed more concessions out of the governments. To bleed this very process dry. They stand by their demand of prior decommissioning. A condition found nowhere in the agreement. A condition alien to its principles. What they are doing is worse than failing to operate an inclusive executive. They are actually preventing its very creation. They are dishonouring the agreement. They are insulting its principles. (Mallon's statement, 15 July 1999, CAIN)

As a result of the failure, the government had to put the process into review.

This particular impasse over decommissioning was broken later in the year as a result of a three-month review conducted by Senator George Mitchell. In December 1999 power was finally devolved to Northern Ireland. The basis upon which it was secured was actually very similar to that which had been unacceptable five months earlier. A carefully choreographed series of events saw the UUP issue a statement indicating they would enter into government with Sinn Féin if the IRA responded positively to a call that John de Chastelain had made for paramilitary groups to engage with his Commission. Sinn Féin also issued a statement which acknowledged 'that decommissioning is an essential part of the peace process'. The party also stated its opposition to the use of violence and its 'total and absolute commitment to pursue our objectives by exclusively peaceful and democratic means', although the statement also noted that decommissioning, 'can only come about on a voluntary basis' (*Financial Times*, 17 November 1999). The day after the parties' statements, the IRA issued its own, which pledged that 'following the establishment of the institutions agreed on Good Friday last year, the IRA leadership will appoint a representative to enter into discussions with General John de Chastelain and the Independent International Commission on Decommissioning' (*Independent*, 18 November 1999). As a result of this carefully choreographed sequence, on 2 December power was devolved to Northern Ireland, the AIA lapsed, Articles 2 and 3 of the Irish constitution were removed and the North–South Ministerial Council and British–Irish Council came into being.

The decision to agree to enter into government with Sinn Féin before decommissioning occurred was undoubtedly a huge risk for Trimble, as it broke the 'no guns, no government' position that his party had stressed since the GFA was negotiated. Quite how problematic it was became immediately apparent when it was widely reported that at least six out of the ten UUP MPs were against the deal and they issued a statement arguing that 'This deal effectively removes the lines between democracy and terrorism and we urge the wider party to stand by our manifesto pledges' (*Irish Times*, 18 November 1999). Willie Thompson MP called on Trimble to resign and threatened to leave the party if the deal was agreed, and his colleague, Jeffrey Donaldson, made his objections clear. 'There is no timetable, no declaration that the so-called war is over, absolutely no guarantee that decommissioning will ever happen. It doesn't give anything like the commitment unionists need to see peace and democracy' (*Independent*, 18 November 1999). Despite the opposition from the majority of his parliamentary colleagues, Trimble managed to get the backing of the party's ruling council on 28 November to enter into government with Sinn Féin despite no decommissioning having occurred. He did this by depositing a post-dated letter of resignation with the UUP's president, Josias Cunningham, which was to be activated in February 2000 if no decommissioning had occurred by that date and the government had not suspended the institutions. He also stated that he would make it a condition of any UUP ministers that they did the same upon taking office. Jeffrey Donaldson subsequently told Trimble's biographer that it was this move that enabled Trimble to get the backing for the deal, which Donaldson had opposed at the meeting (Godson, 2004: 531).

Several factors seem to have contributed to Trimble's decision to jettison his party's previous 'no guns, no government' stance. He believed if the UUP did not alter its position then the logjam could not be broken. It could be argued, as many within his own party did, that this was not the fault of the UUP and so they should not abandon a morally defensible position and allow armed groups into a democratic government. However, the party was under significant pressure to alter their stance on the grounds that not to do so would mean not only no devolved government, but no chance at all of decommissioning, and potentially the end of the peace process. Tony Blair had publicly stated in July, whilst trying to get agreement for his 'Way Forward' document, 'The alternative to this agreement is not decommissioning faster or on different terms, it is no decommissioning at all: ever.' The Prime Minister had also sought to suggest that if the UUP did not alter their stance it would lead to them being blamed for the collapse of the peace process. If Trimble's party refused to enter into government unless there was prior decommissioning, Sinn Féin would have a 'massive propaganda victory of being able to say: we were never even given the chance to get decommissioning but excluded from the Executive. The blame would fall on unionists. It would be a tactical own goal of monumental proportions' (*Sunday Times*, 4 July 1999).

So why was Trimble unwilling to take that risk in July 1999 but persuaded to alter his position in November? It is clear that similar arguments were used privately to him by the British government at the close of the Mitchell review (Godson, 2004: 514). Trimble believed, however, that there was a distinct difference between what he had signed up to in November 1999 to that offered in July. The difference was that the previous deal had been put together by Blair and Ahern, whereas this deal was a result of commitments given by Adams and McGuinness, with whom he had interacted directly during the Mitchell review process. By November, Trimble had begun to trust Adams and McGuinness (Godson, 2004: 508). He argued that if 'you read the Sinn Féin and IRA statement together. We have got what amounts to a commitment to decommission' (*Daily Telegraph*, 19 November 1999). Trimble was perhaps also more inclined to believe that the British government would stand behind the UUP if the IRA failed to deliver as he had more faith in the new NISS, Peter Mandelson, than he had had in Mo Mowlam, whom he had frequently called on to resign. Trimble presented the move as a risk worth taking, arguing that the situation could be presented as win–win for unionism. 'If the IRA defaults, the Irish constitutional claim will have disappeared. The Anglo–Irish Agreement of 1985 will be dead and republican bad faith will be exposed … If this plan works, Ulster Unionists will have secured decommissioning and devolution. The prize is enormous.' He seemed to envisage an electoral penalty for Sinn Féin should the IRA fail to decommission, claiming 'if they're stringing people along' then, 'politically they're wrecked'. He argued that even if the government failed to act if the IRA did not decommission, there would be a price for Sinn Féin. 'It doesn't matter what the governments do or don't do. The electorate aren't going to stand for it' (*Daily Telegraph*, 26 November 1999).

Trimble's decision allowed the peace process to move forward and the creation of the devolved structures and other institutions was widely hailed as a historic moment.

Policing

Decommissioning was not the only difficult issue for unionists. As part of the GFA there was a pledge for 'a new beginning to policing in Northern Ireland' (Belfast Agreement, 1998: 26). The Agreement proposed an international Commission on policing whose proposals 'should be designed to ensure that policing arrangements, including composition, recruitment, training, culture, ethos and symbols, are such that in a new approach Northern Ireland has a police service that can enjoy widespread support from, and is seen as an integral part of, the community as a whole' (Belfast Agreement, 1998: 28). The problems with policing in Northern Ireland were linked not only to the conflict but the wider societal perceptions and suspicions that existed. There had been a historic mistrust from elements of the nationalist community of the RUC. (For a brief overview of perceptions of the RUC in Northern Ireland see McGarry (2000: 173–176).) Thirty years of conflict had exacerbated the mistrust, and due to both the mistrust and the targeting of police officers by republican paramilitaries, by 1998 Catholics made up only 8 per cent of the RUC (The Patten Report, 1999: 82). Effectively one tradition was policing the other; a highly problematic situation for any deeply divided society. The Independent Commission on Policing for Northern Ireland was headed by former Conservative politician (and the last governor of Hong Kong) Chris Patten. The 128-page Patten Report (as it came to be known) was published in September 1999 and recommended 174 changes to how Northern Ireland was policed. The report quoted survey data that stated only between a quarter and a third of Catholics believed that the RUC treated the two communities equally (as opposed to 70 per cent of Protestants) (The Patten Report, 1999: 13–14). It also highlighted problems that symbolic issues, notably the name and badge of the RUC caused for some citizens. 'Many people in Northern Ireland from the Irish nationalist and republican tradition regard the name, badge and symbols of the Royal Ulster Constabulary as associating the police with the British constitution and state. This contributes to the perception that the police are not their police.' But for those of a unionist tradition it was 'perfectly natural that a service provided and funded by the state should signal its provenance'. As a result, the 'name of the RUC, and to some extent the badge and the uniform too, have become politicised – one community effectively claiming ownership of the name of "our" police force, and the other community taking the position that the name is symbolic of a relationship between the police and unionism and the British state' (The Patten Report, 1999: 98–99).

The Commission's analysis of the situation was borne out by the reaction to the recommendations in the report. Patten suggested that the RUC be renamed the Police Service of Northern Ireland (PSNI), a new badge be adopted, and the Union flag no longer flown from police buildings. Much of the subsequent opposition to the report centred upon these symbolic criticisms, although other issues, such as the establishment of a policing board to oversee the PSNI's actions were also contentious, not least because as one of the parties to the Executive, Sinn Féin would have a seat on the proposed board. This was problematic for many unionists given that Sinn Féin had always opposed the RUC and the IRA had actively targeted its members, over three hundred of whom had been killed during the Troubles. Trimble also criticised the plan to amalgamate Special Branch and the Criminal Investigation Department (CID). Patten had suggested that there were problems with Special Branch acting as a 'force within a force'. Many unionists believed this would reduce the ability of the police force to target terrorism. Trimble was highly critical of the Patten Report claiming it was 'the most shoddy piece of work I have ever seen. It makes recommendations without any discussion whatsoever. This is a report that doesn't argue its case.' He objected not only to the symbolic changes, but also to the proposals that to tackle under-representation of Catholics in the police, 50 per cent of all new recruits for a ten-year period should be from a Catholic background. Whilst he noted that under-representation was a problem in the RUC, he suggested that the policy was unnecessary, claiming the issue could be corrected if intimidation of possible Catholic recruits was ended (*Belfast Telegraph*, 10 September 1999). This suggestion was questionable, given that Catholics had only made up 10 per cent of the RUC at the outbreak of the Troubles in 1969 (McGarry, 2000: 179) suggesting that there were wider reasons for Catholic non-participation in the RUC than simply intimidation. (For an interesting wider critique of policing in Northern Ireland from a nationalist perspective, see Mallon (2019: chapter 9).) Trimble spoke for many unionists when he claimed the report was a 'gratuitous insult' to the RUC (*Belfast Telegraph*, 10 September 1999). The dropping of the name was seen as a slight on the service of police officers during the Troubles. The Police Federation's chairman, Les Rodgers, argued that the 'abandonment' of the name was 'a repudiation of the professionalism, courage and sacrifice of our police officers' and the DUP's Peter Robinson described it as the 'greatest ever betrayal of the RUC' (*Belfast Telegraph*, 10 September 1999).

Despite the outrage amongst unionists over the proposed reforms, the British government largely accepted the Patten Report. In January 2000, Peter Mandelson paid tribute to the RUC and noted the sacrifices it had made during the conflict (the force had been awarded the George Cross by the Queen two months earlier). However, Mandelson announced that there needed to be radical change as 'the extreme religious imbalance in the composition of the police in Northern Ireland is simply unsustainable. A normal, peacetime society cannot be policed by a force that is so extremely unrepresentative of the society that it serves' (*Hansard*, 19 January 2000, vol. 342, col. 855). Many of the issues that unionists had protested against, the change of name, 50:50 recruitment but no 'ex-terrorists' allowed to join, the new policing board, effectively combining Special Branch and CID by placing them both under a single assistant chief constable, and a new oath including a pledge to uphold human rights for new recruits, were to be implemented. The question of what the new badge design should be was left for the proposed policing board to decide upon (*Irish Times*, 20 January 2000;

Hansard, 19 January 2000, vol. 342, cols 345–348). It was clear that the unionist campaign against Patten had failed.

Unlike with decommissioning and the creation of the Executive, the ability of unionists to force the government to alter its policies over RUC reform were rather limited. Reform of the police did not require UUP agreement. It was, of course, possible for the party to have taken action similar to that which they did over decommissioning and refuse to sit in devolved government unless the RUC's name and badge were retained, but that was a step which David Trimble was unwilling to take. The link between policing and office-holding was tenuous at best and police reform could take place whether the UUP were in government or not but, as was apparent by January 2000, decommissioning would not take place unless the UUP were in government. There was, as Frank Millar, the former UUP general secretary, then London editor of the *Irish Times* and future Trimble biographer, noted, an 'inevitability' to the Patten reforms given the stress on inclusivity in the peace process. 'With inclusivity would come "parity of esteem". And, when it came to the matter of policing, a blind man on a galloping horse could have seen that that would translate into the end of the identification of Northern Ireland's police service with the symbolism of the British state' (*Irish Times*, 20 January 2000). The reform of the RUC was an emotive issue for Unionism but not one for which, ultimately, Trimble was willing to make a line in the sand. It is also interesting how little attention the issue received in the accounts of the period from the main British politicians who have written on the peace process. Whilst decommissioning is a recurring and extensively discussed issue in their accounts, Patten and RUC reform features far less often. For example, in the index of Campbell's *Irish Diaries* decommissioning has over fifty index entries whilst Patten/RUC reform-related entries have eight. Similarly, the memoirs of Mowlam, Blair, Mandelson and Powell deal briefly with Patten but say far more on decommissioning. The issue of police reform was to continue to be a bone of contention in Northern Ireland for another three years with nationalists believing the British were seeking to water down Patten's proposals up until they were largely fully implemented in the Police (Northern Ireland) Act in 2003. The SDLP's Seamus Mallon called the Act the one 'very hard-won achievement' he would cite from his nineteen years in the House of Commons (Mallon, 2019: 3184).

Collapse and realignment

Any hope that might have been engendered by the progress in 1999 on decommissioning, the establishment of the GFA institutions and moves to implement Patten, was short-lived. Almost the entire decade of the 2000s was to be marked by crises in the peace process, political instability in

Northern Ireland and a notable realignment in its politics. Talk of 'trust' between unionism and republicanism was soon shown to be premature. The period demonstrates that, despite the difficulties that were clearly apparent in negotiating the GFA, if anything, its implementation was even more challenging. Many of the fault lines noted above remained destabilising. The main issue, and the one which accounted for the suspension of the Executive in February 2000 and July 2001 was decommissioning. It was increasingly apparent throughout January 2000 that, despite appointing an interlocutor to the de Chastelain body, no actual decommissioning was on the horizon. Gerry Adams had announced that the IRA was not about to decommission at the end of January and called for the organisation to be given 'time and space' (*Independent*, 27 January 2000) whilst Sinn Féin's Mitchell McLaughlin stated that common sense 'tells us that the IRA are not going to respond to deadlines set by unionists' (*Guardian*, 29 January 2000). The two governments received the report on 31 January, although they delayed its publication in an attempt to avert the crisis. The report noted that whilst the IRA had assured the Commission of their commitment to the peace process and the body recognised the IRA's difficulties over decommissioning, 'our sole task is decommissioning and to date we have received no information as to when decommissioning will start'. The IRA issued a statement on 5 February noting that 'The IRA has never entered into any agreement, undertaking or understanding at any time with anyone on any aspect of decommissioning.' However, it also seemed to acknowledge the need for decommissioning.

> We recognise the issue of arms needs to be dealt with in an acceptable way and this is a necessary objective of a genuine peace process – for that reason we are engaged with the IICD [decommissioning body]. We have supported and will continue to support efforts to secure the resolution of the arms issue. The peace process is under no threat from the IRA. (*AP/RN*, 10 February 2000)

However, this was not adequate as it did not pledge to actually decommission weapons or indicate when the process might begin.

Faced with this impasse, and to prevent Trimble's resignation letter being implemented, the government suspended the institutions. The fear was that if the institutions collapsed it would be far harder to resurrect the process than reactivate suspended institutions. As Blair said, 'It is a choice between pause or bust ... I am not going to let the government of Northern Ireland simply collapse into a black hole' (*Guardian*, 9 February 2000). The Independent International Commission on Decommissioning (IICD) issued a second, more positive, statement the day before suspension, noting the IRA's representative 'indicated to us today the context in which the IRA will initiate a comprehensive process to put arms beyond use, in a manner as to ensure maximum public confidence' but again there was no timetable to do so (*Guardian*, 12 February 2000).

Despite the pressure that Trimble was placed under to withdraw his threat to resign (and so remove the need to suspend the institutions) he refused to do so, and Mandelson activated the suspension. The move was heavily criticised by Sinn Féin who claimed that the British had squandered a last-minute offer by the IRA over decommissioning. Whilst Mandelson subsequently acknowledged that a proposed IRA statement was 'a step forward' as it did appear to commit to decommissioning, albeit if there was a process to 'progressively and irreversibly remove the causes of the conflict', it was 'frustratingly vague on how and utterly silent on when'. Gerry Adams had also said that it could not be passed to Trimble or de Chastelain as the IRA base had not been prepared (Mandelson, 2010: 296). Godson offers a similar account but suggests Adams did agree that the statement could be shown to de Chastelain (Godson, 2004: 575). Under such circumstances, it was not realistic for the British to rescind their stated intention to suspend the institutions (although this did cause friction with the Irish government). As a result of this action the IRA announced they were ending their engagement with the IICD.

The collapse of February 2000 was undoubtedly a significant blow to the peace process. Godson argues that the outcome was 'the greatest victory of any unionist leader in 30 years' but he is highly critical of Trimble for 'underselling' this victory. In narrow terms, it can be seen as a 'victory' in that Trimble had forced the British government to suspend the institutions (a move they were reluctant to do), in the face of huge pressure from Sinn Féin, the Irish government and, to a lesser extent, from the SDLP and the US. Godson portrays the US as comparatively neutral on this issue, 'when the crunch came, the White House was not there, either for Trimble or Blair' (Godson, 2004: 588). Alastair Campbell's account suggests that the US administration was actually pressurising the UK not to suspend, 'Bill [Clinton] was taking Sinn Féin's side, saying Trimble had to get out and sell this' (Campbell, 2013: 256). Godson claims Trimble had also forced from the IRA a last-minute move on decommissioning. However, if it was a victory, it was a minor one. Godson criticises Trimble for failing to make the most of the victory, as Trimble's 'definition of "victory" did not extend to driving the republicans out of the process and trying to form an Executive without Sinn Féin (or even a renegotiation of the Belfast Agreement)' (Godson, 2004: 591). This is a questionable criticism of the UUP's leader. It seems to presuppose that such an outcome was realistic. There is little to suggest that the SDLP, British or Irish governments would have been willing to take either of these steps. The peace process, as has been previously noted, was largely designed to entice the IRA away from violence, create power-sharing devolved government which included Sinn Féin, bring some stability to the region and reduce the issue's impact upon wider British and Irish politics. Although there was increasing frustration with the IRA over decommissioning, in February 2000 this had not reached the level that would persuade the SDLP to sit in a devolved government without Sinn Féin, or persuade the other parties and governments to abandon the GFA and start again.

The institutions remained suspended until May 2000, when another round of talks made some more progress on decommissioning. On that occasion David Trimble was again persuaded to re-enter government with Sinn Féin, despite there still being no actual decommissioning. The breakthrough was the statement issued by the IRA on 6 May. This was, in many ways, similar to that which the IRA had proposed in February; it asserted that 'in the context' of 'full implementation' by the governments of what they had agreed, the IRA would 'initiate a process that will completely and verifiably put IRA arms beyond use'. This was, for the first time, a specific public undertaking by the IRA to decommission weapons. The statement was also a notable advance as they agreed that in the meantime, as a 'confidence-building measure', they would allow a number of their arms dumps to be inspected 'by agreed third parties' who would then report to the IICD (with which the IRA would re-engage). The dumps would be 'regularly inspected', 'to ensure that the weapons have remained silent' (CAIN).

Trimble hailed the statement as 'an important step forward. It means to me that the IRA campaign is finally over' (*Sunday Times*, 21 May 2000). He managed to persuade the members of his party's ruling body, the UUC, to back returning to government by 459 to 403 votes (*BBC News*, 27 May 2000). This second stint of devolved government was also to be time-limited. Trimble announced in May 2001 that he would resign as First Minister if the IRA had not decommissioned weapons by July (*Irish Times*, 9 May 2001), which he subsequently did. The move meant that if a new First Minister could not achieve sufficient support in the Assembly within six weeks it would be necessary to hold new elections or suspend indefinitely and conduct another review of the GFA. Over the following weeks there were a series of talks with the parties, including several days spent at Weston Park in Staffordshire, after which the two governments published their latest 'non-negotiable' plan, 'The Proposals for the Implementation of the Good Friday Agreement'. This sought to persuade the IRA to begin decommissioning by offering a wider package of proposals, which addressed several issues that the republicans claimed were necessary to advance the peace process. These included proposals linked to the normalisation of Northern Ireland also referred to as 'demilitarisation'. Under the plan, the British proposed, in 'the event of a significant reduction in the level of threat as a result of this package being implemented' to close several police stations, army bases and watchtowers. It also pledged to bring in changes to guarantee that those facing prosecution for actions committed during the Troubles (the so-called on-the-runs), 'are no longer pursued'. New legislation to more fully implement the Patten Report on policing was promised. In addition, a review of the Parades Commission would be held, a judge of 'international standing' would conduct an investigation of collusion in a number of high-profile killings, and the establishment of a fund to assist families of RUC members killed in the conflict.

Most of these measures were aimed at appealing to republicans; they were 'successes' which it was hoped would enable them to justify decommissioning weapons. Although the plan had actually little to say on decommissioning, it noted decommissioning was 'an indispensable part of implementing the Good Friday Agreement' (CAIN). The following week, the IICD issued another report which stated that the IRA had recently 'proposed a method for putting IRA arms completely and verifiably beyond use'. The Commission believed that 'this proposal initiates a process that will put IRA arms completely and verifiably beyond use'. The statement was widely praised and described as 'a historic breakthrough' by Bertie Ahern, 'an important step' by Tony Blair and the Secretary of State, John Reid (who became NISS after Mandelson resigned from the government over a non-Northern Ireland related scandal). The editorials of most of the British and Irish newspapers were largely favourable and saw the move as significant progress. The harshest critic of the move was the *Daily Telegraph* whose editorial stated, 'The only thing that is "historic" about Gen de Chastelain's statement is that the British and Irish governments' pathetic gratitude to the IRA for making the most nugatory of gestures has reached new depths' (*Daily Telegraph*, 7 August 2001). However, whilst the move was welcomed by Trimble, he noted that there had still not been any actual decommissioning. It was clearly not going to be a move which would allow him to re-enter government as he had stated in June, 'Words and statements won't be sufficient this time. An eleventh-hour statement from John de Chastelain saying an agreement on the modalities of decommissioning is close, won't carry us through: we need more than that, we need product' (*Sunday Independent*, 17 June 2001).

As the six-week deadline approached, the British government were faced with a dilemma; if they called elections it was far from clear that the UUP would be returned as the largest unionist party, nor indeed that the SDLP would be the largest nationalist one. At the Westminster election of 2001 the UUP won six seats (down from the ten they won in 1997) and the DUP secured five seats (compared with two in 1997). Trimble's party also saw its vote fall by 5.9 per cent to 26.8 per cent whilst the DUP's had increased 8.9 per cent to 22.5 per cent (Hennessey et al., 2019: 63). The DUP had sought

to portray the UUP as surrendering to the republicans. Their election manifesto stated, 'The following were SUPPORTED by the UUP and OPPOSED
by the DUP: • Terrorists in government • The RUC destroyed • Murderers
released • Executive all-Ireland bodies set up' (DUP, *Leadership to Put
Things Right*, CAIN). Similarly, the 2001 Westminster election also saw Sinn
Féin outpoll the SDLP for the first time and the party secured four Westminster seats, compared with the SDLP's three (*Independent*, 11 June 2001).

As a result of the apparent electoral shifts in Northern Ireland, the British
were keen not to have an Assembly election. The way they avoided one was
by John Reid suspending the institutions for one day on two occasions. Each
suspension then triggered a further six-week period to resolve the issue.
However, things came to a head in October when, after a motion in the
Assembly by David Trimble calling for Sinn Féin to be expelled from government failed to achieve the support of the SDLP, the UUP leader announced
all UUP ministers would resign the following week on 18 October and the
DUP followed suit. This crisis, however, had a different outcome in that it
was followed less than a week later by the first act of IRA decommissioning.
On 22 October Gerry Adams issued a statement publicly calling on the IRA
to decommission. 'Martin McGuinness and I have also held discussions with
the IRA and we have put to the IRA the view that if it could make a ground-
breaking move on the arms issue that this could save the peace process from
collapse and transform the situation' (*Irish Times*, 23 October 2001). The
following day the IRA issued a statement which argued the 'political process
is now on the point of collapse. Such a collapse would certainly and eventually put the overall peace process in jeopardy. There is a responsibility upon
everyone seriously committed to a just peace to do our best to avoid this.
Therefore, in order to save the peace process, we have implemented the
scheme agreed with the IICD in August' (*AP/RN*, 25 October 2001). The
IICD also issued a statement noting, 'We have now witnessed an event in
which the IRA has put a quantity of arms completely beyond use. The material in question includes arms, ammunition and explosives' (*Guardian*, 23
October 2001). The move was sufficient for David Trimble to agree to re-
enter government with Sinn Féin.

Explaining decommissioning

The statement that the IRA had taken the decision to decommission to 'save
the peace process' is obviously not the whole story. The peace process had
been in crisis on several occasions since the GFA and these crises had often
been the result of a failure to decommission. On previous occasions the IRA
had been willing to resist pressure from all sides. It was the case that by the
summer of 2001 Trimble was determined to bring down the institutions

rather than remain in government with Sinn Féin whilst the IRA had not commissioned. But, as we have seen, this was not the first time that Trimble had made such a move. Similarly, Trimble's original rationalisation for breaking his 'no guns no government' pledge in November 1999 had proved to be erroneous. Despite his predictions, failure to decommission had not led Sinn Féin to be 'wrecked' politically and not only had the electorate 'stood for it', they had increasingly been willing to vote Sinn Féin, despite the IRA's position. There was widespread speculation that a significant factor in the IRA's first act of decommissioning was less a result of domestic pressures but more a result of the changed political context in the immediate aftermath of the Al Qaida attacks in the United States on 11 September 2001. The BBC journalist, Shane O'Neill argued that 'September 11th had changed attitudes to international terrorism and pressure on the republican movement intensified. It is now clear many in the IRA leadership do not want to be caught on the wrong side of history' (*BBC News*, 23 November 2001). Others, such as the *Daily Telegraph*'s Ireland correspondent, David Lister, also stressed the influence that America had on the IRA's thinking, 'The West's war on terrorism, and the threat this poses to the IRA's financial support in the US, have convinced it that now is the time for action' (*Daily Telegraph*, 23 November 2001).

Whilst the attacks themselves were obviously nothing to do with the IRA, the standing of Sinn Féin in the US had been damaged by the arrest of three Irish republicans in Colombia in August. It was widely suggested that they had been training members of the Revolutionary Armed Forces of Colombia (FARC), a Marxist group that was conducting a terrorist campaign and believed to be linked to the drugs trade. FARC had welcomed the September 11 attacks and the IRA's connection to them led President George Bush's head of counterterrorism to describe the IRA as a 'threat' (*Irish Independent*, 12 October 2001). Others, however, believed that whilst US pressure may have been the immediate catalyst for the decision to begin decommissioning, the IRA was already moving towards that act. Richard English has argued that the 'causal link between 11 September and the subsequent path taken by the IRA towards the actual decommissioning of arms should not be overplayed' (English, 2004: 333). The journalist Ed Moloney suggested that decommissioning had become 'a slow but boring strip tease in which the name of the game became about the Provos extracting an extra dollar bill for every piece of flesh that was exposed' but 'once the dollar bills dried up, the veil had to fall' (*Sunday Tribune*, 28 October 2001). Such arguments are persuasive given the movement towards decommissioning that the IRA had been taking, from apparently asserting that it would not happen, to suggesting it might as a voluntary act on their part, then engaging with the IICD and agreeing for their arms dumps to be inspected. The actual decommissioning of some arms was a logical progression on this trajectory.

What is less clear is whether they were simply using the arms as a bargaining tool to milk every concession out of the process they could, or whether Adams and McGuinness were unable to deliver decommissioning before this period. This is an issue which divides commentators. Those who were most critical of republicanism tended to take the first view. According to this rationale, if the IRA were committed to the peace process, they did not need guns so they should simply have decommissioned much earlier in the process. Such accounts were highly sceptical of claims by Adams and McGuinness that they were not in complete control of the IRA and could not simply deliver decommissioning. Richard English has suggested six reasons why it took so long for the IRA to begin decommissioning. These were: fear of appearing to have surrendered/been defeated; reluctance to be seen to be responding to the public demands of unionists and the British government; concern that it would be taken as an indication that violence (whether future or indeed past) was an illegitimate way to pursue their goals; the need to retain weapons for defensive reasons as sporadic loyalist violence continued; decommissioning would diminish republican leverage and, finally, their refusal to do so led to rancour and division within Unionism (English, 2004: 335). English's list is useful as it illustrates the complexity of the issue, the multiple considerations which were in play for republicans and why it was so difficult to resolve. An additional issue that could also be added to English's list was the inability of Adams and McGuinness to deliver decommissioning in the earlier stages of the peace process. English alludes to this in his third point when he notes that any suggestion that the armed struggle was illegitimate could lead to 'further schism' in the IRA, 'a nightmare for the leadership'. There is evidence which suggests that the republican movement was far from monolithic in this period and that there was a great deal of opposition within the IRA to suggestions that they should undertake decommissioning, and a suspicion of both the peace process and the GFA. In November 1999, Anthony McIntyre, a former IRA prisoner who wrote a PhD on republicanism and became an influential commentator and critic of the Sinn Féin leadership, but was against a return to violence, wrote an interesting analysis of the decommissioning issue. According to McIntyre, not 'one core republican demand' was met in the GFA. The leadership of the movement was increasingly seen as having different lifestyles from the wider membership and this alienation 'congeals around the decommissioning issue'. For McIntyre the last act of control of the base over the leadership was the refusal to hand over weapons (an act he was in favour of, arguing 'long may that veto continue') (*Sunday Tribune*, 14 November 1999).

A related sentiment amongst those who were critical of the peace process within the republican movement, which was influential in the emergence of the breakaway dissident republican groups, was that even if the armed campaign was to be halted, the weapons must never be surrendered or destroyed as these would be needed for a future generation's uprising. Marisa McGlinchey has argued that 'decommissioning was "the choke" for individuals who left the Provisional movement at this point. Decommissioning negated the historic *right* to engage in armed struggle at a future time' (McGlinchey, 2019: 85). Ed Moloney has highlighted that decommissioning was without precedent for republicans. 'Never before in the long and bloody history of Anglo–Irish conflict had an insurgent group voluntarily given up its weapons for destruction, even self-destruction at the behest of its opponents … That was the significance of the Provisional IRA's action on October 23, 2001.' Moloney argues that previous campaigns had ended with an order to dump arms which said the 'guns were being put away only for the time being, the war against Britain would be resumed when conditions improved'. But decommissioning 'said the opposite: not just that this campaign had been brought to an end but that the age-old conflict between Irish republicanism and Britain was over' (Moloney, 2002: 492). Whilst Sinn Féin would strongly dispute such an interpretation (their narrative was that the struggle was entering a new phase, but very much continued), Moloney's observations highlight what a transformative, and therefore difficult, issue decommissioning was. As English has also pointed out, 'contrary to some casual speculation, decommissioning *was* a very important issue' (English, 2004: 334). John Hume had told the SDLP's conference in November 1999, 'Viewed in its own terms, the decommissioning issue has been given an absolutely disproportionate significance. Future historians will ask themselves how on earth this matter came to so dominate a political agenda.' Hume's argument was that the issue was whether guns were being used, but he also made the important point that decommissioning had taken on a wider significance as, 'in another sense the decommissioning impasse is about a lack of trust' (CAIN). It was not just about a lack of trust between unionists, the governments and republicans, it was also, as English and McIntyre suggest, about a lack of trust between elements of the republican movement and the Sinn Féin leadership. There are suggestions in accounts of those who were involved in the negotiations that led to the GFA and sought to deal with the series of crises over decommissioning that followed it, that Adams and McGuinness were unable to deliver on the issue due to wider IRA resistance. Even Trimble's biographer, Dean Godson, whose account is far from sympathetic to republicans, records that he 'knew from senior Irish officials in early January [2001] that Adams et al. did not have the votes in the 'Army Convention' to do anything on arms' (Godson, 2004: 586). Whilst decommissioning may indeed have been used to extract concessions by republicans during the peace process before the first act of decommissioning in October 2001, and would be used to do so subsequently over the next four years, it is too simplistic to argue that it could have been delivered by Adams and McGuinness any time they wished.

Changing attitudes and issues

The mistrust and acrimony engendered by the decommissioning issue was not the only representation of underlying tensions in Northern Ireland after the signing of the GFA. Whilst the peace process had led to hugely reduced violence it had not led to wider inter-communal, or indeed intra-communal, rapprochement. The early 2000s were marked by an intra-loyalist feud. The UVF-linked PUP had two seats in the Assembly and remained supportive of the peace process. However, the UDA/UFF-linked UDP failed to secure any seats. The UDA and the smaller loyalist LVF were increasingly critical of the direction of the peace process. After an increase in activities over several months, on 12 October 2001, John Reid announced that he no longer considered the UDA, UFF or LVF to be on ceasefire. This was as a result, in part, of a bloody feud that had developed within loyalism, particularly between C Company of the UVF on the Shankill Road, led by Johnny Adair, and the wider UVF, who were also feuding with the LVF. These feuds were to run on and off until the mid-2000s. Such intra-loyalist feuds not only increased violence and instability within that community, but also put pressure on the wider peace process and reduced the likelihood of loyalist decommissioning (Shirlow, 2012: 50–52).

Tensions and mistrust were still very much a feature more widely in Northern Ireland in the post-GFA period. Given the length and depth of division within Northern Ireland this was not surprising. The GFA was not designed to be a panacea, the peace process was about stopping the violence and trying to create a blueprint for how Northern Ireland could become a more stable society, which would not happen instantaneously. Inevitably after such a period of conflict, suspicion between the parties and within the wider society was going to remain a significant issue. The problems associated with achieving and securing devolved government had meant that there was increasing suspicion of both the peace process and of its benefits, particularly amongst the unionist community. Survey data clearly and consistently showed falling levels of support for the Agreement amongst the unionist electorate after 1998. The Northern Ireland Life and Times survey (NILT), which was a joint enterprise between Queen's University Belfast and the University of Ulster, included a question on attitudes towards the GFA. In 1999, 55 per cent of Protestants surveyed claimed that they had voted 'yes' in the 1998 referendum in Northern Ireland on the GFA, broadly in line with estimates of the proportion of Protestants who had supported the Agreement in the referendum. However, when asked over the coming years how they would vote if 'the vote on the Good Friday Agreement was held again today' support from Protestants was on a firm downward trajectory; by 2003 only 28 per cent of Protestants stated they would vote Yes. Interestingly there had also been a decline in support from Catholics but 74 per cent said they would still vote 'yes' in 2003. Protestants increasingly believed that the benefits of the Agreement had not been equally distributed. As can be seen in the table below, there was a pronounced feeling amongst the Protestant community that nationalists had been the main beneficiaries of the GFA. Even in the months immediately after the GFA was concluded (when the 1998 survey was conducted) 50 per cent of Protestants believed that nationalists had benefited a lot or a little more than unionists. However, over the next five years, during which time the crises over decommissioning, policing and creating stable devolved government were occurring, this mistrust increased to the extent that, by 2003, 70 per cent of Protestants believed that nationalists benefited more than unionists from the Agreement. This view seemed to be not only widely held but there was also a notable increase in those who believed that nationalists benefited 'a lot more' than unionists, rising from 31 per cent to 53 per cent. This view was far more prevalent within the Protestant than Catholic community. Over the same period the proportion of Catholics who believed that the nationalist community had benefited more than unionists only rose from 16 per cent to 22 per cent, markedly lower than the 70 per cent of Protestants who held such a view. Indeed, the majority of Catholics believed that the two communities had benefited equally (a view that fluctuated from a high of 74 per cent of Catholics in 1999 to a low of 47 per cent in 2001– the only year it fell below 50 per cent). As can be seen below, this was always a distinctly minority view amongst Protestants.

Table 4.1 Protestants' attitues to the GFA, 1998–2003 (%)

	1998	1999	2000	2001	2002	2003
Unionists benefited a lot more than nationalists	1	0	0	1	1	0
Unionists benefited a little more than nationalists	1	1	1	1	1	0
Nationalists benefited a lot more than unionists	31	46	42	52	55	53
Nationalists benefited a little more than unionists	19	13	14	11	12	17
Unionists and nationalists benefited equally	41	32	29	19	19	18
Don't know	8	8	1	0	0	0

Source: NILT, n.d.

These trends were replicated across a variety of other polls conducted in the period. There was a belief within the unionist community that they had been asked to make significant concessions, such as the reform of the RUC, prisoner releases, allowing Sinn Féin into government before decommissioning and the demilitarisation process. David Trimble had been persuaded that such changes were necessary to progress the peace process and had managed on several occasions to persuade the majority of his party's ruling council that this was the case. There were clearly gains for Unionism from the GFA and the peace process: the end of IRA violence, the acceptance by Sinn Féin of the consent principle, the removal of Articles 2 and 3 of the Irish constitution, the replacement of the AIA and, overall, the belief that they had secured the Union. Tony Blair records being asked by a group of unionists, 'what have we really got out of this agreement?' Blair's answer was 'The Union, that's pretty big don't you think?' But the response of the man who asked the Prime Minister the question is illustrative. Blair recalled, 'But he didn't really see it like that. He just saw a string of concessions to bring "the men of violence" to stop what they never should have been doing anyway' (Blair, 2011: 185).

This was part of the problem for unionists. The gains they had secured were ones which either they felt no concessions should have been given for anyway or were not really gains at all. They had long seen the Republic's constitutional claim on Northern Ireland as illegitimate, the principle of consent, and by extension the Union itself, as simply a reflection of democracy and IRA violence as illegitimate. These, for many unionists, were not gains that required reciprocal concessions. Similarly, the AIA, for many unionists, was an outrageous interference in British affairs by a foreign government and should never have been signed by the Thatcher government. Removing it was not something that many felt should incur the price that they'd had to pay. Similarly, for many unionists the 'losses' they had to endure were unacceptable concessions to those who had used or advocated violence (prisoner releases, the perceived slur on the RUC of the Patten Report, and power-sharing with a party allied to an armed terrorist group). Unionism increasingly perceived the peace process in this period as a conveyor belt of concessions to republicans. By October 2000, one of Trimble's most vocal critics within the UUP, Jeffrey Donaldson, was arguing, 'the IRA has eaten all the carrots, but no one is prepared to use the stick' (*Channel 4 News*, 27 October 2000).

Indeed, it was not a view held exclusively by Ulster Unionists. After he left office, Peter Mandelson was critical of the Blair government's approach in this period. Mandelson told the *Guardian* in 2007 that Blair had given too much to the republicans at that stage. 'Weston Park [July 2001] was basically about conceding and capitulating in a whole number of different ways to republican demands – their shopping list. We always called it the Sinn Féin shopping list. It was a disaster because it was too much for them [the UUP]. Too much. That was a casualty of my departure, I would say.' Mandelson's view was that Blair was too willing to make concessions to republicans to keep them engaged with the peace process, or, as Mandelson put it, republicans were 'having too much of the blanket. We've got to allow the unionists to tug it back a bit their way.' He was critical of Blair's overall approach to the peace process at this time claiming, 'One problem with Tony, Tony's fundamental view of Northern Ireland, is that the process is the policy, that as long as the process is being sustained and nurtured and as long as you are giving plenty of evidence that you believe in the process, even if you can do nothing else, that is sufficient policy. The process is the policy, he used to say' (*Guardian*, 14 March 2007).

This idea of the peace process as something that needed to be in perpetual motion is one that was widely shared within British policymaking circles, it was often compared to a bicycle in that there was a belief that if you did not keep it moving it would simply fall over. The problem was, however, could you keep everyone on the bike as you sought to make progress? The former British cabinet secretary, Lord Butler, who had been involved in the early stages of the peace process under both Major and Blair, noted that 'There was a lot to be said for paying a price to keep the bicycle moving. The issue is whether Tony Blair paid too big a price' (*Guardian*, 13 March 2007). Undoubtedly republicans were very often the primary focus of British and Irish governments. In his memoirs Blair is open about this, noting that the 'trouble was Sinn Féin had to be brought in from the cold, and so, inevitably more time, energy and focus were given to them. This caused deep resentment; but it was an unfortunate and inevitable consequence of making peace' (Blair, 2011: 196). He also appeared to have shared this view with the SDLP, telling their deputy leader at a dinner 'The trouble with you fellows, Seamus, is that you have no guns' (Mallon, 2019: 2261).

The deterioration of unionist support for the Agreement and wider unease with the political developments in Northern Ireland was occurring at a time when tensions were evident in particular areas of the region. A high-profile dispute emerged around the Holy Cross Girls' Catholic primary school in North Belfast between June and November 2001. The school was in an interface area of the city. Due to demographic changes, the school itself was in what had become primarily a Protestant area, on the edge of the Glenbryn estate which the children and their parents had to walk beside to get to the school's main gate. Tensions in the area were running high over claims on both sides that houses were being attacked by paramilitaries and the display of loyalist flags and emblems in the vicinity of the school. The dispute itself began when residents of the Glenbryn estate staged a picket outside the school claiming that the school run was being used to mask attacks on their area. Billy Hutchinson of the PUP complained of 'incursions into the area, using the school as a cover' (*Guardian*, 1 December 2003). Over the next three months, images of terrified young girls and their parents running the gauntlet of abuse were beamed around the world, greatly damaging the image of both Unionism and Northern Ireland. At times, the protests were violent, with a blast bomb being thrown at the police during the protests in early September. The Secretary of State, John Reid, argued 'Any legitimate grievances of protesters have been drowned out by this violent sectarian bigotry ... Children should not have to pay the price of the failure of adults to live together in peace' (*BBC News*, 5 September 2001).

The protests demonstrated several aspects of the peace process and the state of politics and relations in Northern Ireland. It was a graphic and very public indication of the continuing suspicion that was a characteristic of areas in Northern Ireland, particularly in interface areas. It also suggested that the failures to make progress at the political level were influencing wider society in Northern Ireland. In his examination of the dispute, Colm Heatley quoted one woman who had been involved in the picket:

> Community relations throughout all of Northern Ireland took a step backward because Protestants felt they weren't getting a fair deal under the Good Friday Agreement. People in Glenbryn kept telling the Government about attacks on their houses and how vulnerable they felt but we weren't being listened to. That is why people protested on the Ardoyne Road, the focus wasn't so much the school itself. You can't detach the Holy Cross protest from the high-level politics that go on in Northern Ireland. People on the streets see politicians at each other's throats, so it's little wonder they give up all hope of resolving local disputes in a peaceful manner. The community in Glenbryn is in decline and it is fearful of Ardoyne. That does encourage a siege mentality. Glenbryn had no choice but to protest and I don't think people should apologise for that. (Heatley, 2004)

However, few outside the local community shared the view that the residents had 'no choice' but to protest and few saw the link between the high-level politics and primary children going to school. But for many who lived in the area of North Belfast, distrust of the 'other' and a fear of being marginalised and targeted (on both sides) provided the backdrop for the dispute. Whilst it was far from the only area which had seen demographic changes alter the composition of streets, or the only area where sectarianism was a problem, North Belfast was one of the areas which had been most impacted during the Troubles. Almost a quarter of all the killings in the conflict happened in the vicinity and it was an area where paramilitary groups had significant influence. There was heightened tension at the time the dispute broke out. The police officer in charge of Belfast, Alan McQuillan, noted,

> North Belfast is a mosaic of sectarian interfaces and Ardoyne is just one of the worst of them. We have had police officers and soldiers camped out at seven fixed points throughout the constituency for 12 hours a day for the last 10 or 12 weeks to stop the communities getting at each other. There have been repeated attacks both ways across the peace lines in this area. On one night on the Limestone Road we had up to 500 people wanting to fight, with my men between them. (*The Times*, 9 September 2001)

Those looking in from the outside were neither cognisant of this wider context nor interested in it. What did interest them was the appalling images beamed around the globe. *The Boston Herald* in America noted, 'What manner of coward targets schoolgirls? Just when civilised people think things in Northern Ireland can't get much worse, they do. Protestant unionists have long criticised the recalcitrance of the IRA and its refusal to turn over its weapons. Yesterday unionists surrendered whatever claim they might have had to the moral high ground.' In Canada, the *Montreal Gazette* argued, 'Such attacks by adults on innocent children are outrageous and inexcusable. The perpetrators look like raving lunatics', and in Germany, *Die Suddeutsche Zeitung* noted 'The idea that mothers and children are subjected to a hail of abuse, spat at and threatened simply because they are Catholic and want to go to school has dragged us down to a new nadir' (*Scotland on Sunday*, 9 September 2001). But whilst it was widely argued that the events had been a propaganda disaster for loyalism and diverted some attention from republicans in light of the Colombian arrests, it was not simply indicative of growing unease with the peace process within loyalist heartlands. The journalist Suzanne Breen noted it could cause potential problems for

> the Sinn Féin and Provisional IRA leadership and help republican dissidents. Ardoyne was always sceptical of the benefits of the peace process ... Several republican supporters yesterday said they were rapidly losing faith in the peace process. "Things were meant to have changed with the agreement, but nothing has changed. Catholics are still fighting for basic civil rights just like they were in the 1960s," one said. (*Irish Times*, 5 September 2001)

The picket was eventually ended in November, but the issue highlighted the continuing tensions and mistrust in Northern Ireland and brought to a wider audience that the GFA had not been the transformative event that many had hoped for.

The end of Trimble, devolution and the peace process?

The moderate centre, which was to have been the foundations for sustained devolved government, was clearly crumbling throughout the early years of the 2000s. The hope that the extreme groups who used violence could be enticed to pursue an unarmed political strategy and play a supporting role enabling the main constitutional parties of the UUP and SDLP to head the new political dispensation in Northern Ireland was slowly becoming unsustainable. Whilst the IRA had been cajoled and persuaded along the road from violence to politics, the journey had taken its toll not just on republicanism but on wider nationalism and unionism. The advances that the DUP and Sinn Féin had made in the 2001 Westminster election showed little sign of abating. Unless something fundamentally altered it seemed increasingly likely that the UUP and the SDLP would not be in a position to be the poles around which devolution was anchored, as they would be the minor parties after the next Assembly elections, which were due in 2003.

Both the SDLP and the UUP were at times angered by the attention that the two governments paid to the IRA. As noted earlier, this was seen by the governments as simply a reflection of the reality of the peace process; the IRA were the ones who needed to be persuaded to disarm and so they were the ones who had to be prioritised. But the long and stalling nature of this persuasion undoubtedly undermined support for the UUP, with Trimble's leadership and decisions attacked by a relentless DUP who portrayed each step taken by him as a further weakening of the Union and a concession to the IRA.

The SDLP's position during this period was difficult. The party believed that their isolation was unacceptable given they were the largest nationalist party and, indeed, one of the key reasons there was a peace process at all. However, although at times the party's leadership was critical of the IRA, it was not willing to agree to remain in government with the UUP if Sinn Féin was excluded for failures by the IRA to decommission. This is something that was suggested periodically, but which the SDLP consistently refused to agree to. Tony Blair noted in his memoirs the impact that this had on the peace process. Whilst he stated that their stance was 'understandable' as they wanted to avoid accusation from Sinn Féin that they were 'selling out', the problem was, as Blair noted, 'it meant that they gave up their trump card. They used to attack me for 'handing Sinn Féin the veto' but actually *they* had, since without Sinn Féin there could be no government with the SDLP' (Blair, 2011: 170).

From the SDLP's position, their stance made sense. If they had agreed to remain in government if Sinn Féin were excluded it is likely that they would have been heavily criticised by Adams and McGuinness. Given that Sinn Féin's vote was clearly increasing despite the IRA refusing to decommission, there was little to suggest that the SDLP would have benefited electorally from such a stance. Although polls did suggest that the nationalist electorate were in favour of decommissioning, the same electorate did not appear inclined to punish Sinn Féin as a result of a lack of progress in this area. This was not just the case in Northern Ireland as Sinn Féin had seen five candidates elected to the Irish parliament in May 2002, a month after the IRA carried out a second act of decommissioning. It was not just the SDLP who were unwilling to try and marginalise Sinn Féin. The Irish government were unhappy with such proposals at times and, according to Jonathan Powell's account, Dublin placed pressure on the SDLP when it seemed they were willing to pledge support for proposed police reform without Sinn Féin (Powell, 2009: 194).

By 2002, however, even the two governments were losing patience with the republicans. The immediate catalyst for the change in tone from London and Dublin was the latest collapse of the devolved government in October 2002. On 3 October the police carried out a raid of Sinn Féin's offices at Stormont amid allegations that republicans were operating a 'spy-ring' from their Assembly base. This followed suspicion that the IRA had been involved in a break-in at the Special Branch's offices at Castlereagh police station the previous March. The raid at Stormont discovered addresses of police officers' homes and the details of the Army General Officer Commanding's car (Powell, 2009: 209). Sinn Féin's head of administration, Denis Donaldson, was arrested and charged with having information likely to be useful for terrorism. In December 2005 it was announced that charges against Donaldson were to be dropped as his prosecution was deemed not to be in the public interest. Shortly afterwards Donaldson admitted that he had been a paid British agent for over twenty years. He was murdered in a cottage in Donegal in April 2006. The dissident group the Real IRA claimed they had killed him.

The episode soon acquired the label 'Stormontgate' after David Trimble made the comparison to the infamous break-in at the Watergate building during the 1972 American election campaign. 'At Watergate, Nixon's cronies only broke into one filing cupboard whereas at Stormont hundreds of files, many of them marked confidential, were stolen. The volume here is greater than Watergate and the aim was the same: political intelligence and dirty tricks' (*Observer*, 6 February 2002). As a result of the events, Trimble told Blair that it was 'now impossible for me to have any further trust' in Sinn Féin and he would resign within a week unless Sinn Féin were excluded from the government in Northern Ireland (Godson, 2004: 799). The British met with the SDLP leader, Mark Durkan, to ask if he would support the suspension of Sinn Féin, and when he refused, the government suspended the Executive (Powell, 2009: 209).

The collapse of the government led to a firmer stance by the two governments towards republicans. Two weeks after the raid, Tony Blair made a speech at the Harbour Commission in Belfast where he stated, 'But the crunch is the crunch. There is no parallel track left. The fork in the road has finally come ... we cannot carry on with the IRA half in, half out of this process. Not just because it isn't right anymore. It won't work anymore.' The Prime Minister argued that the continuing actions of the IRA were detrimental not only to the peace process but to Sinn Féin itself. 'Remove the threat of violence and the peace process is on an unstoppable path. That threat, no matter how damped down, is no longer reinforcing the political, it is actually destroying it. In fact, the continuing existence of the IRA as an active paramilitary organisation is now the best card those whom republicans call "rejectionist" unionists, have in their hand.' He spoke out against continuing punishment attacks by the IRA on their own community, stating 'There can't be two police forces. And as the changes in criminal justice take effect, how can there seriously be calls on the one hand for human rights and on the other, the savage beatings of people without any trial or due process without any rights, human or otherwise.' He concluded by stating 'It's time for acts of completion' (*BBC News*, 17 October 2002). However, the pressure from Blair was not enough to move the IRA. Although in a documentary at the end of October Martin McGuinness did state that 'my war is over', the IRA were unwilling to make such an assertion at that stage (*BBC News*, 30 October 2002). The two governments continued to seek to get a breakthrough over the coming months and put pressure on the IRA to announce the end of their campaign. In April 2003 Bertie Ahern told an Easter commemoration that 'Democratic politics and continued paramilitarism simply do not mix ... Just as incrementalism will no longer work in the process, neither will ambiguity' (*Irish Independent*, 21 April 2003).

Despite the harsher rhetoric, in reality the two governments faced the same limitations with which they had wrestled for the previous five years. They could not proceed with devolved government without Sinn Féin, as the unwillingness of the SDLP to remain in government without the republicans made it impossible to have a devolved power-sharing government. They did not want to declare Sinn Féin in breach of their ceasefire as this would have necessitated their exclusion and collapsed the process. They did not want to wind up the institutions and return to direct rule, as this was what the peace process had been designed to replace. They were not willing to abandon the GFA and reintroduce some form of majoritarian system into Northern Ireland as this would have exacerbated the situation and destabilised

Northern Ireland further. They did not want to govern the area jointly between the two governments, which would have also destabilised the situation, given the likely unionist reaction, and made the issue more central in British and Irish political life, which neither state wanted. So, again, they found themselves having to try and find a way to broker agreement between the main parties to return to government and keep the institutions mothballed, but not formally collapsed, in the meantime.

In March 2003 the governments met with the local parties at Hillsborough to try and negotiate a package that would allow devolution to be restored and elections to be called, which would see the UUP and SDLP returned as the largest parties. The concern was, if elections were called which resulted in the DUP being returned as the main party, then the chances of restoring devolved government would diminish further. Blair was reported as describing the likelihood of a Sinn Féin–DUP deal as 'pie in the sky' (*Guardian*, 2 May 2003). When they failed to achieve a breakthrough, the elections were postponed. There was, however, exasperation with David Trimble in some quarters of the British and Irish governments. Jonathan Powell claims in his memoirs that by the end of 2002 some Irish officials believed that it would be better to hold the elections in May even if it meant the DUP emerging victorious as they would be easier to deal with than Trimble. Indeed, Blair's chief of staff states that this view was also held by the British Secretary of State, John Reid and the NIO, but not by Blair who 'remained obstinately committed to Trimble until the very end' as he believed Trimble was 'still our best hope' (Powell, 2009: 209–210). Blair's suspicion of Paisley and the likelihood that he would do a deal was echoed by an unnamed British government 'source' who argued, 'As long as Paisley is alive, there is no hope of a deal, and even after that, there is no indication things would change … David Trimble may be a prat sometimes, but he's the only prat we've got' (*Guardian*, 2 May 2003). So, the decision to postpone the elections was part of what became known as the 'save Dave' campaign.

A few weeks after the decision to postpone the elections, the British published the details of the proposals they were hoping would be the basis of an agreement by the parties to return to government. They are interesting because they illustrate that whilst the talk had been for the IRA to undertake acts of completion and the focus of the pressure was on them, it was clear that there were also proposed changes which were designed to address concerns of republicans. The proposals called for an end to all paramilitary activity, stressed the need for full decommissioning and proposed a new independent monitoring body to oversee paramilitary organisations' activities. There were also, however, plans for a significant reduction in the size of the army stationed in Northern Ireland to 5,000 (in line with comparable numbers in other parts of the UK) and a reduction in the number of bases in NI; the removal of a number of watchtowers and the de-fortification of police stations; an end to Britain's ability to suspend the Assembly; an amnesty for 'on the runs' (OTRs) and the possibility of devolving policing and justice powers to Northern Ireland (*Guardian*, 2 May 2003 and *Belfast Telegraph*, 2 May 2003). But when these proposals were not accepted, the government postponed the elections.

However, the Assembly elections could not be postponed indefinitely, unless the government was willing to collapse the institutions and revert to direct rule, which was not on the agenda. Sinn Féin, the SDLP and the Irish government were pressing for elections to be held. The period between May and the announcement in October that elections would be held in November was spent in seeking to work out a detailed sequencing of events that would achieve what had proved impossible to achieve a few months earlier: the ability to go into an election with power restored, the IRA embarked upon acts of completion and Trimble's position strengthened. But the events over a 24-hour period were to be a clear example of how the best-laid plans often going awry. As the SDLP leader Mark Durkan commented after the bizarre series of events unfolded, 'What we had this morning was hope. By this afternoon hype, and now this evening it's a debacle' (*CNN News*, 22 October 2003).

The sequence was to be that the British government would announce the date for new Assembly elections, Sinn Féin would make a positive speech and General John de Chastelain would announce a further act of IRA decommissioning, which would effectively signal an end to the IRA's conflict. This would then be welcomed by the Ulster Unionist leader, David Trimble, who would state that, as a result, he was willing to go back into power-sharing government with Sinn Féin. It was intended that this series of events would not only enable devolved government to be returned to Northern Ireland but would result in a strong showing for the UUP in the forthcoming elections, enabling them to remain the largest unionist party. However, although the sequence started out as intended, it fell apart when Trimble announced that there had been insufficient detail in de Chatelain's account on what had been decommissioned to allow his party to agree to return to government with Sinn Féin. According to Trimble, his party 'had made it very clear to the governments and General de Chastelain that what we needed was a transparent report of major acts of decommissioning, the nature of which would have a significant impact upon public opinion and a news conference. Unfortunately, we have not had that.' Gerry Adams rejected such claims by arguing that, 'One man's transparency is another's humiliation' (*CNN News*, 22 October 2003) and insisted that the IRA had kept their side of the bargain.

De Chastelain was limited by his agreement with the IRA regarding the level of detail he could divulge and so could not give the specifics that Trimble argued were essential. There is a large element of farce to this series of events. The sequencing had been agreed as a result of months of talks between the two governments, the UUP and Sinn Féin, talks from which the SDLP had largely been excluded. Mallon asked the key question regarding the episode:

> May I ask the Secretary of State a second question, because my mind boggles at this? For five years, decommissioning has been debated in every nook and corner and every way. Is it not down to this? Did Sinn Féin say in the negotiations that the act of decommissioning would be transparent, and did they renege? Or did the Ulster Unionist party forget to ask them about the confidentiality clause that this Parliament wrote? Can the Secretary of State answer that simply? Can he confirm that it was Sinn Féin deviousness, or was the UUP simply incompetent? (*Hansard*, 22 October 2003, cols 646–647)

Questions can also be raised regarding the competency of the two governments in allowing the sequence of events to be initiated without establishing that it would have a successful conclusion. Why start with the announcement of the election, the only thing over which the government had control, rather than plan to end with that commitment, which could have been withheld if the wider choreography had failed? The answer appears to be more cock-up than conspiracy. Sinn Féin would only agree to the process if there was firm commitment that there would be no further delays in the election date (a position in which they were supported by the Irish government and the SDLP). Jonathan Powell claimed in his memoirs that the IRA were told not to begin decommissioning until the election had been announced. But they expected that the announcement would be made on the Monday, and the British had scheduled it for the following day. This led to John de Chastelain being held incommunicado overnight by the IRA. When he reappeared the next day, he refused pressure from the British government to give details of what had been decommissioned (Powell, 2009: 232–233). The press conference that followed was disastrous due to lack of detail, and Blair suggested it was so bad that it 'should be compulsory viewing for all students of press conferences' (Blair, 2011: 185).

The answer to the question that Mallon raised, according to Godson, is that Trimble chose to make clear to Adams the need for transparency but not to press him for a commitment that it would be provided. The reason was that Trimble did not believe that Adams would give him a clear answer on this point and if they subsequently failed to deliver transparency he had the 'freedom of manoeuvre to pull the plug', which was his 'insurance policy' (Godson, 2004: 795). This is a rather questionable stance for Trimble to take, given what was at stake. By that stage of the process, the unionist electorate were not going to swing back to the UUP on the basis of an impasse and a refusal to go into government with Sinn Féin. Given that the party had already crossed the 'no guns, no government' line, and were perceived as having made too many concessions to Sinn Féin, a perception which the DUP had striven to promote, they needed more than a harsh line on Sinn Féin to succeed in the forthcoming election. The failure to get clarity from de Chastelain, 'did then for David Trimble', and Blair records in his memoirs 'I blame myself for it' (Blair, 2011: 184).

The net result of this failed choreography was that the elections went ahead in November 2003 in circumstances which were hugely stacked against the UUP; there was little chance of 'saving Dave'. The DUP's manifesto urged voters to 'give a mandate to a strong and united Democratic Unionist team and to negotiate a new agreement'. The message the party hammered home was one of concessions to terrorism and compromises by Unionism:

> The destruction of the RUC, the withdrawal of the Army, the release of terrorist prisoners, the elevation of Sinn Féin/IRA members to government office without evidence of the destruction of weaponry, the creation of ever-expanding all-Ireland institutions, the lawless state of our Province, the ever-growing list of breaches of IRA and loyalist so-called ceasefires, the disregard of the views of peaceful and democratic politicians in favour of the spokesmen of terrorist organisations. (DUP, *Campaign03*, 2003)

Paisley claimed that due to 'the policy and actions of the Official Unionists we are closer to a united Ireland than we have ever been' and argued that the UUP was 'seeking your endorsement for a continued programme of appeasement' (DUP, *Campaign03*, 2003). By comparison, the UUP sought to run on a positive message stressing the successful aspects of their record and claiming, 'devolution worked because Ulster Unionists worked'. They noted that they wanted 'to see the Assembly restored, but only when republicans have dealt conclusively with the issues of decommissioning, continued paramilitary activity and the effective winding-up of their private army'. However, most of their election pitch was based on domestic improvements for Northern Ireland rather than on the threat that Sinn Féin posed, in comparison with the DUP's manifesto, which invoked the threat of a united Ireland seven times. The UUP manifesto did not mention the issue (UUP, *Ulster Unionists Manifesto*, 2003).

When the results were tallied, the unionist electorate opted for the DUP's narrative. The UUP's share of the vote actually increased marginally from the 1998 election, rising to 22.68 per cent of the poll (from 21.25 per cent in 1998) but this was more than offset by the rise in the DUP's share to 25.71 per cent (from 18.01 per cent in 1998). Similarly, on the nationalist side, the SDLP lost its position as the main voice of that community, polling 16.99 per cent of the vote compared with the 21.96 per cent they received in 1998 (when the party topped the poll). Sinn Féin outperformed its long-time 'constitutional' rival and secured 23.52 per cent, up from 17.63 per cent five years previously. This move from the mainstream parties to the parties which were seen as more extreme was also evident with the Women's Coalition losing their two Assembly seats. The largest losers though were the small number of independent unionists who were elected in 1998 (no independent unionists were elected in 2003) and the Northern Ireland Unionist Party (NIUP), which emerged from a split within the UKUP in 1999 but lost all four of its seats in 2003. Once the votes were counted, the DUP emerged as the largest party with thirty seats – up ten on 1998 (which subsequently rose to thirty-three after three UUP MLAs defected to the party), the UUP secured twenty-seven seats, actually up one on 1998 (this later fell to twenty-four with the resignations), Sinn Féin gained six seats to finish on twenty-four and the SDLP lost five seats, securing eighteen MLAs.

These results marked a shift in Northern Ireland's electoral landscape and had significant implications for the peace process. It was now no longer possible to build the devolved government around the UUP and SDLP; what was now required was the agreement of the DUP to share power with Sinn Féin. There had been little in the public utterances from the party to suggest that this was a likely outcome. Indeed, their manifesto had listed seven principles, two of which were: 'No negotiating with the representatives of terrorism but we will talk to democratic parties' and 'Those who are not committed to exclusively peaceful and democratic means should not be able to exercise unaccountable executive power' (DUP, *Campaign03*, 2003). Given how they had described Sinn Féin and its relationship with the IRA throughout the peace process, it did not seem that the electoral shift was a boost to the peace process and the chances of restoring devolved government to Northern Ireland.

Conclusion

The period between the securing of the GFA and the replacement of the UUP and SDLP as the largest parties in the NIA in 2003 is illustrative of some of the key underpinning considerations of the peace process and the difficulties which were associated with them. The fact that several difficult issues were set aside to be dealt with after the GFA was finalised was a good conflict management tactic, but it did store up problems that had to be addressed in the difficult period post-1998. The issues of police reform and decommissioning could not have been fully concluded by April 1998, so it made sense to consider these issues subsequently. However, the relationship between decommissioning and the holding of office was unclear in the Agreement. This became such a significant issue because of the lack of trust between the main parties, their views of the legitimacy of the armed struggle, and the significance they and their constituents attached to decommissioning. These differences between the two traditions in Northern Ireland also made the question of police reform hugely problematic. For nationalists, reform of what was an overwhelmingly Protestant force whose relationship with the nationalist community had been problematic for years, was a key indicator of the extent to which the peace process would lead to greater parity of esteem and a fairer society. For unionists, however, the RUC was 'the thin blue line' that had bravely sought to keep order and peace in Northern Ireland in the face of appalling violence by republicans, and the proposed reconfiguration of it was a retrospective slur on its integrity and record. These competing expectations and allegiances led to a further deterioration of trust both within and between political parties and traditions in Northern Ireland. This in turn made it even more difficult to achieve the compromises that were needed to secure the devolved structures and changes that the GFA had mandated.

The period also illustrated well the pragmatism that underpinned the approach of the two governments towards the peace process. As has been noted, Tony Blair's government's approach was not driven by moral considerations of what was right, but rather by practical considerations of what might work. This is not to argue that nothing was unacceptable to the government; considerations over the consent principle and the objectives of reducing the impact of Northern Ireland on British politics were important. But it was pragmatism which was the defining characteristic of the approach under Blair. The primary focus of criticism of the Blair government in this period has been that it made too many concessions to republicans to try and get them to decommission. Certainly some authors, such as Mary Alice Clancy, have suggested that a distinction should be drawn between the peace process, which she defines as the process designed to 'facilitate paramilitaries' in order to get them to 'transition from violence to peaceful means' and the political process which 'describes attempts to get unionists and nationalists to share power in Northern Ireland' (Clancy, 2010: 4–5). For Clancy, the problem was that the British government undermined the political process's quest to secure power-sharing government by their action in the peace process. In reality, the overlap between the two spheres was too great to make the distinction workable. Clancy suggests that any fear that either there would be a significant split from the IRA to dissident groups or that Adams and McGuinness may be replaced by 'hard men' 'had largely disappeared by 1999' and so the implication was that less attention needed to be given to the peace process side and more should have been given to the political dimension (Clancy, 2010: 175). But, as noted above, there seems to have been a genuine belief in both the British and Irish governments that concessions to republicans were needed. Suggestions that it was all simply a ruse by Sinn Féin to get concessions from the government and the UUP are not borne out by the accounts of those involved in the negotiations, or the evidence that appears to have been available at the time. As will be discussed in the next chapter, the arguments that concessions were still needed became less persuasive after 2003, but in the immediate post-GFA period conditions were not conducive to simply 'forcing' decommissioning without regard to the wider political context. The peace process was built on the necessity to engage Sinn Féin, and once they were engaged, and their electoral support was increasing, it became increasingly unlikely that the focus or direction of the British and Irish governments would change; there was no desire in this period to have a fundamentally different 'Plan B'.

Relatedly, it could also be argued that the SDLP (and Irish government) should have put more pressure on Sinn Féin over decommissioning. The UUP were periodically disappointed that Hume and Mallon would not agree to remain in government and support the exclusion of Sinn Féin over the failure of the IRA to decommission and disband. But, again, there were good practical reasons for the party's stance. The SDLP, and John Hume in particular, had been instrumental in creating conditions that led to the peace process, and they were very reluctant to move against Sinn Féin. Although they did at times criticise republicans over decommissioning, they were faced with a situation that made it difficult for them to alter course. The electorate were showing no signs of seeking to penalise Sinn Féin for the IRA's reluctance to decommission and so a stronger stance against Sinn Féin by the SDLP may have pleased unionists but there was no indication that the party would benefit electorally as a result. Indeed, a poll in the run-up to the 2003 Assembly election suggested that a power-sharing devolved government which excluded Sinn Féin was only the favoured option of 4 per cent of Catholic voters (*Belfast Telegraph*, 4 November 2003).

Difficulties were further compounded for the SDLP by the fact that, aside from the decommissioning issue, Sinn Féin's policy positions were not diametrically different from those of the SDLP. As Peter McLoughlin noted 'whilst the SDLP may have lost the electoral battle, the party certainly won the ideological war'. He argues that Sinn Féin's success post-GFA was 'built upon an acceptance of what is, in essence, the SDLP's political programme' (McLoughlin, 2010: 187). As a result, the SDLP's options towards the peace process and Sinn Féin were rather limited post-1998.

The position within Unionism was different, given that the two main parties were not in agreement regarding the GFA or how it should be implemented. It is often suggested that Trimble failed to sell the Agreement sufficiently to the unionist electorate, a charge which republicans frequently levelled against him. However, such a criticism rests on the presumption that the deal was sellable in the absence of movement over decommissioning at a faster rate than the IRA was willing to offer. Undoubtedly Trimble's character made his relationship with key party colleagues difficult (a fact that is widely borne out by accounts of those who dealt with the UUP leader). However, the problems in the peace process during this period were not presentational, and the UUP found itself increasingly losing the support of the unionist electorate. This was accelerated by the DUP's criticism and the narrative of betrayal and perfidy they consistently offered (whilst cleverly not absenting themselves from the structures that were created under the GFA). This criticism, and the ethnic outbidding that the DUP used, meant that Trimble's claims that the GFA was beneficial to Unionism and, indeed the Union, was increasingly questioned by the unionist electorate.

The British and Irish governments did not consider Trimble's precarious position to a sufficient degree until it was too late (hence Blair's reflection that he blamed himself for Trimble's losses in 2003). There are, of course, historical precedents aplenty in Northern Ireland where leaders have gone further than their base would countenance and have subsequently paid the price. The most obvious potential parallel for Trimble was that of his predecessor as UUP leader, Brian Faulkner, and the concessions he was persuaded to make by the British government during the 1973 Sunningdale Conference. As Willie Whitelaw subsequently told the Conservative commentator, T. E. Utley, 'you always told me that I was driving Faulkner too far. My God you were right! But what a damned fool he was to allow himself to be driven.' Indeed, Trimble himself used to invoke this comment when discussing the dangers of being too close to Blair (Godson, 2004: 813). There are undoubtedly similarities between the two in that in both cases the leader of the UUP went further than their base would tolerate and, like Blair in the later period, Willie Whitelaw recorded in his memoirs, 'I probably did not give enough thought to helping Brian Faulkner' (Whitelaw, 1989: 112). However, there are also notable differences given that in 1974 the Sunningdale Agreement ultimately collapsed, and Faulkner lost his position as party leader, in part due to the activities of the Vanguard group within the UUP, of which a young Trimble was a key part. Whereas, although the UUP were replaced as the largest party by the DUP, the GFA survived. But could the government have done more for Trimble in the post-GFA period than they had done for Faulkner twenty-five years before? In hindsight, the pressure that the British (and Irish) government put on Trimble to enter into government with Sinn

Féin before decommissioning began, and to rejoin the government after the various crises noted above, does suggest a lack of appreciation of how difficult Trimble's position was. The commitment that the government had to the peace process and their determination to keep the 'bike' moving, meant that they were unwilling to offer much to the UUP as they saw keeping republicans onboard and the IRA ceasefire intact as the more pressing concern. The governments did not see the issue as either/or and, as in the Sunningdale period, may have presumed that if the UUP leader could be persuaded to accept something, he must believe he could sell it. Indeed, despite Blair noting how he blamed himself for Trimble's 2003 demise, he also noted elsewhere in his memoirs that whilst Trimble 'took the view that I did too little to assist him; I took the view that he never quite stood up for the positive, tending rather to share and sympathise with the unionist propensity to see plots and conspiracies against them' (Blair, 2011: 194). In this case, as in 1973–1974, the belief that the unionist leader would be able to sell what they agreed to would prove false. The British did begin to appreciate the extent of the challenge Trimble faced, hence the decision to postpone the May 2003 scheduled elections, but the farce of the October 2003 choreography meant that it could not be done a second time. Trimble and the UUP, along with Hume and the SDLP, paid a heavy price for the peace process. Their willingness to take significant political risks for peace was instrumental in ending the violence and securing a deal in 1998, but the electorate turned to other parties when the process lurched from crisis to crisis. Whatever the arguments about what should have been done differently, the pragmatism that underpinned the peace process, and the context in which it developed during 1998–2003, make the events comprehensible, if not inevitable or desirable.

5

The reconfiguration of Northern Ireland's politics, from devolution to destruction, 2003–2017

The disparity between Northern Ireland's politics in 2007, and what the rhetoric of some parties, especially the DUP, suggested were likely outcomes in the immediate post-2003 Assembly elections, might require the kind of analysis beloved by Kremlinologists during the Cold War. The peace process in this period saw a movement from apparent resolution to never sharing power with Sinn Féin and demanding a renegotiation of the GFA, to the sight of the new First Minister of Northern Ireland, Ian Paisley, joking with his Deputy First Minister, Martin McGuinness (the famous 'Chuckle Brothers' picture). If a pictorial representation were needed for the difficulty in predicting the outcomes and unintended consequences that conflict resolution processes might result in, it would be hard to beat. A close second may be the 2012 image of Martin McGuinness shaking hands with the Queen of England, Elizabeth II. Although it may have been the case, as previously noted, that some in British and Irish governmental circles had believed that a deal between the DUP and Sinn Féin was the only way to progress the peace process, in 2003 most would have held Blair's view that this was 'pie in the sky'. This chapter examines how the deal was brokered and the extent to which the DUP's agreement to share power with Sinn Féin was the result of a fundamental renegotiation of the GFA or simply an acknowledgement by the party of the changed context that the peace process had created.

The signs of a deal

The changes in the electoral landscape after the 2003 election did not, however, cause a fundamental re-evaluation of the objectives of the peace process. The ambition of creating a situation whereby republicans remained committed to the political struggle over the armed variant, the institutions and bodies created agreed under the GFA were restored and Northern Ireland had stable devolved government, remained the same. Despite the problems in achieving these objectives since 1998, there was no real appetite for a fundamentally different approach by either government, or the main political parties (despite the DUP's protestation that the 'flaws in the Belfast Agreement are so fundamental that it requires to be replaced with a new agreement' (DUP, *Towards a New Agreement*, 2003)). These objectives appeared to remain the most desirable ones for the citizens of Northern Ireland as well. An opinion poll suggested that power-sharing devolved government was the single most popular governing option for the people of Northern Ireland; albeit with a less than overwhelming 35 per cent endorsement. Not surprisingly there was a notable difference in levels of support for restoring power-sharing devolution between Catholics (45 per cent) and Protestants (27 per cent), but even for Protestants the option was the most popular one compared with the offered alternatives of devolved government without Sinn Féin; direct rule; full integration of Northern Ireland into the UK; or a united Ireland (*Belfast Telegraph*, 14 November 2003). The fact that power-sharing remained the most popular outcome is perhaps a surprising one, but it suggests that by 2003 it was not the fear of the possibility of power-sharing devolution that explains the electoral endorsement of Sinn Féin and the DUP. As a result, suggestions such as that by the journalist Siobhán Fenton that the UUP and SDLP's ousting by voters was 'a rational response from a nervous electorate who were still wary of the new power-sharing experiment and felt more comfortable having its detractors at its core', were not convincing (Fenton, 2018: 278). By 2003 it was hard to describe Sinn Féin as a detractor of the power-sharing experiment and indeed even the DUP had partaken in government and taken their seats in the Executive, albeit refusing to sit in meetings with Sinn Féin.

Whilst the objectives of the peace process remained the same, what did (and had to) alter post-2003 was the focus of the efforts to secure these objectives. As previously discussed, the main focus of much of those efforts, particularly by the governments, during the peace process up to 2003, had been republicans. In narrow terms it could be argued that the efforts were a success, as the IRA had remained on ceasefire, had begun decommissioning and Sinn Féin had agreed to serve in a devolved Northern Ireland government, which was hard to see as anything but a partitionist structure. However, whilst wooing the republicans was indeed instrumental to the peace process, the objectives of the peace process could not be delivered solely by the republicans (or even by them with the support of the SDLP, Irish and British governments). For devolution to be restored, it was necessary to have the participation of the main unionist political parties. By 2004, the main unionist political party, the DUP, seemed to be intent on ensuring that the approach that the two governments had used, concessions to republicans, would not continue. Whilst such a rationale may have been in line with the old adage 'the noisiest wheel gets the oil', the position that the DUP took from 2004 meant that more attention had to be paid to persuading them to support the objectives of the peace process. Unionism had got much noisier and therefore a greater focus needed to be given to the DUP than the British had, at times, given to the UUP.

Jonathan Powell's account suggested that even at that stage Blair had not given up on the idea that Trimble was still key as he 'was sceptical that Ian Paisley would ever do a deal'. As a result, Blair 'proposed that our strategy should be to give the DUP enough rope either to reach an agreement or hang themselves politically by obstructing one', the idea being that if the DUP were too obstructive, a further election could be held which the UUP might win (Powell, 2009: 236). However, the DUP were both too shrewd to be simply overtly obstructive and, perhaps more surprisingly, more prepared to do a deal with Sinn Féin than their previous stated positions had suggested. The party's position had been strengthened by the decision in December 2003 of three UUP MLAs, Arlene Foster, Jeffrey Donaldson and Norah Beare to defect to the party. Donaldson and Foster were high-profile members of the UUP, who had been significant critics of Trimble. Their resignation was over the tactics of the party and the concessions that the UUP had made during the peace process. Donaldson said of his new party: 'I am proud to be part of a team capable of providing leadership to the unionist community – not like the leadership of the party I have left. Not like the leadership which has no bottom line, a leadership that does not know how to lead the unionist community.' If the problem for Donaldson was concessions to Sinn Féin, the comments of his new party leader on welcoming him to the DUP would have been reassuring. Paisley noted that, 'There is one issue which we will not be renegotiating and that is the possibility of getting Sinn Féin/IRA back in the government of Northern Ireland. That is not for discussion' (*Guardian*, 5 January 2004).

However, the reality was that by 2004 the DUP were more prepared to share power with Sinn Féin than such statements would suggest. What they needed was to create conditions that would enable them to argue that they had pushed Sinn Féin further down the road to democratic politics and away from their IRA-linked past than the UUP had been able to do and had forced the IRA to cease all activity. They also wanted to be able to argue that they had lived up to their pledges that they would cause a renegotiation of the GFA. As a result, their opposition towards both the peace process and Sinn Féin was not as absolute as many of their voters might have believed it to be. There also appear to have been differences within the party on the issue. As early as the beginning of March 2004, just three months after Paisley had rejected any suggestion of allowing 'Sinn Féin/IRA back in the government of Northern Ireland', two of his senior negotiating team, Nigel

Dodds and Peter Robinson, were indicating something very different to the British government. If the Independent Monitoring Commission (IMC) confirmed that there had been no IRA activity over a six-month period and that decommissioning had been achieved, and if Sinn Féin accepted changes they wished to see to Strands One and Two of the GFA, they would agree to share power with them. It could be argued, as the DUP subsequently did, that such an outcome would be a victory for the DUP and an outcome that the UUP had failed to achieve. However, the fact that they were immediately looking to create a situation that would enable them to return to government with Sinn Féin, appeared to be out of step with their public statements at the time. Dodds and Robinson subsequently indicated to the British that they were having problems convincing Paisley, but within a few weeks they had 'sold' him the plan (Powell, 2009: 239–241).

In their analysis of the DUP, Tonge et al. note the problems that the DUP identified with the GFA and which, by implication, would need to be addressed to make any agreement acceptable to the party. Many of these issues had been laid out in the party's 2003 document *Towards a New Agreement*, the cover of which was an image of a crumpled copy of the GFA stuffed into a bin. These included greater accountability of the NSMC to the Assembly; further reform of the changes of what had been Articles 2 and 3 of the Irish constitution, which the party asserted now simply claimed the people of Northern Ireland rather than the territory; the 'failing' British–Irish Intergovernmental Council; problems with the 'pro-nationalist/pro-agreement' institutions of the Human Rights Commission and Equality Commission; the Victims Commission that had led to the marginalisation of victims and elevation of former prisoners; the provisions on decommissioning that had been 'woefully inadequate'; the 'destruction of the RUC' and the suggestion that Sinn Féin/IRA would join a policing board in the future and 'seek to control the police they once tried to slaughter'; the review of the justice system which had removed the 'British ethos' by abandoning royal symbols and an oath to the Queen; and the release of prisoners which had happened despite there not being a clear end to violence (DUP, *Towards a New Agreement*, 2003; Tonge et al., 2014: 37–38). The party, very clearly and specifically, laid the blame for all of these 'failings' at the door of Trimble and the UUP.

The issues they identified were not, however, all ones that they could realistically expect to alter in any 'renegotiation'. In many cases the failings they cited were irreversible. It was not realistic, for example, that the reforms of the police would be overturned, that prisoners would be sent back to jail, the Irish constitution would be amended again, or that substantial changes would be made to the bodies associated with the equality agenda created under the GFA. Whilst the DUP might suggest that they were demanding movement on such issues (for example, one of the seven principles in the *Towards a New Agreement* document was to 'work to restore the morale and effectiveness of the police force') in reality the party were considered in what they sought to change and what they knew they had to accept. On the latter point, they were keen to portray what they needed to accept as the result of deals already done between the UUP and the British government and on certain points, such as OTRs, insisted that Blair wrote a letter to Paisley 'making it clear that these concessions had been agreed during David Trimble's watch, not theirs' (Powell, 2009: 241). As David Mitchell noted, 'Paisley was in the agreeable position of being able to negotiate a deal without the hot potatoes of prisoners and police; the risk and cost had already been borne by Trimble' (Mitchell, 2015: 156).

In terms of what they then insisted upon in order to agree to enter into government with Sinn Féin, the key issues were first, signs from republicans that their campaign was over, linked to decommissioning, ending of criminal activities and a public acceptance of the police and justice system and, second, changes to the mechanisms of certain aspects of the workings of the Executive and Assembly.

Tonge et al. noted how close the DUP came to doing a deal with Sinn Féin in this period, and that although it did not happen until 2007, 'the essentials of an agreement were in place' in 2004 (Tonge et al., 2014: 35). By 2004, republicans were showing a willingness to fully decommission and to countenance some changes to the structures of the workings of the Executive and Assembly. However, the demands from Ian Paisley at the Leeds Castle talks in Kent in September 2004 that a Protestant clergyman be allowed to witness the decommissioning of IRA weapons along with General de Chastelain and be permitted to take photographs were unacceptable to Gerry Adams (Powell, 2009: 251). According to both Arlene Foster and Jeffrey Donaldson, the notable difference between the DUP and their experiences with the UUP was that Paisley's party was willing to resist pressure to compromise and would walk away from high-profile meetings if necessary. Foster claimed that Leeds Castle showed that the DUP would not agree to something 'just for the sake of the optics. We are just going to leave and say we couldn't reach an agreement because that was much better than giving way and ceding something' (Tonge et al., 2014: 41).

This was coupled with a view within the DUP that they were in a position to pressure Sinn Féin as the republicans had invested so much in the peace process that they were desperate to return to power-sharing government. According to Nigel Dodds, Sinn Féin 'had nowhere else to go'. Jeffrey Donaldson made a similar point. 'Don't underestimate the amount of political capital they [Sinn Féin] had invested in the peace process. They needed the peace process to work. If it didn't work, then the Adams and

McGuinness leadership would have to admit defeat to the hardmen' (Tonge et al., 2014: 43). This is an interesting comment, in part because it seems to implicitly acknowledge that Adams and McGuinness were not in an unassailable position of complete control over the IRA. This was not a position that the DUP had often suggested they believed when Sinn Féin claimed that there may be problems in delivering IRA decommissioning. But it also implies that the DUP were in a stronger position than they actually were. The picture of an insouciant DUP and a desperate Sinn Féin does not quite chime with other accounts. Powell, for example, notes on several occasions that he believed Dodds and Robinson were keen for a deal and that by the time of Leeds Castle, when Paisley returned after a health scare, 'all negativism had switched to a driving desire to conclude the Northern Ireland question before he died' (Powell, 2009: 251). However, the DUP were keen to maintain their image as the party that would pressure Sinn Féin and refuse to compromise with republicans. This went too far, however, when in November 2004, Paisley delivered a speech (apparently arranged by his son, Ian Paisley Jr) designed to reassure his electorate that he would not be involved in a sell-out (Powell, 2009: 259). The DUP leader noted that Gerry Adams had accused the party of seeking to humiliate the IRA on decommissioning. According to Paisley there was 'nothing wrong with that. I think it's a very noble thing. The IRA needs to be humiliated. And they need to wear their sackcloth and ashes, not in a backroom but openly' (Tonge et al., 2014: 44). This, again, demonstrates the difficulty of seeking to reassure one constituency with hard-line rhetoric whilst also seeking to make progress towards a negotiated accommodation that would inevitably involve compromises. Whatever the desire that Sinn Féin may have had to do a deal, they also had a constituency to 'play' to and republicans were determined not to be seen to be conceding to the DUP's demands. As a result, the chance of the IRA agreeing to photographic evidence of decommissioning declined further.

Pressure on the IRA

If the DUP were going to be able to sell a deal that enabled them to enter into government with Sinn Féin, it was necessary that they could do so against a backdrop and actions which indicated that the IRA had effectively ceased to function and no longer posed a realistic threat. A series of events in 2004 and 2005 made this significantly more difficult. In February 2004, IRA members had been caught abducting a dissident republican, Bobby Tohill, from a Belfast pub, and in December 2004 the organisation was believed to have been behind the largest ever bank robbery in the UK when

£26.5 million was stolen from the Northern Bank in Belfast. But it was the events of 30 January 2005 which did the most damage to republicans and increased the pressure they came under. On that date IRA members were involved in a fight in a Belfast city centre bar. After the fight spilled out onto the street IRA members are believed to have pursued the man involved in the original incident, Brendan Devine and his friend, Robert McCartney, who a subsequent IRA statement claimed had not been involved in the original altercation. Both men were stabbed, and McCartney was killed. The scene was subsequently cleaned, and the bar staff threatened and made to hand over the CCTV footage before the police arrived.

After initially issuing a statement denying any IRA involvement, the IRA issued a second statement on 25 February stating that after an internal investigation three IRA volunteers had been court-martialled and dismissed. The killings caused widespread condemnation throughout Northern Ireland and internationally due to a high-profile campaign by McCartney's partner and sisters. The campaign included the McCartneys taking their message to Washington for St Patrick's Day in 2005 and meeting President Bush. Adams's own trip to Washington that year saw his access to key American policymakers far more limited than previously, and the reception he received was far more critical (Clancy, 2010: 149–150). The episode was particularly damaging to Sinn Féin as the McCartney family were republican supporters and Sinn Féin voters. As the journalist Angelique Chrisafis noted, 'For republicans to kill an innocent man and one of their own community was shock enough. But the cover-up, intimidation and lies which residents said continued … despite an IRA statement expelling three of those involved, had badly damaged their standing' (*Guardian*, 28 February 2005).

As pressure mounted on the IRA, they issued a third statement on 8 March which stated that four people had been involved in the killing, two of whom were IRA members. The statement noted that at a meeting with the McCartney family the IRA had 'stated in clear terms that the IRA was prepared to shoot the people directly involved in the killing of Robert McCartney' (CAIN). The family had refused the IRA's offer and stated that they wanted those involved brought to justice via the court rather than an IRA shooting. The position of an IRA on ceasefire, threatening to shoot people by way of justice for a killing, was not one that played well domestically or internationally. By their own admission the IRA knew who was responsible for the murder of Robert McCartney but despite their statement claiming that they had 'ordered anyone who was present on the night to go forward and to give a full and honest account of their actions' no one was ever convicted of the murder.

Tony Blair argued that 'the killing was in many ways the final turning point' (Blair, 2011: 190). This view was echoed later by Bertie Ahern, who argued that it demonstrated to the IRA 'that they could not continue having Sinn Féin doing the talks while they were in the background doing whatever they wanted, so it did crystallise in their minds that they couldn't just carry on doing these things' (Spencer, 2020: 255). It can also be seen as fortunate for the DUP that the deal which had apparently been so close two months previously had not been completed. Had it been, the DUP may have found themselves in the position they had often castigated the UUP for: making concessions to an organisation that was still engaged in criminal and violent activity, a point made by a DUP insider to Tonge et al. (2014: 44).

The failure to do the deal at that stage did not damage either the DUP or Sinn Féin electorally. In the Westminster election on 5 May 2005, the DUP consolidated its position as the main voice of Unionism. The party saw nine of its candidates elected as MPs (up from six in 2001) and secured 33.7 per cent of the vote. The DUP ran on a platform of being the only party that 'can prevent Sinn Féin becoming the largest party in Northern Ireland. It is vital for unionism and democracy that those who refuse to give up paramilitarism and criminality do not become Northern Ireland's leading political party' (DUP, *Leadership That's Working*, 2005). The UUP, however, was almost wiped out, securing only one seat (down from six in 2001) and polling only 17.7 per cent of the vote (compared with its poll-topping 26.8 per cent in 2001). David Trimble lost his own seat and was replaced as UUP leader by Reg Empey. Sinn Féin also consolidated their position seeing five candidates elected (on its traditional abstentionist ticket) but the SDLP fared better than the UUP, securing three seats, the same number as in the previous election.

The end of the armed struggle

Whether as a direct result of the events of early 2005 or not, a momentous breakthrough was finally made on 28 July when the IRA issued a statement read by long-time republican and former IRA prisoner, Seanna Walsh. 'The leadership of Oglaigh na hEireann has formally ordered an end to the armed campaign. This will take effect from 4 p.m. this afternoon. All IRA units have been ordered to dump arms. All Volunteers have been instructed to assist the development of purely political and democratic programmes through exclusively peaceful means.' The statement asserted that the 'armed struggle was entirely legitimate', praised the sacrifices that had been made by republicans and noted that 'many people suffered in the conflict'. It pledged to engage with the IICD to complete decommissioning as 'quickly as possible'. It stated the decision had 'been taken to advance our republican and democratic objectives, including our goal of a united Ireland. We believe there is now an alternative way to achieve this and to end British rule in our country. It is the responsibility of all Volunteers to show leadership, determination and courage' (CAIN). The statement on the end of the campaign was followed by another two months later which asserted that the 'IRA leadership can now confirm that the process of putting our arms verifiably beyond use has been completed' (CAIN).

There appeared to be certain conditions attached to the IRA's declaration of the end of its campaign, primarily the release in advance of the statement of Sean Kelly, the man who was convicted of the Shankill bomb, who had previously been released early after the GFA but rearrested when he appeared to breach his licence conditions. Sinn Féin also wanted the speeding up of the demilitarisation process that had long been discussed. The immediate response to the moves by the DUP was hardly positive. They were highly critical of the IRA statement and although Paisley was relaxed about the proposed statement when told by the NISS, Peter Hain, in advance of it being made, by the time they met again on 3 August, Paisley led 'a furious delegation' that complained about Kelly's release, and two moves linked to demilitarisation, the proposed disbanding of the NI-based Royal Irish Regiment and the dismantling of watchtowers in South Armagh (Hain, 2012: 320–328). Similarly, Powell notes that they were concerned about Paisley's reaction when they told him in advance of the proposed decommissioning process given there was to be no photography and that the process would be overseen by two independent witnesses, a Protestant cleric, Rev. Harold Good and a Catholic priest, Fr Alec Reid, both of whom the republicans had selected. Powell notes that Paisley 'accepted the approach and recognised there was no point in making a fuss about it' (Powell, 2009: 273). However, again perhaps for the purpose of maintaining the view of his having a hardline stance against republicans, once decommissioning was announced Paisley publicly strongly criticised the process. After meeting General de Chastelain, Paisley declared that there was 'a cover-up' and questioned the intelligence estimates that had been provided to General de Chastelain and on which he had based his assessment that all the IRA's weapons had been destroyed. Asked whether he could now see himself sharing power with Sinn Féin, Paisley replied, 'we will not be doing it' (*Guardian*, 25 September 2005).

It was not just the DUP that had been pushing for photographic evidence of decommissioning, the Irish government were also demanding it. This was especially true of the justice minister, Michael McDowell, who had been one of the most vociferous critics of Sinn Féin within the Irish government, notably calling Adams a fascist over IRA criminal activity in the Republic the previous year (Powell, 2009: 239). Once the destruction had occurred, of course, there was little that could be done about the lack of photographic evidence.

The end of the IRA's campaign was a significant event and removed one of the major hurdles to the restoration of devolved government under the DUP and Sinn Féin. In reality, it was an outcome that the republican movement could be said to have been moving towards for at least a decade. The former IRA man, Anthony McIntyre, who by 2005 had become a significant critic of the Provisional leadership, noted his feeling of 'indifference' at the statement ending the armed struggle: 'It is comparable to receiving a death certificate many years after a loved one has died. The raw emotion was vented at the time of the event rather than at the point of its much-delayed announcement' (*Observer*, 31 July 2005).

The pressure that the IRA found themselves under after the events of the late 2004/early 2005 period was indeed considerable, but they had resisted pressure before. What was different in 2005 was that the situation was hindering the progress to where republicans wanted to be. By that stage they had already taken many monumental decisions which meant that, in some respects, the formal announcing of the end of the armed struggle was a logical step. The decision to call the ceasefires in 1994 and 1997, to enter into government at Stormont, to undertake the first acts of decommissioning can all be seen as steps that were clearly moving away from the armed struggle. Whilst on their own none of them were irreversible or absolute, collectively they moved the republican movement further and further away from its military past and towards a political future. The events of July and September 2005 were highly symbolic, and undoubtedly difficult for the organisation, but they were not completely unexpected (indeed as accounts such as Powell's and Blair's suggest, their necessity had been accepted privately by republicans for months). What was less clear at that stage was that the DUP would accept the bona fides of the end of the armed struggle and agree to join Sinn Féin in government.

Back to Stormont via St Andrews

It would take almost two years from the announcement of the end of the armed campaign to the creation of the DUP–Sinn Féin led devolved government. With the issue of decommissioning and the status of the IRA (largely) settled, the focus became the necessity for Sinn Féin to endorse the police service, related demands by Sinn Féin that a date be set for policing and justice oversight to be devolved to the NI executive, and the changes to the nominating process for the First and Deputy First Ministers and how decisions were made in the Executive, which the DUP wanted.

Frustrated by the continuing failure to restore devolution, the British government, supported by their Irish counterpart, unveiled their 'Plan B'. This essentially argued that if the parties could not agree to the restoration of the Assembly and devolved government by November 2006, then the institutions would be wound up. The elections scheduled for 2007 would not be held, salaries and allowances paid to MLAs would cease, and, effectively, direct rule would be given a more permanent footing. But, in addition, the NISS, Peter Hain, hinted there would also be an increased role for the Irish government as 'British direct-rule ministers will work with our counterparts in Dublin on common sense north–south partnerships'. He also listed a number of reforms that would be introduced, such as the abolition of the 11-plus, increased water rates for Northern Ireland and local government reform which would see a significant reduction in the number of local councils. These proposals, which to varying degrees were very unpopular with different parties in Northern Ireland, were clearly designed to try and pressure the parties into reaching an agreement. Indeed, as Hain noted, they could avoid them by doing just that. 'If locally elected politicians don't like all this, the solution lies in their hands: taking their places at Stormont and, for the first time in over three years, earning their salaries by exercising self-government' (*Guardian*, 6 April 2006). Hain stressed in Parliament that whilst other deadlines before may have passed without notable penalties being incurred, this one was different. 'All the parties need to understand that, if midnight on 24 November comes and goes and there is no restoration of the Assembly, the salaries and allowances will stop, and the curtain will come down. It would be the parties themselves that had brought the curtain down, not the government (House of Commons, *Debates*, 26 April 2006.). Blair spoke of it being 'the last chance for this generation to make the process work' (*Guardian*, 27 June 2006).

Much of 2006 was taken up with shuttle diplomacy between the governments and the DUP and Sinn Féin. Once again, as had been the case for much of the period since 1998, the focus was on the two parties whose agreement to enter into government was key. Although the other parties were invited to the large set-piece talks, such as Leeds Castle, in reality much of the work was done in bilateral discussions with key DUP and Sinn Féin politicians. These included several talks in adjoining rooms between Numbers 10 and 11 Downing Street, as the DUP still refused to talk directly to Sinn Féin, though a 'backchannel' for communication did exist between the two parties (Powell, 2009; Tonge et al., 2014: 49). The final push towards an agreement was relatively tortuous, though this was hardly unique given the history of the peace process. There were several problems in achieving the agreement. For republicans, the issue of endorsing policing was seen as very difficult. Indeed, as Marisa McGlinchey noted in her study of dissident republican groups, Sinn Féin's subsequent acceptance of the police was, for many of its critics within the republican movement, 'a step too far'

(McGlinchey, 2019: 153–166). The magnitude of this step was appreciated by some in the British government, with Powell noting that Gerry Kelly and fellow Sinn Féin negotiator, Conor Murphy, told him, 'in many ways it [endorsing the PSNI] would be the hardest decision for republicans to make', though Ahern apparently saw policing as 'Sinn Féin's last card' (Powell, 2009: 280).

For the DUP, however, endorsement by Sinn Féin of policing became the litmus test of its suitability to be in office. With the areas that needed to be addressed relatively clear, the parties met at St Andrews in Scotland in early October to try and thrash out a deal. The talks happened against the backdrop of a positive IMC report published a few days before the parties went to Scotland. The Commission argued,

> We do not believe that PIRA is now engaged in terrorism; We do not believe that PIRA is undertaking terrorist-type training; We do not believe that PIRA has been recruiting … We have no evidence of targeting, procurement or engineering activity … We have no reason to believe that there has been any organisational involvement in or planning of robbery … We believe that what might be described as "military" or "terrorist" intelligence gathering has ended. (*Twelfth Report of the Independent Monitoring Commission*, October 2006: 9–12)

In response, Tony Blair declared 'The IRA's campaign is over. The door is now open to a final settlement, which is why the talks next week in Scotland are going to be so important' (*Daily Telegraph*, 5 October 2006).

The St Andrews negotiations were not really comparable to those that led to the GFA, as what they achieved (and were largely designed to do) was a 'tweaking' of some of the aspects of the workings of the GFA, and some comparatively minor additions. Indeed, the third paragraph of the St Andrews Agreement (STAA) text, which was published a few days after the conclusion of the talks, states that, 'Both governments remain fully committed to the fundamental principles of the [Belfast/Good Friday] Agreement.' It is also notable that the STAA was an intergovernmental agreement between the two governments as to what the solution should look like, as at that stage it was not endorsed by the parties.

The 'headline' outcomes were those that could be seen as meeting the objectives of the DUP. The key demand that Sinn Féin signed up to support policing and the justice system was met. The DUP were also successful in securing changes to the procedure for the nomination of the First and Deputy First Ministers. These changes effectively meant that the largest party in each designation (so the DUP for Unionism and Sinn Féin for nationalism) would nominate the First and Deputy First Ministers respectively. This was seen as important to the DUP as it meant that they would no longer have to be involved in nominating a Sinn Féin member to be Deputy First Minister of Northern Ireland (as was the case under the GFA system). The changes were altered when the legislation was passed so that it was no longer the 'largest party in the largest designation in the Assembly' that nominated the First Minister, but it became the 'largest party' in the Assembly, which meant that Sinn Féin could theoretically secure the First Minister post if they secured more votes than the DUP in future elections, regardless of whether more unionists were returned overall than nationalists. But, as Adrian Guelke noted, this was not something that may have worried the DUP unduly as it enabled the party to use the threat of Sinn Féin capturing the First Minister post to appeal to unionist voters to back them over the UUP in order to block Sinn Féin. Sinn Féin could similarly use the possibility to seek nationalist support ahead of the SDLP, tactics which Guelke suggested might account for the poor showing of the UUP and SDLP in the subsequent Assembly elections (Guelke, 2010: 259). Similarly, changes were made to limit the ability of individual ministers to take decisions unilaterally with increased opportunity to have these decisions made either by the Executive as whole in certain circumstances, or for the Assembly to refer decisions back to the Executive for review if thirty MLAs voted for this to happen. There was also provision for greater scrutiny of the NSMC and BIIGC by the Executive (Dixon, 2008: 310–312; Tonge et al., 2014: 49–50). The agreement also noted that there would be a new pledge of office which would consider commitment to the rule of law. This was subsequently implemented and included the statement that ministers 'uphold the rule of law based as it is on the fundamental principles of fairness, impartiality and democratic accountability, including support for policing and the courts'.

There were also proposals in the STAA which addressed Sinn Féin's demands. These included a proposal for the devolution of policing and justice to the Executive by May 2008, an undertaking that the new pledge of office, 'would require that ministers would participate fully in the Executive and NSMC/BIC (British–Irish Council) and would observe the joint nature of the office of First Minister and Deputy First Minister' (STAA, Annex A). This was to illustrate that the First Minister and Deputy First Minister positions were of equal status and to avoid any attempts by unionists to refuse to participate in the NSMC or BIC, as David Trimble had sought to do at one stage by refusing to nominate Sinn Féin ministers to the NSMC, and proposals for an Irish Language Act.

Despite the fact that neither the DUP nor Sinn Féin formally endorsed the STAA, their acquiescence in agreeing to the timetable for implementation laid out in Annex D of the document was largely taken to indicate acceptance of the proposals. The road towards devolution being reinstated was not a smooth one, even post-STAA, with battles over the sequence of events such as whether it was necessary for Sinn Féin to announce its support for policing before or after the nomination of McGuinness as First Minister, which was scheduled for 24 November, with power due to be devolved back to Northern Ireland in March 2007. The issue was eventually fudged by Sinn Féin agreeing to accept the role of Deputy First Minister and then have their party meeting to endorse policing as long as a more substantive event was planned for 24 March. This, in turn, nearly collapsed when Ian Paisley, who was under substantial pressure within his own party, omitted a line he had agreed with the British government to include in his speech that stated he would accept the role of Deputy First Minister if the STAA was adhered to and implemented. The NIA chair then read out a statement the British had prepared saying Paisley and McGuinness had agreed to be First Minister and Deputy First Minister. Paisley stood to object, just as the loyalist Michael Stone attacked the building in an apparent attempt to kill Gerry Adams and Martin McGuinness (which he subsequently claimed was 'performance art'). The building was cleared and as the hiatus died down, Peter Hain told Paisley that he would have to 'pull the Assembly down. The legislation leaves me no option' if he had not accepted the role of First Minister. Paisley agreed to issue a press statement confirming his acceptance of the position. As Hain noted, 'we were back in business, but it had been perilously close to collapse' (Hain, 2012: 348).

On the back of the progress made at St Andrews, the DUP and Sinn Féin performed well in the Assembly elections with the DUP securing thirty-six seats (up six from 2003) and Sinn Féin, twenty-eight (up four). The UUP's position weakened further with a loss of nine seats from the previous election to eighteen (albeit three of the 2003 intake had defected to the DUP previously) and the SDLP secured sixteen seats (down two), the APNI gained one seat to secure seven, the UKUP lost its only seat whilst the PUP held their one and the Green Party secured a seat in the Assembly for the first time (CAIN).

The DUP's election strategy was, however, even at that post-STAA stage somewhat ambiguous over whether they had agreed to share power with Sinn Féin. Their manifesto proclaimed that they had 'successfully renegotiated the Belfast Agreement' and held out the threat of Sinn Féin topping the poll by claiming that only one 'unionist party is realistically capable of winning more seats than Sinn Féin to stop them being nominated for the post of First Minister'. But the manifesto also suggested that Sinn Féin had not yet committed to supporting the police and so left open the possibility that power-sharing may not happen. They did this by reproducing a DUP pledge from 6 November 2006 that claimed, 'Clearly as Sinn Féin is not yet ready to take the decisive step forward on policing, the DUP is not required to commit to any aspect of power-sharing in advance of such certainty' though by the time of the election Sinn Féin's Ard Fheis had passed the resolution to support policing (DUP, *Getting It Right*, 2007).

In their own manifesto Sinn Féin asserted their 'own historic unilateral initiative on policing' and portrayed the movement on the issue as a positive step that would lead to the transferring of policing oversight to the devolved government. This would mean a 'new beginning to policing will be realised and Sinn Féin will be in a position to hold the PSNI fully to account'. From being in the position during the GFA talks that they would not engage in the talks over Strand One as this would lead to a partitionist structure, it was Sinn Féin that was now portraying itself as the champion of devolution. 'We are ready for government. It is time that British ministers were sent home for good. The Assembly and Executive need to be restored with full powers and we need to start planning for the future' (Sinn Féin, *Delivering for Ireland's Future*, 2007). Somewhat surprisingly, and ultimately unsuccessfully, the UUP ran on a manifesto that did not directly mention the GFA or STAA but argued that Northern Ireland would be ill-served by electing the DUP and Sinn Féin as the largest parties, given they were 'more interested in dividing power between themselves rather than sharing office for the benefit of Northern Ireland' (UUP, *For All of Us*, 2007). The SDLP, by comparison, portrayed itself as the defender of the GFA and argued it had protected it against more excessive changes sought by the DUP at St Andrews (SDLP, *Let's Deliver* Real *Progress*, 2007).

Despite the strong showing by the DUP in the election, the party was internally divided on the question of taking the final decision and entering government with Sinn Féin. This led to one final delay before the restoration of devolved power to Northern Ireland, which should have occurred on 26 March 2007. The British government agreed to the DUP's request for a delay until May in order to try and 'sell' the move to their party, but the price that they had to pay for this was the agreement of Sinn Féin and a public meeting between Paisley and Adams. The DUP had never directly engaged with Sinn Féin throughout the peace process up to that point. This was achieved on 26 March, despite a last-minute row over the seating formation, with Paisley insisting they sit opposite each other, whereas Adams wanted to sit next to Paisley. The compromise of a diamond-shaped table meant that both ostensibly got their wish. The two party leaders met in public and announced their intention to share power. Finally, on 8 May, power was devolved to a DUP–Sinn Féin led power-sharing government, with a relaxed and smiling First Minister Ian Paisley sitting beside the Deputy First Minister, Martin McGuinness. The images of this genuinely remarkable event were beamed around the world and cemented the view of Northern Ireland as the model of conflict resolution, albeit perhaps a little prematurely given some of the challenges that were to come. Peter Hain argued, 'Devolution Day' was 'a joyous occasion when a new Northern Ireland was born' (Hain, 2012: 352–353).

Explaining the restoration of devolution

It is worth noting that by 2007 the more surprising outcome was not the decision of Sinn Féin to share power with the DUP, but the decision of the DUP to share power with Sinn Féin. Sinn Féin had made most of the major and difficult moves at earlier stages of the peace process. From the decision by the IRA to halt its armed campaign in 1994 (and 1997), to agree to share power with unionists at Stormont in 1999 and begin decommissioning in 2001, there was little to stop them practically or ideologically re-entering devolved government with the DUP in 2007. That said, the final steps they had to take, notably the final decommissioning act, the announcement of the end of its armed campaign and the agreement to support policing and justice systems in Northern Ireland, were not insignificant ones for the republican movement. It was less apparent or, arguably, inevitable that the DUP would take the decision to enter the government. Indeed, as Dixon noted, on 12 July 2016, just three months before the St Andrews talks, and two years after the negotiations at Leeds Castle when Robinson had indicated to the British that they were willing to share power with Sinn Féin if the necessary conditions could be created (Powell, 2009: 231–241), Paisley had addressed a meeting of Orangemen. The DUP leader told the brethren, 'No unionist who is a unionist will go into partnership with Sinn Féin-IRA. They are not fit to be in partnership with decent people. They are not fit to be in the government of Northern Ireland, and it will be over our dead bodies that they will ever get there' (Dixon, 2019: 228). So what had changed between July 2006 and May 2007? The case for consistency and achievement by the DUP would rest on several factors. They could claim that their hard-line stance between Leeds Castle and 2007 had forced the IRA to announce the end of its campaign and finally put its arms beyond use (though, as we have seen, they were publicly sceptical that full decommissioning had been achieved). As a result, they could claim to have broken the link between Sinn Féin and the IRA and made the party publicly accept the police service and, as a result, could claim they were not sitting in government with 'unreconstructed terrorists' or indeed with 'Sinn Féin/IRA'. Tonge et al. have argued that forcing Sinn Féin 'to support the Police Service of Northern Ireland in the explicit and unambiguous manner that it did, is probably the most impressive achievement of the DUP' (Tonge et al., 2014: 61). The party could also claim that the changes which they demanded to the structures and workings of the Executive and Assembly had made the devolved government more accountable to the Assembly and, by extension, to the people of Northern Ireland.

The party also suggested that their actions had 'saved the Union' and, in part, been a response to the pressures they found themselves facing due to Peter Hain's 'Plan B'. This was a point that Paisley made several times in defence of the decision to enter into government with Sinn Féin. He told the journalist Stephen Nolan, 'We were told if we didn't do this then it was going to be curtains for our country … How would I have faced my people if I had allowed this country to have the Union destroyed and the setting up of a joint government by the south of Ireland? (*BBC News*, 4 April 2007). He made a similar point to the *Washington Times*. 'If we had gone back on this and not done the deal, we would have been ruled jointly by the United Kingdom and Dublin. No elected representative from Northern Ireland would have had any say in anything that was being done' (*Washington Times*, 13 April 2007). Overall, the defence that the DUP offered of their apparent change in tack was that their actions had ended the threat of the IRA, renegotiated the GFA, made devolved government more acceptable and democratic and averted the Plan B scenario which would have seen Northern Ireland effectively subjected to joint rule between London and Dublin. Overall, as Tonge et al. argued, the DUP's achievement was 'forcing Sinn Féin and the provisional IRA to accept the logic of the peace process: that violence and the modalities to execute it were a thing of the past. The UUP could not do this' (Tonge et al., 2014: 60).

There are, however, problems with several aspects of such claims. In terms of the portrayal of the alternative to doing the deal being 'curtains' for Northern Ireland and 'the Union destroyed', such claims are not sustainable. The proposals related to water charges, ending educational selection and local government reform would probably have been implemented by the British government and would have been highly unpopular with many sections of Northern Ireland's electorate (not least the unionist middle classes). However, it is highly unlikely that the form of direct rule which followed the failure to reach an agreement would have been significantly different to that which preceded the GFA. The British had pursued 'direct rule with a green tinge' since at least the AIA of 1985, and they may well have sought to increase cooperation with Dublin for the same reasons that they had done so previously. This was to try and placate nationalists and limit 'nationalist alienation' in Northern Ireland (for a review of the rationale behind the intergovernmental cooperation see O'Kane, 2007). However, direct rule, with or without a green tinge, was never the favoured option of the British or Irish governments. As has been argued, one of the key driving factors behind the peace process for both states was to try and limit the impact that Northern Ireland had on their own 'domestic' politics. Neither state was keen to abandon this objective or, as a result, the peace process. This seems to have been appreciated by at least some in the DUP at the time of St Andrews. Nigel Dodds subsequently claimed in relation to Hain's threat over Plan B: 'No, I don't buy it, I didn't buy it at the time … the idea that the British government was just going to throw everything up in the air and wipe out the last 15–20 years of policy at the moment when they had Sinn Féin and almost the DUP [agreeing] it was ludicrous in my view.' His colleague Peter Robinson took a slightly different view to Dodds and claimed that they would have ended up with a 'much greener' form of direct rule if the deal had not been done (Tonge et al., 2014: 48). This is still, however, a long way from the destruction of the Union.

The argument that the DUP had no option but to succumb to British pressure also challenges to an extent the narrative that the party had previously sought to present: that whilst Sinn Féin were desperate for a deal and could be pressurised, they themselves were in such a strong position that they were willing to resist pressure to sign up to anything that was not fully on their terms. It is difficult to have it both ways, to be the resolute defenders of the Union and party that would bring the IRA to heel, and to be the party forced to sign up to a deal under the threat of the complete failure of their project by the destruction of the Union.

Claims that the changes to the workings of the GFA negotiated at St Andrews were fundamental or constituted a 'renegotiation' of the GFA are also an exaggeration. Most commentators see the STAA as 'a relatively slight and technical document that did not upset the fundamental architecture and principles of 1998' (Mitchell, 2015: 158). David Trimble's successor as UUP leader, Sir Reg Empey, asked about the intervening period between the GFA and STAA, 'What was it all for? The Belfast Agreement for slow learners?' (*Sunday Life*, 15 October 2006). Trimble himself later described the STAA as the GFA's 'identical twin' (McGrattan, 2010: 173). There are good reasons for such claims, beyond simply the annoyance of UUP leaders at how the peace process panned out. Some of the institutions of the GFA, notably the NSMC and BIIC, were largely unaltered post-STAA, and although some of the changes to how decisions were made within the Executive and the possibility of decisions being referred back by the Assembly to the Executive, did represent changes to how devolved government functioned, it is an exaggeration to argue that these alterations represented a 'renegotiation' of the GFA.

The question of the extent to which the DUP achieved what the UUP could not, in the years 2003–2007, is a difficult one. At one level they certainly achieved what the UUP had not, before 2003, in that the IRA did announce the end of its campaign, completed decommissioning and Sinn Féin endorsed the policing and justice system in Northern Ireland. But this begs the question: is it clear that this only happened because of the DUP? In other words, might it have happened anyway if the UUP had been returned as the largest party in the 2003 election? It is not unreasonable to speculate that it might well have done so, given that all of these issues were on the agenda before 2003. The DUP undoubtedly took a harder line on these issues than the UUP did, and it is certainly the case that the problem that Trimble had faced as a result of 'jumping first' during the 1998–2003 period (in no small part caused by the criticism that the DUP offered of such moves) made Paisley's party determined not to find themselves in the same position. The DUP were firmer on insisting that these steps were taken, but they did not introduce these demands onto the agenda for the first time. Both the issue of Sinn Féin accepting the police service in Northern Ireland and the devolution of police and justice powers to the devolved government, were being discussed in 2002 and were included in the Joint Declaration of April 2003, which was to be the basis of the acts of completion (Cooke, 2015). Furthermore, Sinn Féin and the IRA had accepted that 'violence and the modalities to execute it were a thing of the past' by 2003. What happened between 2003 and 2007 were the public signs of this acceptance, but arguably the previous actions such as the ceasefires, engagement with the decommissioning commission and the acts of decommissioning were indicators of such an acceptance before 2003. The DUP's action may well have accelerated the process, but it is difficult to argue categorically that it would not have happened if not for that party. Indeed, David Trimble noted almost a decade later, in 2016, 'the DUP are still living in the political world we created, you know' (Hennessey et al., 2019: 59).

If the reasons that the DUP have offered for why they decided to go into power with Sinn Féin are not convincing, what other reasons might there be? One issue that has been noted by several commentators is the belief that Paisley had decided that he wanted to end his career as First Minister and leave a positive legacy. This is suggested by Powell's claim that Ian Paisley was more positively inclined to do a deal after his health scare. Moloney's biography of the DUP leader supports this view and cites Paisley's wife, Eileen, as an important influence on him in this regard. One DUP source told Moloney that at the time of St Andrews, Paisley was 'busting to be First Minister' (Moloney, 2008: 448–452). Indeed, Peter Hain claims that whereas previously Paisley's reticence to do a deal had caused 'despair to Peter Robinson and the reformers in the DUP, Paisley had now leapt over them' and Robinson complained to the Secretary of State that Paisley was 'almost being reckless' (Hain, 2012: 350). There may have been something in concerns over his own mortality causing Paisley to be in more of a hurry to do the deal, but, as has been traced in this chapter, there was a cohort at the top of the DUP who had been moving towards this outcome for several years.

The move was contentious within the party and the decision to enter into government did lead to some departures from the DUP, most notably the DUP MEP, Jim Allister, who formed the alternative party, Traditional Unionist Voice (TUV) and for a period sought to pressurise the DUP on an anti-power-sharing platform.

Overall, perhaps the reason that the DUP decided to take power in May 2007 was simply because they could. The context of the peace process and the cost to them of doing so were markedly different by then than they had been for the UUP in 1999. Many of the hard decisions had been taken by the UUP previously and they, rather than the DUP, had borne the costs over prisoners, RUC reform, decommissioning etc. As Sir Reg Empey argued, the DUP had benefited from his party doing 'the heavy lifting with republicans' (*Sunday Life*, 15 October 2006). The narrative that the DUP offered that Sinn Féin had 'nowhere else to go' by this stage of the peace process can also be applied to themselves. Whilst it may not be persuasive to argue that they had to succumb to the pressure Plan B placed them under, it is also the case that there was no 'Plan C' that was achievable which would have been a better outcome for them. What would they have gained by refusing to enter government with Sinn Féin in 2007? It might have prevented them from being criticised in relation to apparent duplicity or, saved the 'tacticians' in the party from being castigated by what Dixon called the DUP's 'populist' wing (Dixon, 2019: 227–229). But the internal discomfort it caused within the party did not damage them electorally in the longer term. They were, perhaps, assisted in this regard in that there was no unionist party to ethnically outbid the DUP in the way that the DUP party had outbid the UUP, although there were concerns for a period that Allister's TUV might manage this.

A devolution once again

It is possible to argue that the peace process was effectively concluded on 8 May 2007. If we view the peace process as a process to entice the main paramilitary groups away from violence and create an agreed devolved power-sharing government in Northern Ireland, then these things had been achieved. As a result, the distinction discussed previously between a peace process and a political process is more applicable to the period post-2007 than it was to the period of the early 2000s. However, the term peace process continued to be widely applied to Northern Ireland's politics over the coming years. This was not only because the term had become a useful shorthand for politics in the region but also because, despite the decisions taken in May 2007, the political situation was far from stable. Whilst devolved power had been returned to Northern Ireland, it was unclear whether it would be stable or permanent, crises were still to be a feature of its politics in the coming years. Also, despite the success in ending the violence of the main paramilitary actors, smaller groups of both the loyalist and republican persuasion continued to employ violence, sometimes with deadly results. The issue of the status and activity of the IRA was also not completely off the agenda.

Several of the key individuals who had been instrumental in the development of the peace process left the stage once the DUP–Sinn Féin government had been achieved, including Tony Blair and his chief of staff Jonathan Powell a month later. The following year Bertie Ahern, whose last official duty was the opening of the Battle of the Boyne visitor centre with Ian Paisley, left office. Paisley himself left around the same time as Ahern. Despite his assertions that he intended to serve his full term of office he announced in March 2008 that he would resign as First Minister and leader of the DUP in May 2008. He was succeeded by his long-time deputy, Peter Robinson, in both posts. Paisley's apparent mellowing in his attitude to republicans and the momentous decision to share power with Sinn Féin was not without a personal cost. In September 2007 he announced he was stepping down as Moderator of the Free Presbyterian Church which he had been instrumental in creating over fifty years earlier. This was believed to be a result of internal pressure by key elders in the church who were angered by the decision to share power with Sinn Féin (Gordon, 2009: 101–109). In February 2008, Ian Paisley's son, Ian Paisley Jr announced his resignation as a junior minister in the NI government due to controversy over his links with a property developer and his alleged role in lobbying on his behalf, including in the final stages of the St Andrews talks (*BBC News*, 18 February 2008; Gordon, 2009: 137–146). The decision not to carry on as First Minister and DUP leader might be understandable given the demands of the role and Paisley's health and age (he was 82 when he stood down). But there were also widespread reports of disquiet within the DUP over his apparent warm relationship with Martin McGuinness (the 'Chuckle Brothers' description was not meant as a compliment when first used). Similarly, rumours suggested that he was damaged by the problems associated with the resignation of his son and the defeat of the DUP candidate at a council by-election in Dromore in February 2007, where the newly formed TUV had taken 19.5 per cent of the first preference votes (see Martina Purdy's article, 'Did he jump or was he pushed?' (*BBC News*, 4 March 2008)).

Dissidents – denying Sinn Féin victory

The deal between the DUP and Sinn Féin in 2007 did achieve something that had eluded the previous UUP/SDLP-led government, comparative political stability. Northern Ireland experienced sustained devolved government between May 2007 and January 2017. However, there were still notable and threatening issues facing Northern Ireland's politics and society post-2007. In the years immediately following the restoration of devolution, problems persisted with the threat of violence, notably from dissident republicans, the continuing unease from elements of unionism regarding Sinn Féin's partici-pation in government and on when and how devolution of policing and justice powers should be achieved.

The reduction of the threat from the Provisional IRA did not mark the end of the threat in Northern Ireland from violent republicanism. There were several 'dissident' republican groups that were active in this period, not all of which supported the use of violence (Frampton, 2010). The three main ones that were pursuing their own armed struggle were the Continuity IRA (CIRA) which emerged from a split in the Provisional IRA in 1986, the Real IRA (RIRA) which emerged from a split in the Provisional IRA in 1997, and Oglaigh na hEireann (ONH) a term that was used by several groups but the most significant faction that used this name emerged from a split in the RIRA in 2002 and was revamped in 2006. Although these groups were not able to sustain a violent campaign comparable to that the Provisionals had waged, they remained a serious threat to the peace of Northern Ireland and, to an extent a political threat to Sinn Féin and the narrative it sought to offer to the republican community.

The most high-profile actions by dissidents since the Omagh bombing occurred in March 2009. The RIRA killed two British soldiers, Patrick Azimkar and Mark Quinsey, at Massereene barracks on 7 March and the CIRA killed PSNI officer, Stephen Carroll, in Craigavon two days later. It was estimated that in the eight months following the killing of Stephen Carroll a further eleven attempts were made to kill PSNI officers without success, although a Catholic police officer, Peadar Heffron, was seriously injured by a car bomb in January 2010. The groups also sought to detonate bombs in Northern Ireland and a report suggested that in the two years up to November 2009 there were over 750 bomb alerts, over 420 of which were considered to be 'viable devices', though not all of these were linked to dissident republicans (*The Times*, 9 November 2009).

Although the dissidents' threat was not comparable to that posed by the Provisional IRA during the Troubles, that was not their aspiration. They did not believe that they were in a position to 'drive the Brits' from Ireland. One purpose of the dissidents was simply to be disruptive. As the journalist Suzanne Breen argued, 'The Real IRA knows it won't force a British with-drawal within a few years, but it believes even infrequent attacks can shatter the normalisation of life in Northern Ireland' (*Sunday Tribune*, 12 April 2009). To a large extent what the dissidents sought to achieve by their use of violence was to ensure that the peace process did not succeed (and so deny 'victory' to Sinn Féin). Their actions in the immediate post-devolution period were disruptive, indicated by the fact that the British decided to deploy the SAS-trained Special Reconnaissance Regiment (SRR) to Northern Ireland in March 2009, and that 15 per cent of MI5's manpower and 60 per cent of its surveillance activity were employed to combat the threat they posed in this period. The threat level in Northern Ireland was upgraded from 'moderate' to 'substantial' in September 2010, its highest level for a decade (*The Times*, 8 March 2009; *Guardian*, 24 September 2010).

The violence used by dissidents, and their claims that Sinn Féin had betrayed the republican cause, was a challenge for the party of Adams and McGuinness, post-2007. Some of those who were at the forefront in making such accusations were former members of the Provisional IRA who had split from the organisation over the peace process (Bean, 2007). Sinn Féin's reaction to the threat caused by the dissidents was to argue either they were not republicans at all and were simply criminals, or that they were republicans but had failed to realise the new situation and were actually thwarting the peace process's advance towards the creation of the Republic. In what was seen as a highly symbolic move, after the Masereene and Craigavon attacks in March 2009, McGuinness stated that the perpetrators were 'traitors to the island of Ireland' (*Irish Times*, 10 March 2009). Similarly, after a RIRA bomb attack in Derry in October 2010, McGuinness told the Conservative Party conference that 'These conflict junkies are attempting to drive a city living very much to the future, back to the past. People in this city are horrified that there are still these neanderthals within our society' (*Guardian*, 15 October 2010). The actions of the dissidents in the immediate period after the restoration of devolved government did not succeed in critically destabilising the new arrangements in Northern Ireland, but they remained a physical threat to Northern Ireland and a political irritant to Sinn Féin for years to come.

Devolution in practice

The fact that devolved government was achieved did not mean that devolved government would be harmonious. The two largest parties continued to have a problematic relationship and distrust remained a notable characteristic between them. Indeed, within eighteen months of Robinson becoming First Minister the entire devolution project was once again in crisis and Sinn Féin were threatening to leave the government and pull down the institutions. The immediate cause of the crisis was the continuing argument about the failure to devolve policing and justice powers to Northern Ireland. Sinn Féin claimed that this was a denial of what had been agreed at St Andrews, when it was proposed devolution of such powers would occur in 2008. The problem was that the DUP leadership, under pressure from elements within the party that were still deeply uncomfortable about sharing power with Sinn Féin, were resistant to the move. The spectre of Martin McGuinness or (former Old Bailey bomber) Gerry Kelly in charge of policing was frequently raised by Jim Allister as part of his new party's attacks on the DUP.

The impasse was finally broken by almost two weeks of negotiations between the two governments and parties at Hillsborough Castle in late January into early February 2010. However, in common with most of the crises during the peace process it was not a solitary issue which divided the parties. The DUP had argued that there was insufficient trust within the unionist community to agree to devolving policing as they were not sufficiently benefiting from the process. The key issue became demands for changes to the Independent Parades Commission which had been established in 1997 to rule on whether parades might need to be banned or rerouted. Unionists had long seen the Commission as an 'unelected quango' that was preventing the Orange Order from marching its 'traditional routes' (Walsh, 2015). The DUP were pushing for the Parades Commission to be abolished to increase Protestant confidence (*Independent*, 29 January 2010).

The talks themselves took place during a difficult time for the DUP. The First Minister, Peter Robinson, had just returned from a six-week self-exclusion from the role (his colleague, Arlene Foster, had been acting First Minister in his absence). Robinson had temporarily stood aside whilst investigations were made in relation to the revelation that his wife (and fellow MP and MLA) Iris Robinson, had secured £50,000 from two property developers to help a 19-year-old man open a café; £5,000 of the funds went directly to Mrs Robinson (*Guardian*, 8 January 2010). It was revealed by the BBC's *Spotlight* programme that Mrs Robinson was having an affair with the recipient and had not disclosed the relationship or her role in securing the funds to either the NIA or to the Council which owned the café's building and on which Mrs Robinson sat as a councillor. Peter Robinson was cleared of any wrongdoing and returned to his roles, Iris Robinson resigned from both Parliament and the NIA. In 2014 the NIA Committee of Standards and Privileges ruled that Iris Robinson had committed a 'serious breach' of the NIA's code of conduct. By then, however, she had retired from politics (*BBC News*, 28 November 2004).

The events around the Robinson scandal were relevant to the impasse over policing and parades as it was widely believed that the DUP did not wish to face an Assembly election against such a backdrop. There were concerns that it might have a negative impact with the party's conservative and, often deeply religious, constituency. The party was facing a notable threat at that stage from Allister's TUV. In the 2009 European Elections, Allister (who was a sitting MEP, having been elected on a DUP ticket in 2004) gained 13.7 per cent of the first preference votes, though he ultimately failed to get elected. Sinn Féin topped the poll for the first time and saw Bairbre de Brún elected on the first count, with the UUP's Jim Nicholson and DUP's Dianne Dodds elected on the third count. Dodds was elected with the smallest number of total votes of the three MEPs and had received just 18.2 per cent of the vote on the first count, compared with the 32 per cent that Allister had received when he was elected as the DUP's candidate in 2004 (CAIN). In light of these results, even those within the DUP who were uneasy with policing powers being devolved to a government which included Sinn Féin, acquiesced to the deal rather than see Sinn Féin force an election (*The Times*, 6 February 2010).

The breakthrough was secured by an agreement that policing powers would be devolved in April 2010 and a decision would be taken later in the year to resolve the parades issue. The post of justice minister would go to someone outside of the main parties (so neutering for unionists the threat that Sinn Féin might gain control of the oversight of policing and the courts). As a result, the nomination of the minister sits outside the usual d'Hondt system and is subject to a cross-community vote. The first justice minister was the APNI party leader and MLA, David Ford. As Ford subsequently argued, he got the role with the backing of the DUP and Sinn Féin in the Assembly, 'not because they loved me, it's because they hated each other, and they hated their tribal rivals' (David Ford, author interview, 15 September 2017). However, the proposed changes to the parades commission foundered in September when the Orange Order refused to back the plans, which the DUP had urged them to agree to (*Belfast Telegraph*, 28 September 2010).

Problems therefore continued in securing stable devolved government even post-2007. Even with the devolution of policing and justice powers in April 2010, which was widely portrayed at the time as the last piece of the devolution 'jigsaw' (*Independent*, 28 January 2010; Cameron, 2019: 308), Northern Ireland's politics and society continued to be buffeted by crises and disputes. This was frustrating as almost twenty years had been spent negotiating what the structures, composition and powers of government should be in Northern Ireland, and what the region's relationship should be with both the wider constituent parts of the United Kingdom and the Irish state. The problem was, however, that the lack of trust between the main political actors in Northern Ireland, and the wider traditions they represented, was not resolved by the peace process. Conditions had been created which persuaded the main groups that had used violence to forgo it in favour of a political approach, and an accommodation was reached on the new governing structures, but there was still widespread suspicion over both the intentions of 'the other' and of who was benefiting most from the new arrangements.

These tensions manifested themselves increasingly in disputes over cultural and symbolic issues often related to the 'parity of esteem' agenda. The peace process had not resulted in a convergence of identities within Northern Ireland. There was still a tendency for many to see the areas that they sought changes in, in zero-sum terms. Unionists believed that areas that nationalists were pressing for changes in, such as those related to parades, protection for the Irish language and increased sensitivity in the flying of the Union flag on official buildings, were really attacks on their British identity and its symbols. Similarly, nationalists took resistance by unionists to the changes they proposed as further evidence that there was a reluctance to see their concerns as legitimate or to treat them as equal to those associated with British identity. Given the bi-national identity at play in Northern Ireland and voting patterns which saw almost no votes transferring across the communal divide, there was little incentive for the main parties to seek to appeal to those from the 'other' tradition. As a result, the parties tended to campaign exclusively within their own ethnonational bloc.

For example, the DUP's 2010 Westminster campaign was clearly focused on appealing to their traditional base. Given that the election was for seats in Parliament rather than the Assembly, it might have been expected that the issues addressed would be either UK-wide or, given that they were now in a devolved power-sharing government, would be geared towards the improvement of Northern Ireland in a holistic sense. However, the 'culture' section of the manifesto is telling. The manifesto noted that, 'The DUP has worked to promote and develop the roles of the Loyal Orders, marching bands and Ulster-Scots heritage.' Specifically, it noted that the party had 'ensured that', 'there would be no Irish Language Act', provided 'greater funding for the Twelfth and other Orange activities', 'reform of the Community Festivals Fund with money being taken from republican festivals and redirected to Orange events', and had 'secured £1 million benefiting 40 Orange Halls'. It was critical of the Parades Commission and also called for the creation of a body to 'encourage discussion and debate around the diversity and development of the British identity past, present and future' (DUP, *Let's Keep Northern Ireland Moving Forward*, 2010). The previous attacks on Sinn Féin in relation to policing and their unsuitability for government were no longer a feature, but the focus of the manifesto was, in part, on what would become known as the 'culture wars'.

Even the discussion of poverty had a partisan focus as the manifesto noted that 'The DUP is particularly concerned about the often-overlooked deprivation within Ulster's Protestant Unionist and Loyalist communities. The long-held myth that poverty was most prevalent within nationalist and republican areas whilst unionist parts of the province were all affluent has been dispelled.' For their part, Sinn Féin's manifesto was less overtly partisan, although they also stressed the cultural dimension and particularly the promotion of the Irish language and calls for an Irish Language Act. They also pledged to work to 'repeal the 1737 Act which prohibits the use of Irish in the courts' and to promote Irish language education and use. They stressed their aspiration to achieve a united Ireland, 'Sinn Féin is a proud Irish Republican Party. Our primary political goals are an end to partition and a new Ireland, a United Ireland.' There did, however, need, 'to be meaningful engagement with unionists about the type of united Ireland they want to live in' (Sinn Féin, *Westminster Manifesto*, 2010). So, although the manifesto of Sinn Féin was less obviously playing to their ethnonational gallery, the focus was still clearly on 'their' constituents and their republican political and cultural agenda. The UUP and SDLP manifestos were less overtly sectarian in their appeal and both sought to criticise Sinn Féin and the DUP.

The DUP suffered an electoral setback when the party leader, Peter Robinson, lost his East Belfast seat to the APNI's Naomi Long. This was, however, thought to be a result of the personal scandals that had hit the Robinsons, and the DUP saw eight other MPs elected. The threat of the TUV was not as significant as some had originally feared, and Jim Allister was convincingly defeated by Ian Paisley Jr in North Antrim (the TUV leader polled 16.8 per cent of the vote to the DUP man's 46.4 per cent). The other notable results of the night were that the UUP failed to win a single seat. The UUP had stood in the election in coalition with the Conservative Party as Ulster Conservatives and Unionists – New Force (UCUNF). This decision had caused the party's only sitting MP, Lady Sylvia Hermon, to resign the whip and stand as an independent. She was re-elected. The move was also criticised subsequently by the then Prime Minister, Gordon Brown. Brown argued that by effectively standing in Northern Ireland the Conservatives undermined the traditional position of British governments being 'honest brokers' and had 'breached' British neutrality on the issue (Brown, 2017: 368). Sinn Féin and the SDLP repeated their 2005 results with five and three seats respectively (though Sinn Féin actually polled more votes than the DUP). Despite the loss of Peter Robinson, the 2010 election indicated that the DUP and Sinn Féin's positions as the two largest parties was entrenched. This was further illustrated in the 2011 Assembly elections when the DUP secured thirty-eight MLAs (up two on 2007), and Sinn Féin achieved twenty-nine (up one). The UUP had sixteen seats (down two) and the SDLP fourteen (also down two). The APNI picked up one seat to secure eight, the TUV only achieved one seat (for Jim Allister) in its first NIA election; the Green Party remained on one seat and the PUP lost their only seat, meaning for the first time there was no representation for a political party associated with loyalist paramilitary organisations in the Assembly (CAIN).

Flagging support

Despite the entrenchment of support for the two largest parties and the successful devolution of the policing powers, disputes continued to bedevil relations within the Executive and more widely in society. Although the devolved structures did manage to last a full term to 2016, there were several issues which continued to cause problems in Northern Ireland. On a positive note, these were less to do with the use or threat of violence, though this did occur occasionally, but were related to three emerging divisive areas: cultural issues and parity of esteem; how the Executive functioned; and the increasing challenge of how Northern Ireland dealt with the legacy of the Troubles period.

The most visible sign of deteriorating communal relations in Northern Ireland was sparked by the flags protest in late 2012 and 2013. In December 2012 Belfast City Council voted to change its policy on flying the Union flag; it would no longer be flown continuously but on fifteen designated days. The decision was a compromise proposed by the APNI as Sinn Féin had originally called for its complete removal. Indeed, the Alliance Party Councillor, Marie Hendron, said after the vote that it was a historic day as for 'the first time in their history both Sinn Féin and the SDLP have voted in support of the Union flag. This proves in a practical way that they acknowledge the constitutional position of Northern Ireland.' This was not the way that many loyalists and unionists saw the outcome. The idea behind the move was to encourage the view of City Hall as a 'shared space' and a neutral environment. However, the decision sparked months of protests in Belfast and subsequently spread to other areas of Northern Ireland, including Newtonabbey and Carrickfergus. Whilst the main unionist parties did condemn the violence, they were also highly critical of the decision taken. After the vote, the DUP councillor, Christopher Stalford, argued,

> Those who started this debate should have known from the outset that it would stir up tension and cause division. I trust as they look back on the damaged relationships, costly consultations and energy expended, they will realise their focus was wrong. Indeed, all those who supported this stripping away of British identity are just as guilty and foolish. (*BBC News*, 3 December 2012)

UUP and DUP activists had been involved in the distribution of 40,000 leaflets in the weeks before the vote, asking, 'A shared future? Shared for who?' which criticised the Alliance Party for 'backing the Sinn Féin/SDLP position' on flags. The leaflets urged people to 'Contact the Alliance Party and let them know we don't want our national flag torn down from City Hall' (*BBC News*, 13 November 2012). The intensity of the row regarding the flags decision was something of a surprise. The move was far from unprecedented, it was the policy at Stormont, the seat of Northern Ireland's devolved government. As the issue loomed, the *Belfast Telegraph* carried an editorial effectively backing the proposed compromise. The leader column noted that the Equality Commission had recommended that the flag only be flown on designated days and had called for 'sense to prevail on the flags issue' (*Belfast Telegraph*, 24 November 2012). There were various suggested reasons as to why the decision provoked such a visible and, at times, violent reaction over the months ahead. It was widely suspected that the UVF were involved in organising and maintaining the protests, particularly given that they tended to be most pronounced in areas where the UVF were strongest. The PSNI's chief constable, Matt Baggott, said he was 'concerned that senior members of the UVF in east Belfast – as individuals – have been increasingly orchestrating some of this violence', and his assistant, Will Kerr, had suggested both the UDA and UVF members were involved in the protests, 'we're now seeing senior members actively involved in orchestrating the violence' (*BBC News*, 28 November 2014). However, whilst loyalists may have been instrumental in organising the protests, there is little doubt that the reason that they were able to do so, at least in part, is that the issue resonated with a belief that had been prevalent in certain circles of unionism. Particularly within working-class loyalism there was a perception that not only had nationalists benefited more from the peace process generally, but that the parity of esteem agenda and the arguments around shared spaces were in fact a thinly veiled attack on signs of Britishness, which were so important to unionist and loyalist identity (Hearty, 2015). As the editor of the *Shankill Mirror* argued, the protests 'were not about the flag, they were never just about the flag. There is deep-rooted disillusionment within PUL working-class communities that they have been left behind by those in power at Stormont' (Edwards, 2017: 328). Aaron Edwards argued that this disillusionment with traditional unionist parties 'ran like a golden thread through the essentially leaderless protests' (Edwards, 2017: 328). (On the issue of changing attitudes within loyalist communities towards the DUP and UUP, see Hearty (2015).)

The perceived attacks on British culture played into the narrative of inequality that was also focused on the parades issue and caused increasing tension between the First and Deputy First Ministers (*Belfast Telegraph*, 17 January 2013). Unionist sensibilities were dealt a blow the year before when, for the first time ever, elections led to nationalists outnumbering unionists on Belfast City Council (twenty-four seats to twenty-one), and Sinn Féin became the largest party (with the APNI holding the balance of power).

The Northern Ireland government invited the former US diplomat, Richard Haass, who had been President George W. Bush's US envoy to Northern Ireland 2001–2003, and the American academic, Meghan

O'Sullivan, to lead a process to try and find a solution to the parades, flags and dealing with the past. The Haass–O'Sullivan talks began against the backdrop of significant parades-related violence when an Orange parade was banned from marching near the Catholic Ardoyne area of Belfast on 12 July.

The Haass–O'Sullivan talks process ran throughout the latter part of 2013 and ended on New Year's Eve. The talks were a serious attempt to resolve the divisions over the three areas. It was also an example of Northern Ireland's parties taking the lead in trying to resolve the impasse, for although the two governments were supportive of the initiative, they were not formally parties to it; it was the creation of the five parties in the Executive. Haass struck a confident note at the outset, saying after the first week of meetings with the parties, 'This is not our first rodeo, we have both been in a number of political processes formal and informal in the Middle East, Asia, Latin America and here (Northern Ireland). Based upon that experience and the quality of the conversations and also our familiarity with the issues I believe there is a real chance to succeed' (*Western People* (Ballina), 20 September 2013). However, despite a lengthy engagement which resulted in Haass and O'Sullivan having a hundred meetings with interested groups and receiving six hundred submissions via a website that was created for the purpose, on 31 December the seventh draft of their proposed agreement failed when the UUP, DUP and APNI refused to endorse it. The process had made a good deal of progress, particularly on the issue of dealing with the past, but less on the issue of parades and little in the area of flags. Although it was embarrassing that such a high-profile initiative, led by prominent American chairs, had failed, for the parties themselves there was little immediate cost (*Belfast Telegraph*, 1 January 2014). The main cost was the increasing divisions that the issues were causing within the NI Executive.

The tensions within the Executive were not solely related to cultural issues and the desire of the parties to simply play to their own constituencies. There were also significant problems around the issue of proposed welfare reform linked to the wider austerity measures that the Conservative–Liberal coalition government had introduced at Westminster. Welfare was a devolved matter in Northern Ireland but there was an expectation that Northern Ireland would implement the welfare cuts that the rest of the UK was experiencing. This led to a crisis within the Executive as Sinn Féin and the SDLP refused to support the legislation. The question highlighted an important but often underappreciated outcome of the mandatory power-sharing structures that the GFA had created in that the system was unlikely to lead to an ideologically coherent government in Northern Ireland. The division over welfare reform further strained relations within the Executive and led the First Minister, Peter Robinson, to write a lengthy article in the *Belfast Telegraph*. The DUP leader contentiously argued that the 'present arrangements are no longer fit for purpose'. The reason he offered was that the 'breadth of the ideological spectrum represented in the Executive does, at times, mean agreement cannot be reached on some initiatives and at other times, in order to secure agreement, unsatisfactory compromises are reached'. Robinson argued that Northern Ireland could not afford to refuse to make the welfare reforms London was insisting upon (not least due to the proposed financial penalties). It was clear, however, that the issue of setting a budget and welfare reform was, for Robinson, symptomatic of a wider problem in relation to the structures and obligations of devolved government. He called for a 'St Andrews 2' type negotiation to review the issues and argued for 'a streamlined Assembly, a reduction in the number of government departments and further normalising our arrangements with a recognised opposition' (*Belfast Telegraph*, 9 September 2014).

Robinson's public criticism of the structures of government in Northern Ireland drew a rebuke from the Deputy First Minister. Whilst there was validity behind his observations regarding the ideological divisions that were likely under a system based upon mandatory power-sharing, the purpose of the peace process, and the resulting GFA and STAA had not, of course, been to create an ideologically coherent Executive. Any move away from the structures mandated under the GFA would be highly problematic for nationalists. The BBC's Northern Ireland editor, Mark Devenport, pointed out that there were only three alternatives to mandatory coalition. First, to take decisions on a majority basis, which would be completely unacceptable to nationalists as it would be seen as a reversion to the old-style majority rule version of Stormont. Second, to introduce a system of voluntary coalition (which could still have the necessity for weighted majority voting etc.), but this would be unacceptable to Sinn Féin who were suspicious that unionists would try and use the change to exclude them and govern with the SDLP. Or, finally, to revert to direct rule to enable the British government to impose the welfare and budget changes they argued were necessary. This option was unattractive as it risked creating a political vacuum in Northern Ireland and there could be no certainty if devolution was suspended as to when it could be reinstated (as events post-2017 would demonstrate) (*BBC News*, 10 September 2014).

The divisive issues of flags and parades, dealing with the past, and the budget and welfare problems were addressed in the process that resulted in the Stormont House Agreement (SHA) in December 2014 and, when this was not fully implemented, the Fresh Start Agreement (FSA) of November 2015. These initiatives were brokered again by the British and Irish governments who felt compelled, albeit reluctantly, to re-engage after the failure of Haass–O'Sullivan. The SHA and FSA included both elements of coercion to try and get the parties to agree to resolve the issues, and elements of incentive, largely in the form of additional financial incentives.

The perception that Northern Ireland's politicians used crises to try and increase the financial demands they made from London over and above what they received under the Barnett funding format, clearly irked Westminster politicians. Gordon Brown is explicit and somewhat bitter about this in his memoirs. He noted that although the parties were often divided, 'as quickly as the two sides could walk out on each other, they could band together when it came to money'. Brown records he 'joked' with his team, slightly adding to Blair's observation in the run-up to the GFA, 'I feel the hand of history on my shoulders and the hand of Peter Robinson in my pocket' (Brown, 2017: 17). This issue clearly also rankled Brown's successor, David Cameron, who recorded in his own memoir that in the run-up to the SHA, he received advice from the Irish Taoiseach's chief of staff on how to handle the talks. 'Prime Minister just tell them they are not getting any more fecking money' (Cameron, 2019: 311). But although the welfare and budgetary issues were largely resolved, primarily by Sinn Féin 'agreeing to accept legislation passed in Westminster rather than Stormont' (Cameron, 2019: 312), issues related to the disagreements over the Parades Commission, the flying of flags and how to deal with the legacy of the past (discussed in the next chapter) continued to cause division and unease in Northern Ireland.

The IRA, opposition and collapse

Whilst beset by the cultural and economic problems, distrust within the Executive was strained almost to breaking point by the killing of a former IRA man, Kevin McGuire, in Belfast in August 2015. McGuire was believed to have been responsible for the killing of another IRA man a few months earlier (*Guardian*, 12 August 2015). The reason that this killing caused a crisis in Northern Ireland was because the PSNI indicated they believed IRA members were involved in the killings. The UUP leader, Mike Nesbitt, announced that his party would leave the Executive, increasing pressure on the DUP. To prevent the collapse of the devolved government, the NISS, Theresa Villiers, called for a report by the PSNI and MI5 into the status of paramilitary groups, which was published in October 2015. The report argued that 'the structures of PIRA remain in existence in a much-reduced form. This includes a senior leadership in the 'Provisional Army Council'. The report argued that 'PIRA members believe' the IRA's Army Council 'oversees both PIRA and Sinn Féin with an overarching strategy' and that the IRA 'continues to have access to some weapons'.

It might have been expected that the report's conclusions would have ended the willingness of the DUP to serve with Sinn Féin in the Executive. However, the government did not collapse. There are several reasons for this. First, the report argued that the oversight by the Army Council had 'a wholly political focus' and claimed that the 'small number' of IRA members who held weapons had done so to prevent them from falling into dissidents' hands and that the 'PIRA's leadership remains committed to the peace process and its aim of achieving a united Ireland by political means'. It also endorsed the view that the IRA leadership had not sanctioned McGuire's killing (*Paramilitary Groups in Northern Ireland Report*, 19 October 2015). Second, on the back of the report, the government launched the process of talks which led to the FSA. In addition to the issues discussed above, the FSA tried to deal with the suggestion that Sinn Féin was still controlled by the IRA's army council. It was agreed to change the ministerial oath of office so those in government had to pledge, 'to accept no authority, direction or control on my political activities other than my democratic mandate alongside my own personal and party judgment'. In addition, they undertook 'to challenge all paramilitary activity and associated criminality' and 'to call for, and to work together with the other members of the Executive Committee to achieve the disbandment of all paramilitary organisations and their structures'.

The issue illustrated how far the DUP had moved from its pre-2007 position. That the party was willing to remain in government after the PSNI and MI5 had stated that the IRA was still in existence and its leadership oversaw Sinn Féin's strategy. Its members had committed a recent murder and that the organisation had not fully decommissioned its weapons in 2005 was, on paper, shocking. But by 2015 the DUP had been in power with republicans for eight years, during which time the IRA had largely not been involved in violence. The episode also tells us something important about the purposes of the peace process. In response to the killings and the debate around the status of the IRA, the former Irish justice minister, Michael McDowell, wrote an article in the *Irish Times*, 'Abolition of the Provisional IRA was never on the cards'.

McDowell was one of the strongest critics of the IRA in the Republic and even he argued that the purpose of the peace process was not the destruction of the organisation. The peace process was designed to move the IRA away from violence and down the political path, rather than arrange for the organisation to be wound up. It was no doubt hoped by those involved that by taking that path the IRA would become less of a threat and less inclined, or able, to return to large-scale violence, but that is not the same as seeking its abolition. The St Andrews process, which McDowell was involved in, also did not demand that the IRA ceased to exist. Indeed, McDowell suggests that the conscious decision not to try and force the IRA to disband was the result of a political calculation. The 'choice was between an IRA that became an inert, unarmed and withering husk or an open-goal opportunity for dissidents to re-form an Army Council as the legitimate heir of the body which had been "treacherously" wound up'. McDowell invoked historical precedent to justify the approach. 'Past splits and schisms in the IRA showed only too clearly that the IRA could more easily metastasize rather than wind itself up. That was seen, and I think rightly, as being the greater evil to be avoided. The governments took the view that an inert, freeze-dried husk of the IRA was preferable to passing the ideological torch to the dissidents' (*Irish Times*, 26 August 2015).

The risk of not demanding that the IRA disbanded was that they might use violence in the future, as the PSNI argued occurred with the McGuire killing. However, by and large, the IRA had increasingly become 'inert' in terms of violence, which might explain the decision of the DUP not to leave the Executive over the August 2015 killing. The party's stance did not damage them electorally, they again saw thirty-eight MLAs returned in the Assembly elections in May 2016, retaining their position as the largest party. Sinn Féin lost two MLAs (primarily due to the rise of the socialist People Before Profit group which took two seats and topped the poll in the Sinn Féin heartland of West Belfast). The UUP seemed to stem their decline with their representation in the NIA remaining at sixteen. The SDLP lost two seats and saw twelve MLAs returned. The Green Party secured one seat, and one independent unionist, Claire Sugden, was elected.

The largest change after the 2016 election was not in terms of the representation of the parties in the Assembly, but in the decision of three of the parties that had previously sat in the government, the UUP, SDLP and APNI to refuse to join the Executive and go into opposition. This was a result of frustration over how the Executive functioned. There was a perception that the two largest parties agreed policy and the direction of government in advance of cabinet meetings and simply, as Mike Nesbitt argued, used the smaller parties 'for cover' whilst the big decisions were taken elsewhere (Mike Nesbitt, author interview, 11 September 2017). David Ford made similar observations about the working of the Executive and noted that it was unusual for an Executive meeting to last more than an hour and they could be as short as fifteen minutes, again because the decisions had already been taken by the two largest parties before the meetings. Ford said that the decision of his party not to take up the justice portfolio after the 2016 election (it was eventually filled by the independent Claire Sugden) was promoted in particular by the decision of the DUP leader, Arlene Foster (who had succeeded Peter Robinson as DUP leader and First Minister in December 2015), to refuse to give up the ability of her party to trigger a petition of concern. The petition of concern required thirty MLAs, so the DUP were the only party large enough to trigger one on their own. A petition meant that governmental decisions would need cross-community support to be passed, making such legislation more difficult to achieve. The DUP sponsored most petitions, having signed 86 of the 115 that were tabled in the 2011–2016 period, including to seek to block legislation that would allow gay marriage and on welfare reform (Smyth, *The Detail*, 29 September 2016). Ford claimed that he approached McGuinness over the issue of DUP use of the petitions (as it would also have been in Sinn Féin's interest to curtail the DUP's use of the procedure) but McGuinness refused to support the request as 'Arlene has got her fundamentalists to deal with' (David Ford, author interview, 15 September 2017).

The SDLP announced that they were also going into opposition as, according to the party's leader, Colum Eastwood, 'It is clear that the DUP and Sinn Féin are determined to put forward a framework that includes no action, nothing that they can be held accountable for or to' (*BBC News*, 15 May 2016). In their statement on the decision, the SDLP were at pains to stress that their decision was not against the principles of the power-sharing GFA. 'Equality provisions and protections for both communities are now enshrined and guaranteed by international treaties and by two governments. Power-sharing between unionism and nationalism remains locked in.' Instead, they portrayed it as a way of evolving politics in NI and the GFA. 'The Good Friday Agreement was always intended to be a living document. It was never meant to be a document frozen in time. The evolution of our political structures is not a vice. A new opposition at Stormont is one such evolution' (SDLP, *The Constructive Opposition*, n.d.).

The new-look governmental structures did not last long and the government/opposition model was never really tested. Eight months after the election, in January 2017, the Deputy First Minister, Martin McGuinness resigned, collapsing the government and, ultimately, the wider devolved structures. It was somewhat surreal that after over two decades wrestling with the issues related to the use of violence, the constitutional question and how to effectively and acceptably govern a deeply divided society, the issue that brought the system to collapse was a row over the creation of a scheme to encourage businesses to move away from fossil fuels and install renewable heating systems (it was later expanded to the domestic sector). The problem with the Renewable Heating Incentive (RHI) was that the payment rates set were overly generous, meaning that the incentives offered to those who registered for the scheme were greater than the cost of the fuel that was burnt. Hence, rather than encourage fuel efficiency, the scheme actually served to encourage users to consume as much fuel as possible, whether it was needed or not, leading to claims of empty sheds and factories being constantly heated (resulting in the scheme being known as 'cash for ash') (*BBC News*, 16 December 2016). Unlike in the British version in use outside of Northern Ireland, there was no mechanism to taper the payments as more was used or as the uptake to the scheme increased; the scheme lacked 'cost controls'. In his detailed account of the crisis, Sam McBride pointed out that 98 per cent of the legislation for the Stormont bill that created the RHI scheme was cut and pasted from the British variant that had gone through Westminster. Most of the changes that were there were technical. However, in one section 'the cut and paste stopped. There were 107 missing words and it was those missing words which at that point were estimated to cost tax-payers £500 million' (McBride, 2019: 136, 886).

The reason that this poorly designed heating scheme led to the collapse of the devolved government was due to the personnel involved and the increasingly fractious relations between the DUP and Sinn Féin. The scheme had originally been created by the Department of Enterprise Trade and Investment (DETI), whilst Arlene Foster was its minister. The problems with the scheme were made public in February 2016, and over the coming months, allegations emerged of a failure by Foster to act on the information she had received from a whistleblower in 2013 and claims that Foster had fought calls for the scheme to be closed as the scale of the costs became apparent. In December 2016, Jonathan Bell, who had succeeded Foster as minister at the DETI, claimed Foster's advisors had sought to have her name removed from documents linked to RHI and two DUP advisors were preventing the scheme being closed in the autumn of 2015 when the costs were rising out of control. Sinn Féin called for an investigation into the issues around RHI and for Arlene Foster to step aside as First Minister whilst it was being carried out, citing the precedent from Robinson's decision to temporarily stand aside in 2010. Foster refused, which led to McGuinness's resignation and the government's collapse. (For a chronology of the RHI scandal see *BBC News*, 2019.)

As well as bringing down the government, the RHI scandal highlighted problematic aspects of how the government and civil service functioned, and of relations between the two main parties. Sam McBride's study is an absorbing account of the crisis, but it illustrates wider issues beyond the RHI and paints a picture of a government beset with problems. The book suggests a culture of suspicion and poor working relations had emerged at the heart of government, notably between some of the special advisors (SPADs) and senior civil servants. Some SPADs, especially Foster's advisor, Andrew Crawford, seemingly had an excessive level of influence on the civil service and other ministers. McBride also suggested that there was a level of political input for the DUP and Sinn Féin over the appointment of politically neutral senior civil servants (notably the top position of the Head of the Civil Service in Northern Ireland), 'which does not exist anywhere else in the UK' (McBride, 2019: 366). The civil service also came in for criticism due to a 'culture of civil servants doing whatever it took to please their ministers' and civil servants and ministers often decided not to keep a record of controversial meetings and information (McBride, 2019: 520–535, 766). McBride suggests that this might, partly, have been a natural reaction by the civil service to the political landscape they faced, as 'even the civil servants with stunted political antennae would have realised that the DUP and Sinn Féin were likely to be in charge for a very long time. In that context, many civil servants bent over backwards to please their ministers. Some officials were reluctant to give their ministers bad news' (McBride, 2019: 587).

There was also a tendency to try and squeeze as much money as possible out of London by both the DUP and Sinn Féin, echoing observations by Brown and Cameron above. McBride talks of the 'crudely grasping attitude of some senior figures in Stormont' (McBride, 2019: 6349). In the early period of the RHI scheme there was a belief that this would be directly funded by the UK government and so was 'free money' with no cost to Northern Ireland's budget (McBride, 2019: 1025). Overall, even though McBride's book is focused upon the specifics of the RHI scandal, what emerges more widely is a portrait of the devolved structures created under the GFA (and marginally amended under the STAA) resulting in a system which was insufficiently robust to deal with the challenges of implementing a complicated but expensive policy. The account suggested that, whilst it was a scandal that primarily impacted upon the DUP, no party and certainly not the civil service, emerges unscathed from the crisis. The legislation was passed through Stormont 'without a single dissenting voice' (McBride, 2019: 1227). For McBride, 'RHI became the prism through which ordinary people came to understand the scale and nature of the dysfunctionality among their rulers' (McBride, 2019: 6328).

Although Arlene Foster's refusal to stand aside whilst an inquiry was undertaken into RHI was ostensibly the reason for Sinn Féin's departure from government, in reality the underlying and growing tensions at the heart of the government were significant factors in the decision. The then UUP leader, Mike Nesbitt, subsequently pointed out that 'when we left the DUP and Sinn Féin alone in the room to get on with it, it didn't last very long. There was nobody to blame, there was no cover, it was just the two parties who clearly hate each other, with a passion' (Mike Nesbitt, author interview, 11 September 2017). The reasons that McGuinness gave for his resignation went beyond the confines of the RHI issue. He stated that he had resigned to 'protest at the DUP's failure to accept the principles of power-sharing and parity of esteem and their handling of the RHI crisis'.

His resignation comments noted his belief that Foster's party were not sincere in seeking to deal with Sinn Féin as co-partners in the Executive:

> Over the last 10 years I have worked with DUP leaders and reached out to unionists on the basis of equality, respect and reconciliation ... Over this period the actions of the British government and the DUP have undermined the institutions and eroded public confidence ... Sinn Féin wants equality and respect for all. That is what this process must be about. Today I tendered my resignation. Today is the right time to call a halt to the DUP's arrogance (*Irish Times*, 10 January 2017)

It had been apparent that there were divisions in the Executive. The problems over parading and flags protests had caused tension, the decision by Peter Robinson in 2013 to withdraw support for a proposed peace centre at the site of the former Maze prison had deeply angered Sinn Féin, and the refusal of the DUP to agree to the introduction of an Irish Language Act was an increasing source of resentment for both Sinn Féin and the SDLP. Such an Act had been included in the STAA, but the DUP subsequently claimed never to have agreed to implementing it. Given that, officially, the STAA was an intergovernmental document rather than an all-party agreement, the status of the commitment given by the DUP to such an act can be questioned (*The Journal*, 28 January 2017). But Sinn Féin and the SDLP believed that they had received such an undertaking at St Andrews and this was taken as yet another example of the DUP refusing to allow progress on the parity of esteem agenda. Former Sinn Féin minister, Gerry Kelly, stressed the importance of the refusal of the DUP to agree to an Irish Language Act in the decision to leave government. He argued the 'hatred of the language and the people who speak it was a very big straw that broke the camel's back' for Sinn Féin. He also argued that the apparent accommodating approach of his party to staying in power with the DUP despite these problems was causing 'increasing anger' in the republican community (Gerry Kelly, author interview, 12 September 2017). The picture that emerges is of a divided government with very poor relations between the leadership of the parties and significant differences in relation to many of the main cultural and social issues they had to deal with. The RHI crisis brought these divisions to the fore and ultimately led to the collapse of the system.

Evaluating the decade of devolved government

The acrimonious collapse of the government in January 2017 obviously influences the perception of both the record of the government and the parties that formed it. There is, however, evidence that casts the period of devolved government in a more benign light. There were some symbolically significant firsts such as the handshake between Martin McGuinness and Queen Elizabeth II in Belfast in June 2012, something that would have been previously inconceivable and a remarkable indicator of how far the republican movement had come.

There is also evidence of more legislative competency than might have been expected. In an assessment of the performance of devolved government between 2011 and 2016, Sean Haughey indicates that the performance was better than is often perceived. In terms of the amount of legislation passed, the NIA's sixty-seven bills are significantly more than the twenty-eight bills the Welsh Assembly passed in the period and comparable to the Scottish Parliament's seventy-nine bills. Indeed, in terms of primary legislation, the NIA passed more bills than either of the other two institutions. The record on committee and private members bills was also improving towards the end of the period, which Haughey noted as a 'welcome development' and an indication of 'a more confident, more policy active legislature' (Haughey, 2019: 706). This level of comparative activism did not translate into a particularly favourable view of the devolved institutions in Northern Ireland, even before the RHI scandal and their collapse. The NILT poll sampled people between 2007 and 2015 on their views of the achievements of the NIA. Throughout this period the most common view was that the Assembly had achieved 'a little', ranging from a high of 54 per cent in 2009 to a low of 44 per cent in 2014. This can be seen as a 'positive' view of the NIA and is arguably more positive than how it is presented by Haughey, when he argues that the view was that the survey showed they believed it had produced 'little' rather than 'a little', which is what the survey asked. Few had a distinctly positive view of the NIA, however, with the view that it had achieved 'a lot' usually only making it into low double figures. Perhaps surprisingly, the most positive view of the achievements of the NIA was in 2007, when it had only just been restored; 17 per cent believed it had achieved 'a lot', presumably by the parties agreeing to return to devolved government. This rosy view of the NIA was short-lived as a year later only 7 per cent of those surveyed believe it had achieved 'a lot', the lowest figure in the period surveyed. A notable core of Northern Ireland's population held a highly negative view with, on average, over 20 per cent believing it had achieved 'nothing at all' (again this ranged from a low of 8 per cent holding this view in 2007 to a high of 40 per cent in 2014) (NILT, n.d.: 2007–2015 surveys).

Whilst the public's opinion on the Assembly is mixed, it is worth noting that support for having power-sharing devolved institutions in Northern Ireland remained consistently high in polls. For example, the ESRC-backed Northern Ireland General Election Survey led by Jon Tonge recorded

55 per cent support for the NIA and Executive in 2015, 64 per cent in 2016 and 65 per cent in 2017; there were variations in levels of support between those of different religions, however, with Catholics tending to have more positive views of the devolved structures than Protestants (UK Research and Innovation, n.d.). The 2020 survey showed that, even after the RHI scandal, 81 per cent of people wanted to see the devolved government restored (*Belfast Telegraph*, 18 February 2020).

Overall, the success and public opinion of devolved government is something of a curate's egg. But what is clear is that the transformation that took place in Northern Ireland's politics and the peace process between 2003 and 2017 was both remarkable and frustrating. It was frustrating given that both the start and the end of the period found Northern Ireland without devolved government and relations between its two largest parties highly strained. But it was remarkable given that there had been a decade of power-sharing, comparatively stable government in the interim and the immediate reasons for the collapse had less to do with the traditional fault lines of Northern Ireland's politics and society than might have been expected. If it was extremely hard to envisage the 'pie in the sky' of DUP–Sinn Féin led power-sharing being achieved back in 2003, it would have been impossible to imagine that it would have collapsed over a heating scandal, having weathered the storms it faced in the intervening years. But, as has been discussed, whilst the fault lines may not have been deep enough to result directly in an earthquake which would collapse the Executive, the tremors they continued to cause undermined its foundations. The continuing lack of trust between the main parties and the different agendas and objectives that concerned them had to be addressed to restore devolved government. It would take three years to do so, and the challenge was compounded by the issue of Brexit, which once again put the constitutional question back on the agenda.

6

Governing the present, dealing with the past and learning lessons for the future

The collapse of the devolved institutions in January 2017 led to another extended period of uncertainty in Northern Ireland before the parties eventually agreed to their restoration in January 2020. This period of governmental flux coincided with a period of turmoil in British politics as the state sought to grapple with the decision in the referendum on 23 June 2016 to leave the European Union. Whilst Brexit was clearly a UK-wide decision, it raised particular challenges for Northern Ireland. At the same time, the debates and divisions related to the parity of esteem agenda and the disagreements over how to deal with the legacy of the Troubles continued to cause problems for the region. This chapter will examine the debates and outcomes of these issues before evaluating how successful the peace process has been, and what the prospects for politics in Northern Ireland may be.

Brexit

Brendan O'Leary has noted that the term 'Brexit' was, in fact, inaccurate, given that it suggests that Northern Ireland would not be involved. In reality, as he notes, it should have been UKEXIT. 'The Irish, North and South, though not the Scots, would have less objection if it was just Brexit that was being considered' (O'Leary, 2019: 353). But there was no doubt that the Brexit referendum result (as it was universally known) did have significant implications for Northern Ireland, and Northern Ireland had significant implications for Brexit. This was nicely summarised/satirised by the Irish border itself, which had its own twitter account, @BorderIrish. On 8 February 2018, it posted an image of a negotiating table with people deep in talks but ignoring the large elephant that was also in the room, with the image captioned, 'There's me at the Brexit negotiations'. As the debate raged over the UK's exit from the EU it became increasingly difficult to ignore that particular elephant. Northern Ireland had voted against leaving the EU in the Brexit referendum, by 55.78 per cent to 44.22 per cent. The headline

figure, however, masked a division within Northern Ireland along ethnonational lines, with Protestants and Catholics having notably different attitudes on the issue. John Garry's NIA Election study polling in 2016 indicated
that 85 per cent of Catholics had voted Remain, compared with only 40 per
cent of Protestants. Results were broadly similar if you used the self-
designation of unionists (34 per cent Remain) and nationalists (88 per cent
Remain); for those who saw themselves as 'neither', polling suggested a
70/30 Remain/Leave split (Garry, 2016). The difference might not be surprising given that the DUP (the largest party in Northern Ireland) cam-
paigned for Brexit. However, party attitudes on Brexit did not split straight
down sectarian lines as all the other main parties, including the UUP, cam-
paigned for Remain. For many nationalists, leaving the EU would mean
weakening the link with the Republic of Ireland, which would remain in the
organisation, and tie them closer to Britain.

The unionist attitude was slightly harder to explain. There was more of a
class analysis in play for Unionism, as there was a link between socio-eco-
nomic factors and educational level. Garry's analysis suggested that whilst
there was comparatively little difference in Catholic voters' support for
Remain regardless of level of educational achievement, this was not the case
for Protestants. In this regard the voting pattern of Protestants was more in
line with the 'left behind' thesis, which suggested that those with the lowest
levels of skills and educational achievement were least likely to support the
European project (Garry, 2018). In Northern Ireland, the support for Leave
was generally much stronger in working-class loyalist areas than in the more
affluent Protestant-majority constituencies. The DUP had long had a strong
Eurosceptic streak, but their stance did potentially put them at odds with a
core of their traditional base, unionist farmers and the business community.

Brexit itself was not, of course, an issue that was directly related to the
factors that had been the focus of the peace process. It was a UK-wide issue
and, as noted, had split the parties in Northern Ireland in a way not traditionally seen. However, Brexit was also an issue with significant implications
for the peace process and the politics of Northern Ireland. As a result of the
Brexit vote the relationship between the north and south of Ireland and
between the UK and the Republic of Ireland would be subject to change.
Once the UK left the EU the border, the significance of which the peace process had been so successful in diluting, would be fundamentally altered.
A frontier that had been increasingly less visible, both in terms of infrastructure and in its ability to be a divisive issue in the political life in Northern
Ireland, would once again be the key dividing line in British–Irish relations.
As a result of their common membership of the EU, the related customs
union and the creation of the single market in 1992, there was little obvious
friction for people or goods crossing between Northern Ireland and the

Republic; the customs posts that used to exist on all 'authorised' border crossings had long gone. In parallel with this, the decline in violence that had resulted from the peace process meant that the security installations that had been such a feature of border crossing (and the cratering or blocking of all non-authorised crossing points), had also largely been removed. The fear was that once the UK left the EU, this increasingly invisible border would once again become highly visible as it would now not only be the point at which Northern Ireland ended and the Republic began but would also become the international border between the UK and the EU. Given the determination of the Conservative British government for the UK to leave both the single market and the customs union, there would need to be some way of regulating goods and people that moved between the EU and the UK. It was this which led to speculation that the border would have to be significantly altered and the invisible and fluid nature of its existence would be fundamentally changed.

It was the fear that the border would require infrastructure, which would need to be protected, which was the focus of the security-related concerns. The PSNI's chief constable observed in February 2018, 'Anything that makes the police predictable in places where terrorists are active of course raises the threat and increases harm to my officers ... I think it would be poor use of police resources if we are going to have to protect physical infrastructure at the border' (Fenton, 2018: 241).

To counter this fear and to alleviate concerns that Brexit might undermine the peace process, it was the stated position of the British and Irish governments along with the EU, that there would not be a 'hard border', i.e. one which needed infrastructure. The problem was, however, if the UK left the single market and customs union, unless the EU and the UK could agree a free trade agreement which allowed for completely tariff-free movement of goods, it was hard to see how this could happen, given the need for checks on goods being transported from the UK to the EU (Republic of Ireland). A way needed to be found that would do several potentially incompatible things: maintain the economic integrity of the EU (and UK), allow trade and movement between the two parts of Ireland and between Northern Ireland and Britain in an unfettered manner, avoid the need for any infrastructure on the Northern Ireland border and ensure, as the unionists demanded, that Northern Ireland would not be treated differently from the rest of the United Kingdom.

The DUP's position was significantly strengthened in relation to Brexit as a result of the ill-judged decision by Theresa May to call an election in June 2017 in the expectation of strengthening her majority and, as a result, her negotiating position over Brexit with the EU. The outcome was in the other direction, as the Conservatives lost thirteen seats with Labour picking up thirty-two seats; the overall result was a hung parliament. In the Northern Ireland poll, the big winners were the DUP, which saw its Westminster haul increase from eight seats to ten. Sinn Féin also did well picking up three seats to see seven candidates elected. These gains were made at the expense of the UUP and the SDLP. The UUP lost the two seats it had managed to reclaim in 2015 and was once again without representation in Parliament, whilst the SDLP lost its three seats and, for the first time during the peace process period, had no MPs at Westminster. This meant that the two 'extreme' parties held all the Westminster seats except North Down, which the independent Lady Sylvia Hermon retained. However, as a result of Sinn Féin's traditional refusal to take its seats at Westminster, ten of the eleven voices from (Remain voting) Northern Ireland were pro-Brexit DUP MPs.

Since there was a hung Parliament, the DUP found their ten votes effectively meant they held the balance of power. In the aftermath of the election, the DUP agreed to go into a 'confidence and supply' arrangement with the Conservatives. In return for propping up May's minority government the DUP extracted an additional £1billion for Northern Ireland. The deal did attract criticism, some of which focused upon the nature of the DUP themselves, and whether given their socially conservative views on areas such as abortion and gay marriage they were a suitable party for the Conservatives to rely on. Others questioned whether it marked a departure from British neutrality in relation to Northern Ireland and was a threat to the GFA, or if, given their new-found relevance and influence in Westminster, the deal might make the DUP more reluctant to agree to restore power-sharing at Stormont?

Despite the confidence and supply agreement, as negotiations continued between the British government and the EU on the withdrawal deal, tensions became apparent between May's government, the DUP and some hard-line Brexiteers both inside and outside the British cabinet. In order to try and resolve the challenge of how to prevent a hard border on the island of Ireland if there was no free trade deal between the EU and the UK, the May government proposed 'the backstop'. This was effectively an insurance policy. The original proposal was for a Northern Ireland only backstop, whereby Northern Ireland would remain in the single market and the customs union (meaning that there would be no need for border checks or a hard border), whilst the rest of the UK could negotiate their own trade deals with non-EU states. This was vehemently rejected by the DUP as it treated Northern Ireland differently from the rest of the UK. As the plans emerged in December 2017 Arlene Foster issued a statement asserting, 'We have been very clear. Northern Ireland must leave the EU on the same terms as the rest of the United Kingdom. We will not accept any form of regulatory divergence which separates Northern Ireland economically or politically from the rest of the United Kingdom' (*Derry Journal*, 4 December 2017*)*. In addition, the DUP believed that the plans would cause trade problems between Northern Ireland and the rest of the UK. This became the infamous 'red line' for the DUP. A few months later Foster reiterated this graphically when she told the BBC, 'There's only ever been one red line and it is this, there cannot ever be a border down the Irish Sea, a differential between Northern Ireland and the rest of the UK … The red line is blood red – it's very red' (*BBC News*, 4 October 2018).

As a concession to the DUP, May had altered the British position on the backstop to stipulate that if there was not a trade deal, the whole of the UK would remain in close regulatory alignment with the EU. This was, however, unacceptable to many of the hard-line 'Brexiteers' in her party, particularly those associated with the Conservative backbench European Research Group (ERG). The Conservative politicians who opposed the backstop did so on the grounds that it might be used to 'trap' the UK in the customs union and prevent the UK negotiating its own trade deals, leading to 'Brexit in name only'. Due to their shared interest in blocking May's proposed deal, the DUP and the hard-line Brexiteers, such as the ERG and high-profile individuals who had quit May's Cabinet, including the former Foreign Secretary, Boris Johnson, and former Brexit Secretary, David Davis, combined to help defeat May's proposed Brexit bill on three occasions. On 24 May 2019 Theresa May announced she was resigning as Prime Minister once a successor was selected by the Conservative Party. This was the day after the Tories had lost fifteen of its nineteen European Parliament seats and finished fifth in the poll.

Such was the apparent importance of the DUP and the need for their endorsement of any proposed Brexit deal, that some members of the ERG appeared to make their support for any bill contingent on the DUP backing it. In March 2018 Jacob Rees-Mogg had stated that he was taking his lead on May's proposals from the DUP, 'My only condition is the position of the DUP. I won't abandon the DUP because I think they are the guardians of the union of the United Kingdom' (Reuters, 27 March 2019). This was not, however, a position that was to be maintained, and once May was replaced by Johnson as Prime Minister, the DUP's importance as guardians of the Union was apparently not as important after all and it was no longer imperative to stand beside them.

The debates over the backstop and what form Brexit should take highlighted strains beyond Westminster. The issue had notable implications for British–Irish relations. One clear benefit of the peace process had been significantly improved relations between the British and Irish states. Northern Ireland, which had for so long been a source of division between the two, had actually become something of a unifying factor. Since at least 1985 and the AIA, the two states had increasingly cooperated to seek to resolve the conflict, or at least to make it less violent and disruptive of their own 'domestic' politics. Brexit, however, had the potential to undermine this cooperation as, for the first time, the two states would be in a different relationship with the EU, and potentially have to take steps to regulate trade whilst working to different standards in key areas such as agriculture and food production. It had implications for all three strands that the peace process had largely resolved: north–south, east–west and within Northern Ireland. The Irish Taoiseach, Leo Varadkar, told an American audience, 'To me, Brexit is a threat to the Good Friday Agreement simply because it threatens to drive a wedge between Britain and Ireland, between Northern Ireland and the Republic of Ireland, and potentially between the two communities in Northern Ireland' (*Guardian*, 14 March 2018).

The insistence by the Irish government that they would not deal directly with the UK government over issues related to Brexit but would only work as part of the wider EU structures caused frustration in London (Connelly, 2018). The Tánaiste, Simon Coveney, was explicit on this approach, telling the Irish Parliament, 'I will address again the issue of having separate or secret negotiations. We believe it would be a strategic mistake to change in this regard. We are not having separate negotiations with the United Kingdom. That is the reason the European Union fully supports us and why we have had its support until now.' Ireland was highly critical of the suggestion that a solution could be to make the backstop temporary. Coveney stressed, 'Our position has been very clear on a time-limited backstop. If it's time-limited, and you can't answer the question what happens at the end of that time period, then it's not a backstop at all' (*BBC News*, 2 October 2019).

This Irish stance frustrated the newly installed Boris Johnson government in Downing Street. The journalist James Forsyth received communication from 'a contact in Number 10', which was widely reported to be Johnson's chief advisor, Dominic Cummings. The message suggested that the Irish were using their position on Brexit to trap Northern Ireland and undermine British attempts to achieve Brexit. 'It's clear he [Varadkar] wants to gamble on a second referendum and that he's encouraging [EU's Chief Negotiator] Barnier to stick to the line that the UK cannot leave the EU without leaving Northern Ireland behind. There are quite a few people in Paris and Berlin who would like to discuss our offer, but Merkel and Macron won't push Barnier unless Ireland says it wants to negotiate' (Forsyth, 2019).

Others, such as David Trimble, portrayed the threat to the GFA as coming not from Northern Ireland or Britain's stance, but from the Irish government itself, and he sought to issue a warning to Dublin for their own good, in rather condescending language. Trimble told the House of Lords that the good British–Irish relations that the GFA had achieved, is now being threatened and it's being threatened not by us in Northern Ireland but it's being threatened by Brussels and Dublin. Particularly folk in Dublin, they need to think again about who their friends really are. I know the EU are hinting to them or saying to them that they will look after them, but the EU does not have a good record in looking after small countries and I think Dublin should take that on board. (*Irish News*, 11 October 2018)

This somewhat brushed over questions of how well the small Northern Ireland had been 'looked after' by Britain, something which at times had been very much the focus of unionist criticism. Others, such as Lord Bew were critical of the Irish government's stance, and Britain's insufficiently robust response to it. He argued that the 'UK Government has allowed the Irish Government to weaponize the 1998 Good Friday Agreement in a way that prevents compromise on the backstop. This partial reading of the Good Friday Agreement risks generating further difficulties for the peace process in Northern Ireland.' For Bew the British had for too long been willing to concede too much influence to the Republic over Northern Ireland and the key was to insist that the backstop was temporary (Bew, 2019: 3).

The Irish government's argument was that Brexit was a threat not only to the GFA but also had serious implications for the Irish economy. The UK accounted for 13.9 per cent of Irish exports and 25.7 per cent of their imports, and 66 per cent of Irish exports to the EU went through the UK (House of Commons, NI Affairs Committee Report, March 2018; Connelly, 2018). The Irish government believed that they had a vested interest in ensuring that Brexit, which they had not wanted and had no responsibility for, did not undermine their economy or the peace process.

It was inevitable that Brexit would have an impact upon British–Irish relations, not least because at a practical level officials and ministers of the two states had met frequently at EU gatherings and at their margins. There were some signs that the Irish and British governments were aware of this potential problem and the two governments convened a meeting of the BIIC in July 2018, the first for over a decade. New structural arrangements would need to be utilised given that cooperation between the two states would continue to be an important part of underpinning peace and progress in Northern Ireland. Simon Coveney acknowledged this after the BIIC meeting.

British ministers and Irish ministers simply won't be meeting in the future in the same way and as frequently as we have done for more than four decades now and so we have instructed senior officials to come up with definitive proposals on how an Irish government and British government in the future can have structured and interactive dialogue at cabinet level in the same way that France and Germany have, for example. (*BBC News*, 25 June 2018)

But a related point was that whilst they might need to cooperate over Northern Ireland, there would potentially be future frictions between the UK and Irish Republic as a result of differing obligations that the EU membership may place on Dublin. The point was raised by former First Minister, Peter Robinson, in July 2018.

> There is no question that the two governments will continue to claim everlasting friendship and affection complete with copious commitments to maintaining their unique bond, but any lucid thinker will realise that the more remote the new relationship becomes the more it will involve a greater level of competition which will cause the gap to grow ... It is easy to imagine circumstances, in the future, where the Republic takes up cudgels alongside the other EU states which are hostile to the United Kingdom's interests. (*Belfast Telegraph*, 27 July 2018)

Whether there is the employment of cudgels, the point stands that there is likely to be disputes between the two states over issues in the future. Of course, disputes between the two states are hardly without precedent, but there are notable differences here. These will now take place in a different context and altered power dynamics. This is unlikely to be an insurmountable challenge, but it will take some adjustment.

The selection of Boris Johnson as the new Conservative leader and Prime Minister had a significant impact upon both Brexit and the DUP's influence at Westminster. Johnson had been one of those who was highly supportive of the DUP when their interests coincided, for example the desire to stop May's Brexit deal from passing through Parliament. Johnson had addressed the DUP's conference in November 2018 and told the faithful, 'Without you it is likely that the mighty engine of the UK economy would have stuttered and stalled. And indeed if it was not for you then there is a risk that the Union itself would have been placed in jeopardy.' He outlined his unbending opposition to the Brexit deal and the backstop that May was proposing. A central reason for his opposition was, apparently, the impact it would have on Northern Ireland.

> If we wanted to do free trade deals, if we wanted to cut tariffs or vary our regulation then we would have to leave Northern Ireland behind as an economic semi-colony of the EU and we would be damaging the fabric of the Union with regulatory checks and even customs controls between GB and NI – on top of those extra regulatory checks down the Irish Sea that are already envisaged in the Withdrawal Agreement. No British Conservative government could or should sign up to anything of the kind ...

He asserted that he hoped the DUP and Conservatives would continue to work together, 'as proud and passionate unionists backing our Union against all those who would seek to divide us' (*BBC News*, 24 November 2018).

Yet once he became Prime Minister, he would indeed seek to junk the backstop but his mechanism to do so would be by crossing Foster's 'blood red line' and effectively having the customs border in the Irish Sea, which the year before he had asserted to the DUP that no British government could sign up to.

The deal that Johnson got through Parliament in October 2019 meant that if there was no trade deal before the end of the transition period of December 2020, Northern Ireland would stay in the EU single market for goods but would legally remain in the UK customs area. The result was that goods moving from Britain to Northern Ireland would be subject to EU customs unless it was demonstrated that they were for use in Northern Ireland and not possibly moving onwards into the EU. This would need to be done before the goods arrived in Northern Ireland, given the commitment not to have infrastructure on the border with the Republic. There was also speculation that checks would similarly need to be made on goods passing from Northern Ireland into Britain. Johnson himself rejected these claims. Speaking to business people during the election campaign in Northern Ireland he assured them they 'absolutely would not' have to complete extra paperwork and if they were asked to do so they should phone him and 'and I will direct them to throw that form in the bin' (*Guardian*, 8 November 2019). Yet, six months later, the government admitted that the Northern Ireland Protocol (as the deal which replaced Theresa May's proposed backstop was known) necessitated additional checks on goods crossing the Irish Sea whether there was a trade deal or not, with plans for checks at Belfast, Warrenpoint and Larne ports (*Guardian*, 13 May 2020).

There was a time limit on the new arrangements. In the run-up to its four years of operation there would be a vote in the NIA to decide whether MLAs wanted the arrangements to persist. The DUP had argued this should be subject to the cross-community support mechanism, which would mean it needed the approval of 60 per cent of MLAs and at least 40 per cent of those designated as unionist and nationalist, which would effectively have given unionists a veto. However, the British government ruled that it only required the support of a simple majority of MLAs to be renewed for four years (if it reached the threshold of cross-community support it would be renewed for eight years). There was no necessity, however, to secure Northern Ireland's agreement to the Protocol before it was implemented. Despite the pledges that had come from the ERG and the Brexiteers in the Conservative Party for two years, they rowed in behind Johnson's deal over the vociferous rejection of it by the DUP. Sammy Wilson stated that Johnson, 'has not honoured the pledges he made to us. He sought flexibility from us, and the other side of the bargain was that he would ensure that Northern Ireland would come out on the same terms as the rest of the United Kingdom' (*Belfast*

Telegraph, 18 October 2019). From the DUP's perspective the deal was unacceptable on several fronts: Northern Ireland was treated differently from the rest of the UK; it left it closer aligned to the EU's (and therefore the Republic's) rules and regulations for goods; it potentially increased costs to businesses trading with not only the EU but also, crucially, within the UK market if they exported to Britain; and it would create the unacceptable 'border' in the Irish Sea. There was a further twist in September 2020 when the government announced that it was planning to pass legislation to enable it to opt out of parts of the Protocol. The NISS, told Parliament, 'Yes, this does break international law in a very specific and limited way. We're taking the powers to disapply the EU law concept of direct effect' (*Guardian*, 8 September 2020). The proposals were widely condemned (including by his four predecessors as Prime Minister) and led the EU to begin legal action against the British government (*BBC News*, 1 October 2020). So why did the Brexiteers and Johnson agree to a deal that was so unacceptable to the DUP? The reasons clearly lie in considerations that were primarily focused on Britain (if not England) rather than Northern Ireland. The new deal served to remove the necessity for Britain to potentially remain aligned to EU rules in the event of there not being an agreed trade deal with the UK. This was a driving consideration for those who demanded a complete break from the EU. The mechanism for the new Protocol to be renewed after four years enabled them to argue that they had made it temporary and subject to NIA agreement, but this did little to assuage the DUP, and the Northern Irish business community were angered by what they saw as a deal that would increase their costs. At one level it can be argued, as Tony Connelly noted, that 'History will show that Johnson had little choice. The EU was simply not going to tolerate a customs border on the island of Ireland. For both sides, the threat of "No Deal" undoubtedly introduced a sharp incentive to get a deal done' (*RTE News*, 14 December 2019). Negotiations were teetering on the precipice of Britain tumbling out of the EU without a deal and having to trade under WTO terms, something which would have had significant implications for all sides' economies. But the depth of the ideological support, from the hard-line British Brexiteer to the DUP's fears of Northern Ireland being treated differently to the rest of the Union, proved to be shallow. The DUP overplayed their hand in opposing what many believed was actually the better deal for Northern Ireland under May in the presumption that a Conservative government of a different hue would be more responsive to (and in line with) their preferences.

There were signs that key figures, such as Johnson himself, were not as committed to Northern Ireland or as concerned by its plight as the DUP, despite warm words, whilst May was trying to get her deal through Parliament. When Foreign Secretary, a recording of comments by Boris

Johnson emerged indicating his views of the importance of Northern Ireland to the Brexit debate. According to Johnson, concern over the border issue was 'pure millennium bug stuff'. The border was 'so small and there are so few firms that actually use the border regularly, it's just beyond belief that we're allowing the tail to wag the dog in this way' (*The Journal.ie*, 8 June 2018). This view was somewhat surprising and dismissive of the problems of dealing with a land border between what would be two different jurisdictions with potentially different regulations, tariff rates and customs rules that had no trade agreement. It was a border that was over 500 km long, had an estimated 208 crossing points and ran down the middle of at least eleven roads, including a motorway (*Irish Examiner*, 26 April 2018). Yet this clearly held few fears for Johnson who pointed out, 'There's no border between Islington or Camden and Westminster ... but when I was mayor of London we anaesthetically and invisibly took hundreds of millions of pounds from the accounts of people travelling between those two boroughs without any need for border checks whatever' (*BBC News*, 18 February 2018), a comparison which was greeted with some criticism and derision. The reality, which perhaps the DUP had not appreciated whilst being wooed by Johnson and the ERG, was that for those whose overriding priority was a complete break with the EU, the DUP were useful given the Westminster arithmetic and their opposition to May's soft version of Brexit. However, their priority was never the plight of Northern Ireland nor indeed the Union. Faced with the chance to support the DUP or secure a 'cleaner' Brexit, most had no hesitation in doing the latter. This misunderstanding of what constituted the threat to the Union was summed up well after Johnson's 'betrayal', by former UUP leader, Mike Nesbitt. He observed that for decades Unionism had seen Irish nationalism as the worry: 'it's actually English nationalism which is posing the existential threat to the future of the union' (*Guardian*, 13 December 2019). Once Johnson managed to get backing for his Brexit proposals, he secured agreement from Parliament for a general election in December 2019 and achieved a 78-seat majority; the DUP were no longer needed to prop up the new Conservative government.

Back to Stormont

The general election of 2019 threw up some significant results in Northern Ireland. As well as losing their influence at Westminster, the DUP lost two seats in Northern Ireland and saw their tally fall from the historic high of ten back to eight and their share of the vote fall by 5.4 per cent compared with the 2017 election (though they remained the largest party from Northern Ireland). One of those who lost their seat was the veteran DUP figure Nigel

Dodds, who lost his North Belfast seat to Sinn Féin. Despite this victory, Sinn Féin saw its own share of the vote drop by 6.7 per cent and lost the Foyle constituency to the SDLP leader, Colum Eastwood, who had stressed that he would be sitting at Westminster if elected, unlike his abstentionist Sinn Féin opponent, and secured an impressive 17,000 seat majority, leaving Sinn Féin with an unchanged seven MPs (and an unchanged abstentionist policy). The SDLP had a good election overall, seeing its share of the vote increase by 3.1 per cent and two MPs returned to Westminster. The UUP saw its vote rally slightly by 1.4 per cent but still failed to secure a seat. Along with the SDLP, the other big winner on the night was the Alliance Party. Against expectations they won in North Down, the seat that the independent unionist MP Sylvia Hermon had vacated, and one which the DUP had high hopes of winning. The result in North Down was significant. In 2017 the DUP's candidate was Alex Easton, who secured 38.1 per cent of the vote and lost out to Hermon by just 1,000 votes. In that election the APNI candidate was Stephen Parry, who secured just 9.3 per cent of the vote. In 2019 the DUP candidate, Alex Easton, was beaten by the APNI's Stephen Parry, who secured 45.2 per cent of the vote and a winning margin of almost three thousand (*Irish Times*, 13 December 2019). In terms of overall share of the vote, the APNI was the third largest party in Northern Ireland, outpolling both the SDLP and UUP. The 2019 general election was the first time ever that a majority of Northern Ireland's Westminster MPs had not been unionists, a difficult psychological barrier to cross (though practically irrelevant given that only three of the non-unionist MPs would take their seats).

Whilst the 2019 election results in Northern Ireland were something of a surprise, in some respects it continued a (short) trend that had been apparent in Northern Ireland in the immediate period. The APNI's strong showing at the Westminster election was not without precedent, given the party's performance in the local and European elections earlier in the year. In the local elections the party had secured fifty-three seats, which was a gain of twenty-one (the SDLP also saw its number of councillors rise, picking up seven; the DUP lost eight, Sinn Féin were unchanged, but the UUP lost thirteen). In the European election, Alliance's performance was even more impressive. The party secured 18.5 per cent, making it the third largest party in that election, and securing its leader, Naomi Long, a European Parliament seat for the first time in its history, at the expense of the UUP. By way of comparison, the APNI's candidate in the 2014 election had received 7.1 per cent of the first preference votes.

There are various possible reasons for the electoral results that occurred in 2019. Christopher Raymond has noted that the APNI performed most strongly amongst university-educated voters, and also in constituencies with more Protestant voters. As a result, he argued, it squeezed out the UUP (Raymond, 2019), though there is also evidence that a significant number of

DUP voters diverted to the Alliance in the general election, with a poll suggesting 18.6 per cent of Alliance voters had voted for the DUP in the previous Westminster vote (*Irish News*, 6 March 2020). It was also widely speculated that the surge in the Alliance (and potentially SDLP) vote might be a result of increasing frustration in Northern Ireland at the political stalemate. Northern Ireland faced serious problems by the end of 2019, not least in relation to its health service. In the run-up to the general election, nurses in Northern Ireland voted to go on strike for the first time ever. There were 3,000 unfilled nursing posts in Northern Ireland, and a 2017 pay deal at Westminster was not implemented in Northern Ireland due to a lack of a functioning executive (*BBC News*, 2 December 2019). A Nuffield Trust report suggested that waiting lists in Northern Ireland were the worst in the UK with 130,000 people waiting more than a year for an operation and 1 in 5 people in Northern Ireland were on a waiting list, compared with 1 in 12 in England and Scotland (*Irish News*, 30 January 2020). It was against this backdrop that the Alliance (and the SDLP), who had been highly critical of the DUP and Sinn Féin's failure to agree a return to Stormont, achieved their electoral progress.

In the weeks before the general election, the NISS, Julian Smith, reconvened all-party talks to restore Stormont and announced that failure to agree to return to devolved government by 13 January would result in fresh Assembly elections (*Belfast Telegraph*, 27 November 2019). The threat of new elections was taken to be aimed at the DUP and Sinn Féin, whose recent electoral performance might make them reticent to have Assembly elections in the short term. The talks in December and early January between the five main parties and the two governments achieved a breakthrough and an agreement to restore devolved government. The deal that was finally thrashed out saw some of the main issues which had divided the parties for three years, particularly those related to the parity of esteem agenda, 'fudged' in the 62-page agreement, *New Decade, New Approach*. The issue of an Irish Language Act, which had been an increasing source of division since the Sinn Féin and the SDLP thought it had been agreed at St Andrews was such a fudge. The long-standing nationalist demand for a stand-alone act did not materialise, but there was to be 'An Office of Identity and Cultural Expression to promote cultural pluralism and respect for diversity, build social cohesion and reconciliation and to celebrate and support all aspects of Northern Ireland's rich cultural and linguistic heritage'. On the Irish language specifically, there would be an Irish Language Commissioner 'to recognise, support, protect and enhance the development of the Irish language in Northern Ireland and to provide official recognition of the status of the Irish language in Northern Ireland'. The agreement also stated that any MLA could conduct business in Irish and a simultaneous translation service would be available. Similarly, a translation hub would be created to support the Executive's departments, public and local bodies for business conducted in Irish. However, to offset these proposals, the agreement also stated that there would be a separate Commissioner 'to enhance and develop the language, arts and literature associated with the Ulster Scots/Ulster British tradition in Northern Ireland' (*New Decade, New Approach*, 15–16).

Such a move allowed both nationalists and unionists to claim success. Nationalists had seen the Irish language's status acknowledged and steps to promote its use introduced, whilst unionists could claim to have prevented a stand-alone Irish Language Act, which prominent unionists, such as the Orange Order figure, Rev. Mervyn Gibson, had argued would be used to, 'further the Irish identity in a way that puts it above the British identity' (*The Irish Times*, 10 January 2020). The creation of a parallel Commissioner for Ulster Scots/Ulster British tradition enabled Arlene Foster to claim that these proposals were an 'entirely different construct' to what had previously been proposed. 'This is a deal that recognises that we live in a shared society, this is a deal that recognises that no one identity should be placed over another' (*Irish News*, 10 January 2020).

Other aspects of the agreement dealt with issues related to how Stormont functioned. The DUP agreed to changes in the petition of concern process which meant that it could no longer be triggered by a single party; the use of petitions should be reduced, and only invoked, 'in the most exceptional circumstances' (*New Decade, New Approach,* Annex B). There was also a commitment to change the rules so there could not be another long period without a functioning government. If a First or Deputy First Minister resigned and a replacement was not approved by the NIA, then the Secretary of State must call an election after 24 weeks if the situation was not resolved (*New Decade, New Approach*, 24).

The issue that had originally brought the Executive down, the refusal of Arlene Foster to stand aside whilst an inquiry was undertaken, was not a feature of the discussions. The RHI issue was referenced in the agreement, but only to note that the scheme would be closed and replaced by a more effective one; that the UK government would 'carefully review the findings' of the (ongoing) inquiry and the Executive would create a subcommittee to consider the findings of the RHI inquiry and propose reforms 'to rebuild public confidence' (*New Decade, New Approach*, 12). Annex D of the agreement was an outline of a possible programme for government and covered a wide range of policies and areas to be addressed. This suggested an ambitious and proactive period of government was intended (if it could be implemented). The British government also pledged a new financial package if the government was restored. There was to be specific support to help address the healthcare crisis; additional investment in public services; money for infrastructure problems and funds related to Northern Ireland's 'special circumstances', with ten areas specifically mentioned including mental health support, a culture and community fund, tackling deprivation and also paramilitarism (*New Decade, New Approach*, Annex A).

The restoration of the devolved institutions to Northern Ireland was a welcome outcome and one for which the NISS, Julian Smith, and his Irish counterpart, Simon Coveney, received a good deal of credit (*Guardian*, 13 January 2020); somewhat surprisingly, Smith was sacked in Johnson's reshuffle a month later. The speculation was that this was linked to his previous criticisms over Johnson's threat to leave the EU without a deal and/or proposals for a new body to examine previous murders in Northern Ireland and the fear that it might lead to further prosecutions of former security services members (discussed below) (*Financial Times*, 13 February 2020). The sacking drew strong criticism from many of the parties in Northern Ireland, and implicit criticism from the Irish government. The Taoiseach, Leo Varadkar, described Smith as 'one of Britain's finest politicians of our time' (*Irish News*, 13 February 2020).

The fact that the parties found a way round (if not necessarily a solution to) many of the issues that had so divided them for three years was a notable achievement. The potentially comprehensive programme for government might serve as the impetus for a period of government to address some of the key problems that Northern Ireland continued to face. However, an element of caution is needed. The poor relations that had been evident at the heart of the previous devolved government and the suspicion between the two main parties as to the bona fides and intention of the other were far from guaranteed not to be a feature of the reconfigured government. Primarily the same main players were at the top table and many of the same issues would be landing on that table over the coming years. Whilst the suggested programme of government indicated that key areas had been identified that needed to 'improve wellbeing for all', it is worth remembering that this was not the first Programme for Government that a Northern Ireland Executive had issued. The 2011 variant had run to 60 pages and the draft version issued in 2016 had been 112 pages long. It was not a lack of a proposed programme that was the problem in governing Northern Ireland, but an inability to successfully implement it.

The challenges ahead (and behind)

Overcoming identity

Several challenges faced the government of Northern Ireland post-2020. Although the government had been restored there remained significant question marks regarding how it would work and whether there would still be a tendency for the main parties to continue to focus on their own constituencies. The lack of cross-community voting in Northern Ireland has long made this a sensible choice for the parties, but this does not necessarily lead to coherent government. Whilst elections remain sectarian headcounts there is an incentive for the parties simply to deliver for 'their' community rather than address what Northern Ireland actually needs. (For an example of this, see Feargal Cochrane's discussion of the 'sectarian "carve up" between the main parties' in relation to the housing development of the former Girwood army barracks in North Belfast (Cochrane, 2013: 284–286).)

In many respects the constitutional question has been less pressing since the peace process and the GFA. Bertie Ahern stated in 2005 that the 'constitutional question is now settled. The use of violence to achieve a united Ireland is a thing of the past' (*Irish Times*, 4 November 2005). Yet this has not led to an apparent shift in voting across the communal divide. The 2019 Northern Ireland general election survey found that 0 per cent of Catholics voted for either the DUP or UUP whilst 0.2 per cent of Protestants said they voted for either Sinn Féin or the SDLP. The survey also illustrated the huge disparity between how followers of each religion viewed the leaders of the parties from across the communal divide (Tonge, *Belfast Telegraph*, 18 February 2020). As a result of these attitudes, attempts to reach across the divide by party leaders are unlikely to be fruitful. This was illustrated in the 2016–2017 period when the UUP leader Mike Nesbitt and the SDLP's Colum Eastwood made steps to form something of a partnership. Colum Eastwood addressed the 2016 UUP conference. There was an attempt to portray the decision by the two parties to go into opposition as a new departure in Northern Ireland's politics. As Nesbitt told the conference, 'Vote me, you get Colum. Vote Colum, you get me. Vote Colum and me, and you get a whole new middle ground politics, dedicated to making Northern Ireland work, whatever our motivations' (*The Newsletter*, 25 October 2016). In the run-up to the 2017 NIA election, Nesbitt caused some debate when he announced he would give his second preference to the SDLP over the DUP, a move that was unpopular with some in his party. In the election itself the UUP did not appear to benefit from the stance. Whilst the party's share of the vote was marginally up (0.29 per cent) it lost six seats (albeit in an Assembly that had reduced in size from 108 seats to 90). The result was perceived as disappointing and Nesbitt announced his resignation in its wake. The election itself came on the back of Sinn Féin's withdrawal from the Executive, a stance that served the party well as its vote rose 3.89 per cent and it only ended up with one seat fewer in the smaller Assembly (twenty-seven) than it had secured in the 2016 NIA election. The SDLP also performed well, returning the same number of MLAs (twelve) as it had the year before, despite the fewer number of seats on offer. The election overall was poor for Unionism as the DUP lost ten seats, leaving them with twenty-eight, and for the first time, Unionism did not hold the majority of seats in a devolved Northern Ireland legislature (CAIN).

The 2017 election was rather acrimonious as relations between the two largest parties were very strained with the RHI scandal and the collapse of the Assembly. Arlene Foster had attacked Sinn Féin in the run-up to the vote, stating she would never agree to an Irish Language Act, and noting that, given more people spoke Polish as their first language in Northern Ireland than Irish, maybe there should be a Polish Language Act instead. She said she had no intention of rewarding 'bad behaviour, and to capitulate to manufactured demands'. Her conclusion was that, 'If you feed a crocodile it will keep coming back for more' (*BBC News*, 6 February 2017). Nesbitt subsequently argued that it was this stance by Foster that had been the reason for the election result as it had energised Sinn Féin support. 'That crocodile comment really did serve as a lightning rod that incredibly energised nationalists and republicans. That was the real quote of the election and the real consequence was the result that put Sinn Féin just a seat behind the DUP … I did not energise a single one of those additional voters' (*BBC News*, 16 March 2017).

Speaking a few months after he left office, Nesbitt elaborated on the problem of the impact of identity on Assembly elections in Northern Ireland and how, in the privacy of the polling booths, these concerns trump considerations over more practical worries:

> For 364 days of the year people are interested in why the waiting lists are getting longer for the health service; why children are underachieving at school, but on polling day, it's about identity. It's about a recognition that 'them 'uns' will have a big strong bloc – from the unionist perspective it's going to be Sinn Féin – so therefore we must cancel it out by voting DUP, the biggest of the unionist parties. And I do mean cancel them out. Not so that together they will have a strength to deliver, it's to cancel them out.

He noted that there was some chance this might be less in play in Westminster or the EU elections, but not in Assembly elections (Mike Nesbitt, author interview, 11 September 2017). Electoral results and polling data would seem to support this suggestion. The electoral bounce that the APNI has experienced in recent times could be offered as a challenge to this. Similarly, one might highlight the fact that an increasing proportion of voters no longer fit the traditional, binary, unionist/nationalist identity pattern. In the most recent NILT survey in 2018, 50 per cent saw themselves as 'neither' unionist or nationalist, the highest it had ever been (and significantly up from the 33 per cent that saw themselves in these terms in 1998, when the GFA was concluded) (NILT, n.d.). However, this apparent weakening of ethnonational identities has not had a significant impact on voting patterns or outcomes. In the 2017 NIA election almost 85 per cent of voters supported a party that explicitly associated itself as either nationalist or unionist – DUP, Sinn Féin, UUP, SDLP, TUV and PUP. It remains to be seen whether there will be any significant electoral alteration in the coming years or if the current identity-based electoral allegiances can deliver more stable and less sectarian-focused government at Stormont.

Brexit and its impact on the Union

Another challenge for Northern Ireland is how to deal with Brexit. This is an issue which does cut across community lines. The restoration of the Assembly at least gave Northern Ireland a platform to consider the options and seek to devise the policies on how to cope with these challenges. Also the fact that the SDLP and APNI have representation at Westminster means that there is an alternative voice to the pro-Brexit DUP at Westminster (though given that the UK has now left the EU, the remain/leave axis is no longer the central one on which Brexit-related discussions will turn). Given the size of the Conservative majority at Westminster, the views of Northern Ireland's eleven attending MPs are unlikely to be key to what happens in negotiations with the EU or in the future direction of the UK's economic or political trajectory. The issue of what the customs and trade relations between Northern Ireland and the rest of the UK and Northern Ireland and the Republic/EU will be in the event of a failure of the UK to negotiate a comprehensive trade agreement with the EU has serious implications for Northern Ireland.

One (unintended but predictable) consequence of the Brexit vote has been that the issue of a united Ireland has moved further up the political agenda. In the immediate aftermath of the vote, Martin McGuinness called for a border poll on a united Ireland (*Independent*, 24 June 2016). The call was not widely taken up by other nationalists, with the SDLP's leader arguing that the time was not right, and a poll should only be called when it could be won (*Newsletter*, 27 June 2016). The Irish government similarly remained firmly opposed to a poll on unity, with Simon Coveney regularly arguing that a poll would only serve to be further division whilst the issue of Brexit was unresolved (*Irish Times*, 18 November 2019). However, on other occasions, Coveney had noted that 'I would like to see a united Ireland in my lifetime – if possible, in my political lifetime' (*Irish News*, 24 November 2017*)*. The Taoiseach, Leo Varadkar, had also acknowledged that Brexit had possible implications for the United Kingdom, noting, 'I think for unionists – and I take no pleasure in this – it also creates risks for the Union itself because it asks Scotland and Northern Ireland to leave the European Union even though the majority of people in both those countries voted not to do so' (*Guardian*, 14 March 2018). Polls by the Universities of Cardiff and Edinburgh suggested that for many in Britain, Brexit was far more of a priority than the peace process or Northern Ireland more generally. Around 75 per cent of Conservatives said they would support the collapse of the peace process as long as Brexit was delivered, as would 87 per cent of Leave voters within Northern Ireland (*Belfast Telegraph*, 8 October 2018). A follow-up survey in 2019 suggested 74 per cent of Leave voters in England and Wales and 59 per cent of Leave voters in Scotland believed the break-up of the Union would be acceptable to secure Brexit (Northern Ireland-specific data was not included in that poll) (Universities of Cardiff and Edinburgh, 2019).

Such comments and data showed that the issue of the constitutional status of Northern Ireland was back on the agenda post-2016 in a way it had not been post-1998. There is a danger in focusing upon such poll data in that it might implicitly suggest that the EU's role in the peace process was larger than it actually was. Although some have stressed the importance of the EU to the peace process (see for example, Hayward and Murphy, 2018; Tannam, 2018) the role of the EU on the peace process was less directly important than many of the other domestic factors discussed in this book. (On the limitations of the international dimension to the peace process see O'Kane (2007: 185–186) and O'Leary (2019: 293–294).) But this did not mean that the UK's departure from the EU would not have a notable impact on Northern Ireland and on British–Irish relations more widely, given that for the first time the two states would be in a different relationship to the main pan-European regional organisation. The extent to which Brexit would, however, make a united Ireland likely is open to debate. O'Leary in his *Treatise* clearly believes that Brexit has serious implications for Northern Ireland's place within the UK and suggests that the Irish government should consider creating a ministry for Irish unification. In part, O'Leary bases these arguments on economic considerations. He predicts that a future united Ireland would be economically more beneficial for both nationalists and unionists in Northern Ireland and also notes Brexit's threat to the Union, as a future Scottish independence referendum may well influence thoughts in Northern Ireland towards unity. O'Leary's arguments are interesting, not least because he discusses a possible future united Ireland in more complexity than simply presuming it will be a 32-county unity state; he considers the different forms unity may take (O'Leary, 2019: 312–324).

The debate over a united Ireland as a result of Brexit has widened with Seamus Mallon, in his autobiography, suggesting that the bar for unity needed to be set higher than 50 per cent+1, and arguing that nationalists needed to persuade a majority of unionists to back a united Ireland, something which drew sharp criticism from Gerry Adams, amongst others, on the grounds that it would entrench a unionist veto on unity (*Belfast Telegraph*,

23 May 2019). The issue has also prompted a debate within Unionism too. Peter Robinson caused a heated reaction when he suggested that Unionism should prepare for the possibility of Irish unity. Whilst asserting he did not believe that voters would elect to leave the UK, he argued that Unionism should consider the possibility. 'Walking towards that scenario without preparation is madness. I own my house; I don't believe it's going to be burnt down, but I still insure it' (*The Times*, 28 July 2018). The comments resulted in a spat with his erstwhile DUP colleague, Sammy Wilson, who accused Robinson of encouraging the republican cause by even considering the possibility of a vote. Robinson replied by suggesting that those who took such a line 'have not just buried their heads in the sand, only the soles of their feet are visible above the surface'. The former DUP leader asked, 'Do they not realise that the battle is raging? We live in a society divided by identity, so to some extent the Union is always under fire. But surely, nobody could be so chloroformed that they don't recognise that the opponents of the Union are charging our lines like seldom before. The battle for the Union is on' (*Newsletter*, 3 August 2018).

The re-emergence of the constitutional question due to Brexit led to renewed polling as to whether people would vote for a united Ireland. The results of the polls were somewhat mixed. In June 2018, a BBC poll suggested that 28 per cent stated that Brexit had made them more likely to vote for a united Ireland and suggested a border poll could be 'a close fought campaign' with 45 per cent voting to remain in the UK, 42.1 per cent voting for a united Ireland and 12.7 per cent undecided (it was this poll that was the backdrop to Robinson's comments) (*BBC News*, 8 June 2018). But the NILT survey was published shortly afterwards and suggested that 55 per cent would vote to remain in the UK and only 22 per cent would opt for a united Ireland (*BBC News*, 13 June 2018). A year later, Lord Ashcroft's poll had 45 per cent favouring the Union and 46 per cent opting for a united Ireland, and without 'don't knows' it was 51 per cent–49 per cent in favour of a united Ireland (*The Journal*, 11 September 2019). The most recent poll, the 2019 Northern Ireland general election survey, had a 52 per cent–29 per cent divide in favour of the Union and when the 'don't knows' were removed it was 65 per cent–35 per cent for the Union. But, as the head of the survey, Jon Tonge, noted, there was a 2 per cent rise in favour of a united Ireland since the 2017 election survey (*Belfast Telegraph*, 18 February 2020). Whilst this is not an exhaustive list of the polls on the issue over the last few years, it does illustrate that the data on unity vs union is far from clear or consistent. The polling methods used and the size of the sample perhaps account for the discrepancies; the academic polls of NILT tend to ask a larger sample and the Ashcroft poll was conducted online, whereas the election survey was face-to-face.

Overall, it is not entirely clear whether Northern Ireland's position in the UK is more precarious post-Brexit. It is also not clear whether, as O'Leary suggested, future economic prosperity might be a significant factor in increasing the likely willingness of unionists to back a united Ireland. O'Leary himself noted that the attempt by the former Irish Taoiseach, Garret FitzGerald, in the 1980s to launch a constitutional crusade that would change elements of the Republic of Ireland's society to make it more appealing to unionists, failed. He suggested that even an 'abundance of condoms, abortions, and divorces would not have altered unionists' attitudes toward either the AIA or Irish unity' (O'Leary, 2019: 105). O'Leary was right to point out that there was a complexity towards unionist rejection of a united Ireland and that it was related to more than practical considerations about the social differences between the two states. These also extend to economic factors, so it remains to be seen what, if any, impact an economic downturn in Northern Ireland after Brexit would have on unionist attitudes towards unity, and when. Also, the substantial proportion of Catholics who have traditionally been content to remain in the Union would need to be factored into any predictions of Irish unity. Catholic support for remaining in the Union has polled in the region of 40 per cent in most of the NILT surveys in recent years (NILT, n.d.).

The question of whether Brexit is likely to lead to a united Ireland is debatable. The available evidence does not really support such a conclusion. But there are some important points to note. Almost all surveys which have examined the issue do seem to suggest that Brexit makes unity more likely (even if it does not make it likely). What is also clear is that Brexit has put the constitutional question back on the agenda of Northern Ireland's political debate, a question that, although it had not necessarily been settled, had at least been muted by the peace process. If Brexit is not as traumatic or disruptive as many fear, perhaps as a result of a comprehensive trade deal between the UK and the EU, then the question may once again slide down the agenda, but at the time of writing this is far from certain. It may be the case that Brexit, an issue which was not related to the peace process or favoured by the majority of people in Northern Ireland, will remain one of the most destabilising challenges for Northern Ireland's political structures, economy and relations with neighbouring states for a considerable period to come.

Dealing with the past

The challenge of how to deal with the legacy of the violence suffered in Northern Ireland during the Troubles has remained a divisive issue throughout the peace process. Over 3,700 people were killed in the conflict and more than 40,000 people were estimated to have been injured (McKittrick et al., 1999). The majority of the murders never resulted in a successful prosecution. As a result of the violence and the failure of the families of most of those who died to see justice served, there are a great many people in Northern Ireland dealing with the grief and anger of having lost a loved one and with the ongoing physical, emotional and mental health issues related to their experiences. The question of how to deal with these problems has been on the political and societal agenda throughout the peace process. There have been several attempts to draw up a plan to deal with these legacy issues.

Whilst the GFA was being negotiated, the former NIO civil servant, Sir Kenneth Bloomfield, was leading a commission into the issues and published suggestions in his report *We Will Remember Them* in 1998. Subsequently Denis Bradley (who had been a member of the backchannel and later sat on the policing board in Northern Ireland), along with former Archbishop of Armagh, Robin Eames, were tasked to lead another commission 'The Consultative Group on the Past' which reported in January 2009. However, problems continued to bedevil dealing with the past and as a result the issue was also examined as part of the Haass–O'Sullivan process in 2013, the Stormont House Agreement of 2014, Fresh Start in 2015 and the talks that led to the restoration of devolved government in 2020.

What is striking is the overlap between the findings and proposals of many of these reports. Most of the reports have suggested the 'creation of an architecture' to enable people to 'contend with the past' (Haass and O'Sullivan, 2013: 20). Generally these have suggested a new mechanism to investigate unsolved murders, and in most recent variants free-standing from the PSNI; a mechanism for truth recovery, whereby those involved in violent acts can provide information which will be passed on to the family of the deceased (usually with some form of undertaking that any information provided in this way will not be used in future prosecutions); an oral archive project to recover stories of the Troubles period; continuing legacy inquests (related to killings by state forces during the Troubles); and a review and improvement of the services available to those who are suffering mentally and physically as a result of the Troubles. However, despite the general terrain having been well mapped, there has been comparatively little progress in building this architecture.

A number of difficulties have beset the attempts to make progress, many of which are related to political considerations rather than practical ones. Discussing the Eames–Bradley Report (as it became known) with the Northern Ireland Affairs Committee of the House of Commons, Denis Bradley observed that 'the past is the "third rail", as I think they describe it in American politics. If you touch it, you get burnt!' (Northern Ireland

Affairs Committee, 2009: EV9). One of the main reasons for the ability of the past to continue to burn in Northern Ireland is that it is still very much an issue in debates on the present and has implications for the future. Because there is no consensus on what happened during the Troubles and who was to blame, it has been difficult to agree how to deal with it. There is a tendency for groups in Northern Ireland to wish to see the focus of the debate on the past placed on the actions of the 'others' and so limit the criticism and damage that they themselves might receive for the events of the past. For unionists and the British government, the focus should be primarily on those who were most responsible for the killings in the period. Paramilitaries were responsible for 90 per cent of deaths during the Troubles and just under 60 per cent of all killings were carried out by republicans. The state accounted for around 10 per cent of all killings. This is a notably different situation to many other conflict zones and a reason why the experiences of how other states have dealt with their conflicts may not be that instructive for Northern Ireland. As Henry Patterson has pointed out,

> there is a major difference between Northern Ireland and the vast majority of international examples of truth recovery processes: whereas in the South African and Latin American examples, which are those most referred to by those making the case for a local truth commission, it was the state and its agents which were responsible for the vast majority of deaths and traumatic events, in Northern Ireland it was paramilitary organisations that killed the vast majority of victims. (*Newsletter*, 22 November 2016)

However, there is a perception in unionist and government circles that republicans are seeking to shift the focus primarily onto the killings by the state and wish to downplay the killings by those associated with their armed campaign. (For a critique of republican strategy see McGrattan (2018).) As a result, the issue of the past has become a political battleground rather than simply a question of law and order and investigating criminal activity or seeking to produce a definitive historical account of what happened when.

In some respects, this is a legacy of the peace process itself. The heavy strand of pragmatism and compromise that underpinned the approach from the outset meant that peace was, to a large extent, prioritised over justice. The difficult decisions taken in the early stages regarding dealing with republicans, issues such as decommissioning, prisoner releases and attempts to find a way to deal with the 'on the run' republicans might have aided the attempts to woo the IRA away from violence, but they blurred the line between political expediency and criminal justice.

This tension between pragmatism and justice has bedevilled attempts to deal with the past. Republicans have largely focused upon the legacy inquests and demands that state killings be investigated, whilst unionists have focused on demands that the far more numerous killings by non-state actors need far more attention. This view has, at times, been echoed by the British government. Theresa May commented in the House of Commons in 2018 on the 'unfair situation' that 'terrorists are not being investigated. Terrorists should be investigated and that is what the government want to see' (*Hansard*, 9 May 2018, vol. 640, col. 677).

In addition to the tension between pragmatism and justice, there is also a potential tension between justice and truth. The architecture that has been proposed has indicated routes for both to be addressed. The justice mechanism would be provided by the proposed Historical Investigations Unit, and the truth issue addressed by the suggested Independent Commission on Information Recovery (ICIR). The problem with the justice mechanism is that, given the time that has elapsed since many of the killings were committed (in some cases decades), it is highly unlikely that there will be many prosecutions. Peter Shirlow has pointed out that the Historical Enquiries Team, which was an earlier body tasked with reviewing the unsolved Troubles killings, only managed to secure two convictions and eleven prosecutions from its review of 1850 cases (Shirlow, 2018: 422). Although there will be some high-profile cases, such as the prosecution of 'Soldier F' for his part in the Bloody Sunday shootings in Derry in 1972, such cases will very much be the exception rather than the rule. Such cases have also prompted a campaign to introduce legislation that would grant immunity for prosecution for former soldiers and police officers, which has been heavily criticised by nationalists in Northern Ireland. Also, under the GFA, any individual associated with a paramilitary group that is convicted of a killing during the Troubles would serve a maximum of two years. Ostensibly to deal with these issues, in March 2020 the British government announced a new approach that would significantly reduce the number of outstanding cases that would be subject to a 'full-blown' investigation. A 'swift' assessment of such cases would be undertaken by a new independent body. If there was not believed to be 'new compelling evidence and a realistic prospect of a prosecution' then the cases would be closed. An NIO spokesperson noted that once 'cases have been considered there will be a legal bar on any future investigation occurring. This will end the cycle of reinvestigations for the families of victims and (army) veterans alike and a legal bar on future investigation of the cases.' The proposals attracted widespread criticism when they were announced in the nationalist community and from the Irish government (*BBC News*, 18 March 2020). Given the slow and divisive history so far on dealing with the past, it is unclear whether these proposals will either come to fruition or be more successful in dealing with the issues than those previously suggested for criminal investigations of Troubles-related killings.

If 'justice' is unlikely to be widely available, there is an argument that the mechanisms that are designed to secure truth for the families of those killed might at least help them come to terms with the past. Again, in this regard, the architecture looks, on paper, a possible route to help such people. There are, however, potential problems with the proposed mechanisms. The ICIR would require the cooperation of the individuals who carried out the killings and the organisations they were associated with. This is not certain to happen. Given the desire of organisations to continue to insulate themselves from blame, it is questionable how forthcoming such groups would be in their interaction with the ICIR and whether they would encourage/allow individuals to engage in the process. Individuals might also be reticent to come forward in case they could be identified, and their actions come to a wider knowledge. This point was made by Tom Roberts, a former UVF prisoner who now works with EPIC, a group helping loyalist ex-offenders. Roberts noted that, 'they'd be pointing at you walking down Royal Avenue; it's a very small society here ... People draw analogies sometimes with South Africa. South Africa is a vast country (nearly 60 million people), we're less than two million people, to a degree everyone knows who everyone is anyway' (Tom Roberts, author interview, 2019).

Dealing with the past in Northern Ireland has remained an area where too little progress has been made. The problems noted above, which is far from an exhaustive account, are serious challenges individually, and a rather formidable package collectively. One potential problem is that the approach to dealing with the past has largely been that all strands need to be implemented at the same time (to avoid any group securing the changes they wish to see but managing to block those they do not support). However, given the ongoing difficulty in achieving this, Northern Ireland continues to struggle with the legacy of the conflict, not least in practical areas related to mental health and trauma services. There appears to be near unanimity that the past needs to be dealt with, and comparatively little support for ideas of effectively drawing a line under it. There is a logic to such an approach, as outlined by David Rieff in his work *In Praise of Forgetting*. Rieff suggests that in certain situations, particularly in conflicts where there was no 'clear winner' it is not necessarily cathartic to attempt to deal with the past; 'there comes a time when the need to get to the truth should no longer be assumed to trump all other considerations' (Rieff, 2016: 86–89). (For an interesting counterargument, see Beiner (2018).) Whatever the logic of an attempt to seek a fundamentally different way to deal with the past or effectively seek to draw a line under it, support for such an approach does not appear to be gaining traction in Northern Ireland. The issues related to the legacy of the conflict will continue to cause problems for the governance of the present and have wider implications for both community relations in Northern

Ireland and the health of the population; this is likely to remain a significant challenge for the foreseeable future. If a period of sustained and successful government can be achieved in Northern Ireland, it may be the case that a more cooperative political atmosphere may lead to a breakthrough on the issues, allowing the architecture to be constructed. However, the record in this area in the past two decades is not encouraging.

Evaluating the peace process

The issue of how successful the peace process has been is not straightforward. Views on it are, perhaps, analogous to Gary Larson's *Far Side* cartoon 'The four basic personality types'. In the cartoon's first frame, a person is looking at a glass of milk and proclaims in an excited fashion, 'The glass is half full!'; in the second, someone looks unhappy whilst proclaiming, 'The glass is half empty'. A third person looks at the container anxiously and rambles, 'Half full ... No! Wait! Half empty! ... No half ... what was the question again?', whilst in the final frame an irate-looking man is protesting, 'Hey! I ordered a cheeseburger!' One can look at the peace process and come to similar conclusions. If you think that the peace process has led to a better, more peaceful and stable Northern Ireland, you can be personality type one. If you remain more concerned about the continuing instability and underlying divisions in contemporary Northern Ireland, you can position yourself as personality type two; torn between the two positions, you may be type three; and if you lament a Northern Ireland where terrorists are in government or alternatively a Northern Ireland where republicans abandoned a legitimate armed campaign to right an outrageous wrong, then you can be classed as personality type four.

The problem, of course, is that just like those gazing at the milk, evidence is available to support all the positions. However, many of the positions that are most critical of the outcomes of the peace process may be based on a misunderstanding of its purpose. As argued in the preceding chapters, the peace process was never primarily about achieving good governance in Northern Ireland, nor overcoming the divisions that have characterised the region and its politics for decades. Such outcomes were desirable and might have been hoped to emerge in the longer term, but the immediate objectives of the peace process were to end the violence, entice those who were pursuing an armed campaign into the political realm and create a more stable Northern Ireland. As a result, the primary focus of the peace process (and particularly of the two governments' approach to it) was the IRA. This was because they were the organisation who were, for most of the Troubles period, responsible for much of the violence and so the key to securing the objectives of peace. Whilst by 1993 the loyalists were killing more people than republicans, their violence was widely perceived to be a reactive response to republican violence, so if the IRA could be persuaded to give up their armed struggle, then there would be the foundation for securing the wider objectives of the peace process. If one examines the outcomes of the peace process in relation to the suggested objectives of the main actors outlined in Chapter 1, then a case can be made that it was successful.

For the British government, the suggested objectives were to uphold the principle of consent; significantly reduce if not eradicate the violence resulting from the conflict; restore devolved government to Northern Ireland; and prevent the issue from disrupting/impeding the wider British political agenda to a problematic degree. Writing at the start of the 2020s, these objectives have largely been achieved. Some have been met more fully than others, not least devolution has been more sporadic than British governments intended, and as a result Northern Ireland has periodically continued to impinge upon the wider British political agenda to an undesired degree. But, overall, the British government would see the peace process as a success.

For republicans it was suggested that the objectives at the outset of the peace process were to end the violence on relatively favourable terms, increase their influence and advance politically, and make progress towards a united Ireland. The peace process has enabled republicans to fulfil these objectives to a large degree. The terms under which the IRA ended its violence, as we have seen, were originally contested both by the IRA itself, given claims that the British were not fulfilling what they believed they had been 'offered' if the violence was halted, and by the British, given problems of 'permanence' and decommissioning. But after the stop/start problems of the ceasefires in the early years of the peace process, the ending of the violence did not split the movement to the extent that some had feared, or threatened, and the move certainly helped them to fulfil their second objective of increasing their influence and advancing politically. The electoral rise and influence of Sinn Féin has been one of the outcomes of the peace process that was not widely anticipated at its outset, and few were predicting their emergence as the largest nationalist party. This electoral rise has not just been confined to Northern Ireland, as evidenced by their topping the poll in terms of votes in the February 2020 general election in the Republic, where they came within one seat of being the largest party in the Dáil (*Guardian*, 11 February 2020). In 2020 the party was the second largest in terms of electoral representation north and south of the border, a position that was unimaginable at the start of the 1990s. In terms of making progress towards a united Ireland, as noted in the discussion above, the picture is far from clear. However, at the risk of being overly simplistic, it is probably fair to say that a united Ireland is more likely in the early 2020s than it was in the early

1990s. It is hard to argue that republicans were making more progress in the early 1990s towards uniting Ireland by militarily driving the British from Ireland, than they are politically in the early 2020s by purely political methods. This is not to argue that a united Ireland is inevitable or even likely, but it is to argue that they are closer to achieving this objective as a result of almost three decades of a peace process than they ever got as a result of three decades of armed conflict.

The objectives of the SDLP at the outset of the peace process period were identified as persuading the IRA to end their violence, embarking on progress that would lead to all-party talks and advance nationalism's interests. On the first two of these objectives the outcome of the peace process was in line with the SDLP's wishes. The SDLP was instrumental in creating and promoting the context in which the peace process emerged. The willingness of the SDLP, and particularly John Hume, to engage with Sinn Féin was an important factor in the movement of republicans towards their ceasefire. Hume's engagement helped bring them in from the cold and persuade them that an alternative to the armed struggle might be worth pursuing. The support that the party gave Sinn Féin, particularly in the early stages of the peace process, and their refusal to enter into devolved government without them in the years immediately after the GFA was important. On the objective of advancing nationalism's interest, in some terms it could be argued that this was met, as nationalism found itself with a guaranteed place at the heart of a devolved power-sharing government and the existence of an active equality agenda that sought to redress the problems that the SDLP believed persisted in Northern Ireland. The party was also, of course, committed to a united Ireland so the observations above on this point are also applicable to the SDLP (whose main difference from Sinn Féin was not in their aspiration for a united Ireland, but in their fundamental and consistent rejection of the use of violence as a legitimate tool to achieve it). What the peace process did not ultimately do, however, was advance the interests of the SDLP as a political party. Their decline as Sinn Féin grew, was something that, again, was not anticipated in the early days of the peace process. It remains to be seen whether the improved results in the recent elections mark a sustainable upsurge in the party's fortunes, but the party has paid a heavy price for the risks they took to help create and advance the peace process.

The picture for unionists is slightly less clear-cut. The suggested objectives for Unionism at the outset of the peace process were to protect the Union, limit the role of Dublin in Northern Irish affairs, secure devolved government and, for the UUP, limit Sinn Féin's role and bring about the end of the IRA campaign, and for the DUP, prevent republicans' participation in government. On the overriding objective of protecting the Union, a case can be made that Unionism has been successful. The debate regarding the likelihood of a united Ireland emerging has been rehearsed already in this chapter, but the fact is that Northern Ireland has remained in the United Kingdom and recent polling indicates it is likely to do so for the foreseeable future. The changed context, and potentially increased threat to the Union which Brexit has created is clearly not related specifically to the peace process, so it would be unfair to evaluate this issue when discussing whether Unionism has been successful in meeting its objectives. On limiting the role for Dublin in Northern Ireland, again this has been something of a mixed bag for Unionism. Increased Irish 'interference' in Northern Ireland has been something that has sporadically been used as a threat against them during the peace process, most obviously as part of Hain's Plan B. But with devolution once again restored, the threat has, to an extent, ebbed again. The peace process and the GFA negotiations did necessitate unionists agreeing to the institutionalised role for the Irish government in certain areas, notably the NSMC, but this was preferable for unionists to what they faced under the AIA, where they believed that Dublin had a bigger influence on events in Northern Ireland than the elected leaders of Unionism. The GFA also resulted in the claim on Northern Ireland being removed from the Irish constitution. Thus, the objective of limiting the role of the Irish Republic can be seen as a success. Similarly, in terms of the objective of achieving the end of the IRA's campaign and therefore the threat posed by the IRA, this was achieved. However, the area of minimising/preventing Sinn Féin's role is obviously one that was not achieved. The UUP could not prevent Sinn Féin's entry into government before the decommissioning of the IRA's weapons, and far from preventing them from sitting in government, the DUP ended up sharing power with Sinn Féin and jointly running the Office of the First Minister and Deputy First Minister with the party. Of course, the defence offered can be that Sinn Féin and the republican movement were very different by 2007 than they had been at the outset of the peace process. Again, though, the outcome was not one that many anticipated whilst Ian Paisley was consistently pledging never to share power with terrorists and berated David Trimble for doing so. Similarly to the SDLP, the UUP as a party paid a heavy price for the risks it took during the peace process.

Loyalists' objectives were identified as defending the Union (by violence if necessary) and developing a political analysis and voice which better represented their community. In relation to the objective of defending the Union, the observations noted above in relation to Unionism would also apply to loyalists. However, loyalists would also claim that their willingness to use violence was instrumental in protecting the Union and also a contributory factor in the IRA's decision to move away from the 'armed struggle'. In relation to the objective of developing political analysis and a voice, in the early period of the peace process they had notable success in this regard.

The parties associated with the UFF and the UDA/UFF, the PUP and UDP, played an important role in the negotiations that led to the GFA and secured representation in the first NIA. The PUP was more successful in terms of election to the NIA subsequently, and managed to keep a presence in the Assembly until 2011 and have managed to maintain a presence at local council level (notably in Belfast) since. However, the feuding that occurred within loyalism during the peace process was disruptive and the small loyalist political parties have also been susceptible to the ethnic outbidding practised by the DUP, which has become the main party in the working-class urban areas where loyalism is at its strongest.

The Republic of Ireland can also claim to have largely met its objectives as a result of the peace process. The desire to reduce violence, improve the plight of nationalists living there and get them to settle down in Northern Ireland were largely achieved. The AIA was superseded but, as discussed above, an Irish dimension was a notable feature of the GFA. Similarly for the British, although the frequent crises did mean that the Irish government had to remain engaged in Northern Ireland, the peace process reduced its ability to impact on the politics of the South (at least until Brexit).

A desirable outcome?

On its own terms, the peace process has been largely successful. The Northern Ireland of the 2020s is fundamentally different from that of the 1990s. However, in some respects, although the significant political violence that defined the Troubles period is, thankfully, a thing of the past, some of the underlying problems that faced the region in the 1990s are still apparent today. The societal divisions and tensions along ethnonational lines that were the backdrop to the origin, development and longevity of the Troubles have not been eradicated. However, the political inequities and overt discrimination that accompanied its origin and development have been. Although the peace process can be argued to have been successful in terms of what it sought to achieve, this is not the same as arguing that what it achieved was a necessarily desirable, let alone an ideal, outcome. The sectarian basis of much of Northern Ireland's society and politics remains problematic. For some, it is the ethnonational basis and focus of the peace process that both explains, and contributed to, the form of divided peace that the process has resulted in. Cillian McGrattan has critiqued accounts which perpetuate 'the myth that the Northern Ireland conflict was ethnic' and has argued that 'even in an ethnically divided society such as Northern Ireland, ethnic divisions need not be the driving force behind political change and outcome' (McGrattan, 2010: 187, 185). The result of the peace process in Northern Ireland has indeed been to entrench ethnonational divisions by making them the basis of the governing structure. A process that was originally expected to result in the 'moderate' centre being the primary beneficiaries and drivers of the new devolved structures, concluded with those parties being marginalised. The victors of the peace process were the parties who had objected most strongly to the proposed new institutional structures. Those who claimed the GFA as a consociational success heralded the system as merely reflecting the realities of the divisions that were in place in Northern Ireland and argued that the success of the 'extreme' parties did not necessarily mean that politics would become more extreme. These parties might not act in the way that outbidding theory would predict. 'Ethnic tribune' parties, they argued, may be elected because voters want 'ethnonational interests protected' but may actually support more moderate policy positions (Mitchell et al., 2009: 416–417). However, the instability of Northern Ireland politics and the behaviour of the parties in government during the peace process does not, so far, support this analysis. (For a critique of the consociational underpinning of the peace process see Taylor (2006) and Dixon (2011).)

It remains to be seen whether the ethnonational character and behaviour of the governing parties in Northern Ireland can be changed without alterations to the structures of the agreements and institutional procedures, such as the rules on communal identification and voting in the Assembly. This appears unlikely in the foreseeable future. Whether the recent rise in the non-sectarian Alliance Party continues or has any impact on the way government is run in Northern Ireland, and the perennial problem of mistrust between the main actors in government, may be important.

There are, however, good reasons for the decisions that were made during the peace process, and it needs to be borne in mind that the outcome was far more a result of ad hoc decision-making than the implementation of a detailed plan. In hindsight, as previously discussed, some of the decisions appear questionable or ill-advised, but in many cases they were taken during crises and with imperfect information available. The peace process was messy, at times chaotic, and its outcome has left Northern Ireland with significant challenges, which it is not entirely clear that it is best equipped to meet. But it has also left Northern Ireland far more peaceful and more equitably governed and egalitarian than it once was. The glass is at least half full.

References

Agreements and reports

Anglo–Irish Agreement (AIA) (15 November 1985)
Belfast Agreement/Good Friday Agreement (GFA) (10 April 1998)
Common Sense. Northern Ireland – An Agreed Process (1987)
Downing Street Declaration (DSD) (15 December 1993)
New Decade, New Approach (January 2020)
Northern Ireland Affairs Committee (2009)
Paramilitary Groups in Northern Ireland Report (2015)
St Andrews Agreement (STAA) (October 2006)
The Task Force Report. An End to Drift (1987)
TUAS document (1994)
Twelfth Report of the Independent Monitoring Commission (2006)

Books, journals and websites

Adams, G. (2003) *Hope and History: Making Peace in Ireland* (Dingle: Brandon).
Ahern, B. (2009) *The Autobiography* (London: Hutchinson).
Alonso, R. (2007) *The IRA and the Armed Struggle* (Abingdon: Routledge).
Aughey, A. and C. Gormley-Heenan (2011) *The Anglo-Irish Agreement: Re-thinking its Legacy* (Manchester: Manchester University Press).
BBC News (2019) Timeline: Renewable Heat Incentive Scandal. Available at: www.bbc.co.uk/news/uk-northern-ireland-38301428 (accessed 5 October 2020).
Bean, K. (2007) *The New Politics of Sinn Féin* (Liverpool: Liverpool University Press).
Beiner, G. (2018) *Forgetful Remembrance* (Oxford: Oxford University Press).
Bew, P. (2007) *Ireland, The Politics of Enmity, 1789–2008* (Oxford: Oxford University Press).
Bew, P. (2019) *The Backstop Paralysis: A Way Out* (London: Policy Exchange).
Bew, J. and M. Frampton (2012) 'Debating the "Stalemate": A Response to Dr Dixon', *The Political Quarterly* 83 (2): 277–282.
Bew, J., M. Frampton and I. Gurruchaga (2009) *Talking to Terrorists: Making Peace in Northern Ireland and the Basque Country* (London: Hurst).
Bew, P. and G. Gillespie (1996) *The Northern Ireland Peace Process 1993–1996* (London: Serif).

Bew, P. and G. Gillespie (1999) *Northern Ireland. A Chronology of the Troubles, 1968–1999* (Dublin: Gill and Macmillan).

Blair, T. (2011) *The Journey* (London: Arrow Books).

Bloomfield, K. (1998) *We Will Remember Them*, Report of the Northern Ireland Victims Commissioner (Belfast: The Stationery Office, Northern Ireland).

Brown, G. (2017) *My Life, Our Times* (London: The Bodley Head).

CAIN (Conflict Archive on the Internet) (n.d.) Available at: https://cain.ulster.ac.uk/ (accessed 5 October 2020).

Cameron, D. (2019) *For the Record* (London: William Collins).

Campbell, A. (2011) *Power and the People, 1997–1999* (London: Arrow Books).

Campbell, A. (2013) *The Irish Diaries (1994–2003)* (Dublin: The Lilliput Press).

Clancy, M. (2010) *Peace Without Consensus: Power Sharing Politics in Northern Ireland* (Dublin: Irish Academic Press).

Cochrane, F. (2013) *Northern Ireland: The Reluctant Peace* (Padstow: Yale University Press).

Connelly, T. (2018) *Brexit and Ireland: The Dangers and Opportunities and the Inside Story of the Irish Response* (London: Penguin).

Cooke, D. (2015) 'The Joint Declaration and Memory'. In G. Spencer (ed.), *The British and Peace in Northern Ireland* (Cambridge: Cambridge University Press), pp. 147–176.

Cusack, J. and H. McDonald (2000) *UVF* (Dublin: Poolbeg Press).

Dingley, J. (ed.) (2009) *Combating Terrorism in Northern Ireland* (Abingdon: Routledge).

Dixon, P. (2008) *Northern Ireland: the Politics of War and Peace* (2nd edition) (Hampshire: Palgrave Macmillan).

Dixon, P. (2011) 'Is Consociational Theory the Answer to Global Conflict? From the Netherlands to Northern Ireland and Iraq', *Political Studies Review* 9 (3): 309–322.

Dixon, P. (2012) 'Was the IRA Defeated? Neo-Conservative Propaganda as History', *The Journal of Imperial and Commonwealth History* 40 (2): 303–320.

Dixon, P. (2013) 'An Honourable Deception? The Labour Government, the Good Friday Agreement and the Northern Ireland Peace Process', *British Politics* 8 (2): 108–137.

Dixon, P. (2019) *Performing the Northern Ireland Peace Process* (Basingstoke: Palgrave).

Duignan, S (1995) *One Spin on the Merry-Go-Round* (Dublin: Blackwater Press).

Edwards, A. (2011) 'Deterrence, Coercion and Brute Force in Asymmetric Conflict: The Role of the Military Instrument in Resolving the Northern Ireland "Troubles"', *Dynamics of Asymmetric Conflict* 4 (3): 1–16.

Edwards, A. (2017) *UVF: Behind the Mask* (Newbridge: Merrion Press).

Elliot, M. (ed.) (2007) *The Long Road to Peace in Northern Ireland* (Liverpool: Liverpool University Press).

English, R. (2004) *Armed Struggle: The History of the IRA* (London: Pan Macmillan).

Farren, S. (2010) *THE SDLP: The Struggle for Agreement in Northern Ireland, 1970–2000* (Dublin: Four Courts Press).

Fenton, S. (2018) *The Good Friday Agreement* (London: Biteback Publishing).

Finlay, F. (1998) *Snakes and Ladders* (Dublin: New Island Books).

Forsyth, J. (2019) 'How Number 10 view the state of negotiations', *Spectator* (www.spectator.co.uk/article/how-number-10-view-the-state-of-the-negotiations, accessed 5 October 2020).

Frampton, M. (2010) *Legion of the Rearguard: Dissident Irish Republicanism* (Dublin: Irish Academic Press).

Garry, J. (2016) 'The EU Referendum Vote in Northern Ireland: Implications for our Understanding of Citizens' Political Views and Behaviour'. Available at: https://kess.org.uk/2018/11/19/the-eu-referendum-vote-in-northern-ireland-implications-for-our-understanding-of-citizens-political-views-and-behaviour/ (accessed 5 October 2020).

Garry, J. (2018) 'Public Opinion in Northern Ireland. Brexit and the Border', *UK in a Changing Europe*, 12 February 2018. Available at: http://ukandeu.ac.uk/public-opinion-in-northern-ireland-brexit-and-the-border/ (accessed 15 February 2018).

Godson, D. (2004) *Himself Alone* (London: Harper Collins).

Gordon, D. (2009) *The Fall of the House of Paisley* (Dublin: Gill and Macmillan).

Guelke, A. (2010) 'A Consociational Democracy or Anglo–Irish Conflict Management?'. In A. Lecours and L. Moreno (eds), *Nationalism and Democracy: Dichotomies, Complementaries, Oppositions* (Abingdon: Routledge), pp. 247–261.

Haass, R. and M. O'Sullivan (2013) *Proposed Agreement 31 December 2013*. Available at: www.northernireland.gov.uk/publications/haass-report-proposed-agreement (accessed 21 June 2014).

Hain, P. (2012) *Outside In* (London: Biteback Publishing).

Haughey, S. (2019) 'Worth Restoring? Taking Stock of the Northern Ireland Assembly', *The Political Quarterly* 90 (4): 705–712.

Hayward, K. and M. Murphy (2018) 'The EU's Influence on the Peace Process and Agreement in Northern Ireland in Light of Brexit', *Ethnopolitics* 17 (3): 276–291.

Hazelton, W. (2000) 'Encouragement from the Sideline: Clinton's Role in the Good Friday Agreement', *Irish Studies in International Affairs* 11: 103–119.

Hearty, K. (2015) 'The Great Awakening? The Belfast Flag Protests and Protestant/Unionist/Loyalist Counter-memory in Northern Ireland', *Irish Political Studies* 30 (2): 157–177.

Heatley, C. (2004) *Interface: Flashpoints in Northern Ireland* (Belfast: Lagan Books). (Chapter on Holy Cross dispute). Available at: https://cain.ulster.ac.uk/issues/interface/docs/heatley04.htm (accessed 9 September 2017).

Hennessey, T. (2000) *The Northern Ireland Peace Process* (Dublin: Gill and Macmillan).

Hennessey, T., M. Braniff, J. McAuley, J. Tonge and S. Whiting (2019) *The Ulster Unionist Party: Country Before Party?* (Oxford: Oxford University Press).

Leahy, T. (2020) *The Intelligence War against the IRA* (Cambridge: Cambridge University Press).

Major, J. (2000) *The Autobiography* (Hammersmith: Harper Collins).

Mallie, E. and D. McKittrick (1996) *The Fight for Peace* (Abingdon: Hodder and Stoughton).

Mallie, E. and D. McKittrick (2002) *Endgame in Ireland* (London: Coronet Books).

Mallon, S. (2019) *A Shared Homeplace* (Kindle edition: The Lilliput Press).

Mandelson, P. (2010) *The Third Man* (London: The Harper Press).

Matchett, W. (2016) *Secret Victory: The Intelligence War that Beat the IRA* (Belfast: Matchett).

McBride, S. (2019) *Burned: The Inside Story of the 'Cash-for-Ash' Scandal and Northern Ireland's Secretive New Elite* (Kindle edition, Newbridge: Merrion Press).

McGarry, J. (2000) 'Police Reform in Northern Ireland', *Irish Political Studies* 15 (1): 173–182.

McGlinchey, M. (2019) *Unfinished Business: The Politics of 'Dissident' Irish Republicanism* (Manchester: Manchester University Press).

McGrattan, C. (2010) *Northern Ireland 1969–2008: The Politics of Entrenchment* (Basingstoke: Palgrave Macmillan).

McGrattan, C. (2018) '"The Possibilities are Endless" Republican Strategy to Deal with the Past and Transitional Justice in Northern Ireland'. In J. Dudgeon (ed.), *Legacy: What To Do about the Past in Northern Ireland?* (Belfast: Belfast Press), pp. 42–64.

McGrattan, C. and D. McCann (eds) (2017) *Sunningdale, the Ulster Workers' Council Strike and the Struggle for Democracy in Northern Ireland* (Manchester: Manchester University Press).

McKearney, T. (2011) *The Provisional IRA* (London: Pluto).

McKittrick D., S. Kelters, B. Feeney and C. Thornton (1999) *Lost Lives* (Edinburgh: Mainstream Publishing).

McLoughlin, P. J. (2010) *John Hume and the Revision of Irish Nationalism* (Manchester: Manchester University Press).

Millar, F. (2004) *David Trimble: The Price of Peace* (Dublin: The Liffey Press).

Millar, F. (2009) *Northern Ireland: A Triumph of Politics* (Dublin: IAP).

Ministry of Defence (2007) *Operation Banner: an analysis of military operations in Northern Ireland.* Available at: https://www.vilaweb.cat/media/attach/vwedts/docs/op_banner_analysis_released.pdf (accessed 5 October 2020).

Mitchell, D. (2015) *Politics and Peace in Northern Ireland* (Manchester: Manchester University Press).

Mitchell, G. (1999) *Making Peace* (London: William Heinemann).

Mitchell, P., G. Evans and B. O'Leary (2009) 'Extremist Outbidding in Ethnic Party Systems is Not Inevitable: Tribune Parties in Northern Ireland', *Political Studies* 57: 397–421.

Mitchell Report (1996) Available at: https://cain.ulster.ac.uk/events/peace/docs/gm24196.htm (accessed 5 October 2020).

Moloney, E. (2002) *Secret History of the IRA* (London: Penguin).

Moloney, E. (2008) *Paisley: From Demagogue to Democrat?* (Dublin: Poolbeg Press).

Moloney, E. (2017) 'An RUC Special Branch View of the Peace Process', *The Broken Elbow*, 21 May 2017. Available at: https://thebrokenelbow.com/2017/05/21/an-ruc-special-branch-view-of-the-peace-process/ (accessed 5 October 2020).

Morrison, D. (1999) *Then the Walls Came Down: A Prison Journal* (Dublin: Mercier Press).

Mowlam, M. (2003) *Momentum* (London: Hodder and Stoughton).

Murray, G. and J. Tonge (2005) *Sinn Féin and the SDLP* (Dublin: The O'Brien Press).

NILT (Northern Ireland Life and Times survey) (n.d.) Available at: www.ark.ac.uk/nilt/results/polatt.html (accessed 5 October 2020).

Neumann, P. (2003) *Britain's Long War* (London: Palgrave).

O'Cleary, C. (1999) *Ireland in Quotes* (Dublin: The O'Brien Press).

Ó Dochartaigh, N. (2009) '"The Contact": Understanding a Communication Channel between the British Government and the IRA'. In J. J. Popiolkowski and N. J. Cull (eds), *Public Diplomacy, Cultural Interventions and The Peace Process in Northern Ireland* (Los Angeles, CA: Figueroa Press), pp. 57–72.

Ó Dochartaigh, N. (2011) '"Together in the Middle": Back-Channel Negotiation in the Irish Peace Process', *Journal of Peace Research* 48 (6): 767–780.

Ó Dochartaigh, N. (2013) 'The Longest Negotiation: British Policy, IRA Strategy and the Making of the Northern Ireland Peace Settlement', *Political Studies*, Online Version, 24 November 2013.

O'Donnell, C. (2007) *Fianna Fáil, Irish Republicanism and the Northern Ireland Troubles 1968–2005* (Dublin: Irish Academic Press).

O'Kane, E. (2006) 'When Can Conflicts be Resolved? A Critique of Ripeness', *Civil Wars* 8 (3/4): 268–284.

O'Kane, E. (2007) *Britain, Ireland and Northern Ireland since 1980* (Abingdon: Routledge).

O'Kane, E. (2010) 'Learning from Northern Ireland? The Uses and Abuses of the Irish Model', *British Journal of Politics and International Relations* 12 (2): 239–256.

O'Kane, E. (2015) 'Talking to the Enemy? The Role of the Back-Channel in the Development of the Northern Ireland Peace Process', *Contemporary British History* 29 (3): 401–429.

O'Leary, B. (2019) *A Treatise on Northern Ireland Vol III: Consociation and Confederation* (Oxford: Oxford University Press).

Patten Report (1999) *A New Beginning: Policing in Northern Ireland. The Report of the Independent Commission on Policing for Northern Ireland* (HMSO). Available at: https://cain.ulster.ac.uk/issues/police/patten/patten99.pdf (accessed 5 October 2020).

Patterson, H. (1997) *The Politics of Illusion* (London: Serif).

Patterson, H. (2011) 'Republicanism and the Peace Process: The Temptations of Teleology'. In A. Aughey and C. Gormley-Heenan (eds), *The Anglo–Irish Agreement. Rethinking its Legacy* (Manchester: Manchester University Press), pp. 94–108.

Patterson, H. and E. Kaufmann (2007) *Unionism and Orangeism in Northern Ireland Since 1945* (Manchester: Manchester University Press).

Powell, J. (2009) *Great Hatred, Little Room: Making Peace in Northern Ireland* (London: Vintage Books).

Raymond, C. (2019) 'Alliance Ends 2019 as the Third Largest Party', *Queen's Policy Engagement*, 20 December 2019. Available at: http://qpol.qub.ac.uk/alliance-ends-2019-as-the-third-largest-party/ (accessed 4 January 2020).

Reiss, M. B. (2010) *Negotiation with Evil: When to Talk to Terrorists* (New York: Open Road Media).

Reynolds, A. (2010) *My Autobiography* (Dublin: Transworld Ireland).

Rieff, D. (2016) *In Praise of Forgetting* (London: Yale University Press).

Rowan, B. (2008) *How the Peace Was Won* (Dublin: Gill and Macmillan).

Seitz, R. (1998) *Over Here* (London: Phoenix).

Sharrock D. and M. Devenport (1997) *Man of War, Man of Peace?* (London: Pan Books).

Shirlow, P. (2012) *The End of Ulster Loyalism?* (Manchester: Manchester University Press).

Shirlow, P. (2018) 'Truth Friction in Northern Ireland: Caught between Apologia and Humiliation', *Parliamentary Affairs* 71: 417–437.

Sinn Féin (1988) *The Sinn Féin/SDLP Talks January–September* (Dublin: Sinn Féin).

Sinn Féin (1993) *Setting the Record Straight* (Dublin: Sinn Féin).

Smith, M. L. R. (1997) *Fighting for Ireland* (London: Routledge).

Spencer, G. (2015) *From Armed Struggle to Political Struggle* (London: Bloomsbury).

Spencer, G. (2020) *Inside Accounts, Volume II* (Manchester: Manchester University Press).

Swift, J. (2020) 'The Long Road to Peace', *Dublin Review of Books* 131 (March).

Tannam, E. (2018) 'Brexit and British–Irish Relations', *RUSI Journal* 163 (3): 4–9.

Taylor, P. (1998) *Provos: The IRA and Sinn Féin* (London: Bloomsbury).

Taylor, P. (1999) *Loyalists* (London: Bloomsbury).

Taylor, R. (2006) 'The Belfast Agreement and the Politics of Consociationalism: A Critique' *The Political Quarterly* 77 (2): 217–226.

Thatcher, M. (1995) *The Downing Street Years* (London: Harper Collins).

Tonge, J., P. Shirlow and J. McAuley (2011) 'So Why Did the Guns Fall Silent? How Interplay, not Stalemate, Explains the Northern Ireland Peace Process', *Irish Political Studies* 26 (1): 1–18.

Tonge, J., M. Braniff, T. Hennessey, J. McAuley and S. Whiting (2014) *The Democratic Unionist Party: From Protest to Power* (Oxford: Oxford University Press).

UK Research and Innvation (n.d.) Available at: www.ukri.org (accessed 5 October 2020).

Universities of Cardiff and Edinburgh (2019) Available at: www.cardiff.ac.uk/news/view/1709008-future-of-england-survey-reveals-public-attitudes-towards-brexit-and-the-union (accessed 5 October 2020).

Walsh, D. (2015) 'Northern Ireland and the Independent Parades Commission: Delegation and Legitimacy', *Irish Political Studies* 30 (1): 20–40.

Whitelaw, W. (1989) *The Whitelaw Memoirs* (London: The Aurum Press).

Zartman, I. W. (2000) 'Ripeness: The Hurting Stalemate and Beyond'. In P. C. Stern and D. Druckman (eds) *International Conflict Resolution After the Cold War* (Washington DC: National Research Council Press).

Interviews with author

Denis Bradley, Vice Chair Northern Ireland Policing Board, 2001–2006; Co-Chair, *Consultative Group on the Past* 2007–2009 (24 June 2019)

Sir John Chilcott, Permanent Secretary at the NIO, 1990–1997 (20 March 2001)

David Cooke, Head of Division, NIO, 1990–1993; Associate Political Director, NIO, 2002–2004 (25 July 2019)

Sean Duignan, Irish Government Press Secretary, 1992–1995 (25 May 2000)

David Ford, Northern Ireland Justice Minister, 2010–2016 (15 September 2017)

Gerry Kelly, member of Sinn Féin's negotiating team during Belfast/Good Friday Agreement talks; MLA, 1998– (12 September 2017)

Mike Nesbitt, UUP Leader, 2012–2017 (11 September 2017)

Albert Reynolds, Irish Taoiseach 1992–1994 (26 May 2000)

Tom Roberts, former UVF prisoner working with EPIC (27 June 2019)

Party manifestos and reports

DUP, *Campaign03* (2003)

DUP, *Towards a New Agreement* (2003)
DUP, *Leadership That's Working* (2005)
DUP, *Getting it Right* (2007)
DUP, *Let's Keep Northern Ireland Moving Forward* (2010)
SDLP, *Let's Deliver* Real *Progress* (2007)
SDLP, *The Constructive Opposition* (n.d.)
Sinn Féin, *Delivering for Ireland's Future* (2007)
Sinn Féin, *Westminster Manifesto* (2010)
UUP, *Ulster Unionists Manifesto* (2003)
UUP, *For All of Us* (2007)

Index